THE KAISER

THE KAISER

WARLORD OF THE SECOND REICH

Alan Palmer

WEIDENFELD AND NICOLSON
LONDON

Copyright © 1978 by Alan Palmer

First published in Great Britain by
Weidenfeld and Nicolson
11 St John's Hill   London SW11

ISBN 0 297 77393 3

Printed in Great Britain by
Cox & Wyman Ltd
London, Fakenham and Reading

Contents

Illustrations

Author's Note

Any author writing about the German and British Dynasties at the close of the nineteenth century is inevitably faced by problems of nomenclature: Augustas, Fredericks, Victorias and Williams abound in royal and princely confusion. For the sake of simplicity I have accordingly, from time to time, employed familiar names in the course of my narrative – 'Dona', 'Fritz', 'Vicky' etc. I would like to emphasize that this usage on my part is not intended to imply disrespect, either to their memory or to the institution of monarchy.

It is my pleasure to express gratitude to H.R.H. Prince Louis Ferdinand of Prussia for allowing me to quote unpublished comments by his grandfather, Kaiser William II. These comments appear in a book which came into my possession through the kindness of Mr A. W. H. Nicolson, whom I would also like to thank. The Marquess of Salisbury generously allowed me to quote from the papers of his great-grandfather, which are now housed once more at Hatfield. Elizabeth, Countess of Lindsey and Abingdon, kindly permitted me to use extracts from letters written by her father, Major-General the Hon. Edward Stuart-Wortley, which are preserved in a file on the *Daily Telegraph* Incident of 1908 in the Bodleian Library, Oxford. I am also grateful to Lady Lindsey and Abingdon for the interesting information she sent me about Highcliffe Castle.

I would like to thank Mr Martin Gilbert and Dr D. G. Williamson for helping to clarify specific points concerning, respectively, Churchill's staff in 1940 and Rathenau's relations with the Kaiser. My thanks are also due to Mr R. H. Harcourt Williams, librarian and archivist at Hatfield House, and to Mr R. M. Coppock of the Naval Historical Branch at the Ministry of Defence for their kind assistance. I have made much use of the Bodleian Library and I am grateful for the ready help I received there from Mr D. S. Porter, Mrs Mary Major and many other members of the library staff. I am also indebted to the staffs of the London Library and the Public Record Office, especially to the section housed at that time in Portugal Street. Mr John McLaughlin gave welcome advice and encouragement and my old friend Mr Desmond Perry kindly assisted me with my German correspondence. My warm thanks go to Mrs Mary Cumming, who typed the manuscript speedily and helped me through her interest in the subject matter, and to Mr Benjamin Buchan, who is responsible for selecting the illustrations and preparing the book for publication. My wife, Veronica, discussed the book with me stage by stage, took notes for me on our visits to Doorn and other places associated with the Kaiser, compiled the index and read the page proofs, saving me from many slips: I deeply appreciate her constant help and support.

A.W.P.
Woodstock: November 1977

Preface

No ruler has been so lauded and reviled by the British public as Queen Victoria's firstborn grandson, Kaiser William II. His birth was welcomed in London as though he were an English rather than a Prussian prince. As he grew older, the Queen granted him a succession of honorific innovations: he became the youngest foreign Knight of the Garter, the first sovereign from overseas created an Admiral of the Fleet, the first given the colonelcy of a British regiment. Although Victoria deplored the wild words and impulsive gestures with which he disturbed Europe, he remained deeply attached to his grandmother, hurrying to her deathbed in 1901, supporting her with his one sound arm through the last hours of her life. Nine years later he offered a hand of friendship to his cousin, George V, as they stood together before the catafalque of his uncle, Edward VII, in Westminster Hall. On such occasions the London crowd, as sentimental as himself, saw in William one of their own royal family, while he wrote privately back to Berlin describing his emotional pride in being able to look upon Windsor as 'my second home'. As late as July 1911 he was cheered in the London streets, receiving a standing ovation when he went to the theatre.

By 1915, of course, he had become the most hated man in England. Four years later he experienced the last of his 'firsts': he became the first emperor arraigned in a peace treaty for 'a supreme offence against international morality'; and he was threatened with trial before a commission of judges from the five Great Powers victorious in the war he was alleged to have unleashed. For many people the catastrophe of 1914–18 remains 'the Kaiser's War', just as its successor is 'Hitler's War'. This identification of his person with the great disaster was encouraged by many of the political memoirs of the interwar period. Bülow and others readily blamed William for the bankruptcy of policies which they had imposed upon him. Hostile critics seized on his flight to the Netherlands as proof of his inadequacy as a ruler. It was convenient for writers of the Left and the new Right to have a Hohenzollern scapegoat on whose delight in martial speeches they could pour such withering scorn. He was cast as the fall-guy of imperialism: there are many who still see him in this role. Others, however, regret his downfall and the collapse of the monarchical system in central Europe. For several years – most recently in 1973 – an 'In Memoriam' notice appeared in *The Times* each January on the anniversary of his birth, praising the Kaiser's record as an opponent of both the Nazi and the Bolshevik ways of life. It is not always easy to recognize the All-Highest autocrat of Potsdam in the modern dress bestowed on him by some sympathizers. But was he, for that matter, readily recognizable in mourning at Osborne in 1901 or in mufti at Highcliffe in 1907? Throughout his reign and his exile William behaved as though he were dominating the gallery of life immediately around him. This was an illusion. He thought he stood out as a portrait: in reality, he was a mirror, catching the image of what he himself perceived.

This elusive quality – unexpected in someone whose caricature is so firmly etched on the mind – must intrigue any biographer. 'I am what I am and I cannot change', the Kaiser once told Bülow in a moment of pique. But what was he? And why?

1. Thus Win all Men's Applause

Thursday, 27 January 1859, was a wintry afternoon in Berlin, light snow falling on a muffled crowd who had gathered expectantly beneath naked limes and chestnuts down Unter den Linden. Throughout the last two days gunners had stood by at the old palace of the Prussian kings, ready to let the world know when a child was born to the 'English Princess' Victoria, eighteen-year-old wife of Prince Frederick William: the battery in the Lustgarten would fire thirty-six rounds for a girl, a hundred and one for a boy. That afternoon, almost on three o'clock, the first of the saluting cannon broke the midwinter stillness of the city. It rattled the windows in the small palace at the corner of the Oberwaldstrasse, where the doctors were gathered around Princess Victoria's bed, and almost a mile away it shook the rooms in the Wilhelmstrasse where Victoria's father-in-law, Prince-Regent William, was in conference. The Regent broke off his conversation, hurried downstairs, hailed a public *Droschke*, and ordered it to take him to his son's palace. The cab was beneath the arch of the Oberwaldstrasse before the thirty-seventh gun let him know he had a grandson, third in line of succession to the Prussian throne. Soon the news was telegraphed to the Princess's mother and father at Windsor; and, as they rested after a late luncheon, Queen Victoria and the Prince Consort learnt that they too had now become grandparents for the first time. The baby was officially styled Prince Frederick William Albert Victor, names which in themselves linked the royal houses of Prussia and Great Britain. He was known in the family as 'Willy'. Eventually, seventeen years after Germany was proclaimed an empire in 1871, he became Kaiser William II. The world remembers him, with little sympathy or understanding, as *the* Kaiser.

In Berlin and in London there was rejoicing that evening and the next. Despite the bitter cold, Prince Regent William and his consort,

Augusta, went on to the palace balcony and waved contentedly to the jubilant crowd below. There were cheers for Prince Frederick William when he emerged from the Oberwaldstrasse to ride the few hundred yards to his parents' residence. At Windsor, toasts were drunk, not only by the family, but by the household and domestic staff as well. In England people still thought of the new mother as the Princess Royal, eldest child of the sovereign and special favourite of her consort. At the princess's marriage, almost exactly a year before, the Poet Laureate had obliged Her Majesty with two extra stanzas for the national anthem: 'God bless our Prince and Bride, God keep their lands allied', the choristers had sung. Now, the birth of a son to the Princess Royal inspired less elegant turners of verse than Tennyson. When the curtain fell at one London music-hall on the first evening of the future Kaiser's life, the audience stood as the principal comedienne sang:

> Hail the auspicious morn,
> To Prussia's throne is born
> A royal heir.
> May he defend its laws
> Joined with Old England's cause
> Thus win all men's applause,
> God save the Queen!

Never before in English history had the birth of a foreign prince aroused so much interest and enthusiasm. *The Times*, which had for several years been unsympathetic to Prussia, frowned magisterially at such display of public sentiment. On Friday morning the leading article warned readers not to attach undue significance to dynastic connections in assessing political prospects: but it added: 'Our own excellent Sovereign will not have her joy diminished by the reflection that the event which connects her more closely with a great Continental Throne is looked upon by the world as a guarantee of those principles which render her own dynasty secure in the affections of her people.' Happily the general mood in London was less portentous. When the House of Commons reassembled in the following week, the member for North Devon, Charles Trefusis, in moving the address on the Queen's Speech, hoped the birth of a royal grandson in Berlin would 'prove a happy augury of peace'; and the leader of the Opposition, Lord Palmerston, looked forward to a time when the newly born prince would serve 'as an ornament and advantage to the country of his birth and to the lineage from which he has sprung'.[1]

Within a few days of receiving the good news from Berlin, the Queen became aware that 'Vicky' – as the princess was known in the family – suffered considerably during a long and tortuous confinement. For several hours the life of mother and child hung in the balance, not least because of the strange pre-natal position of the baby. At one moment the doctors seemed in such despair that a private message advised the leading Berlin editors to have their presses set up obituary notices for the princess. The battle for her life continued while the cannon were firing their ceremonial salvoes, and the infant was left in the care of a German midwife, Fraulein Stahl, who made his lungs function at the last minute by administering a sharp smack. Only after the crisis had eased around the mother's bed was it seen that the baby's left arm was misshapen. At first it was assumed that the dislocation of the elbow joint and the shoulder socket might be healed by orthopaedic treatment. Nothing was said of the child's disabilities in any communication to Windsor, even though Queen Victoria sent an anxious telegram asking, 'Is it a fine boy?' Sir James Clark, the Queen's principal physician, returned from Berlin in the middle of February and told her about the defective arm, while reassuring her over the general state of Vicky's health. There still seemed no reason why the prince's injury should not be cured in the course of time.

More than sixty years later, the Kaiser himself wrote: 'One definite disability I did suffer from. At birth my left arm had received an injury unnoticed at the time, which proved permanent and impeded its free movement.'[2] The physical and psychological effects of this crippled arm undoubtedly left their mark on his character and therefore, indirectly, on the tragic history of the twentieth century. But it is probable that William himself, and many commentators, exaggerated the significance of the withered arm and neglected its causes. Had the arm itself – and only the arm – been injured by the child's violent birth, there would have been some ground for the medical optimists who recommended gymnastic exercise and electrical treatment. Yet, in reality, the damaged left arm was merely the outward physical form of a deeper disability. When Princess Victoria was five months pregnant she tripped over a chair leg in the old palace at Berlin and (as she wrote later) 'fell with violence on the slippery parquet'. Rightly or wrongly, she believed that this accident – about which she said little at the

time – was responsible for 'all my misfortunes and baby's false position'.[3] In the early months of William's life, the doctors discovered that
a neck injury had been caused in birth because the head was already
tilted abnormally to the left. The damaged neck influenced the func-
tioning of the cervical nerve plexus, thus leading to paralysis of the left
arm. At the same time, the hearing labyrinth of the left ear was harmed,
so that the young prince suffered, even as a child, from deafness on one
side. As he grew older it became clear that his balance was also affected,
presumably by damage to that part of the brain which lies closest to the
inner ear. Determination and will-power enabled William, in the
course of time, to conceal his bodily handicaps from casual eyes; but it is
impossible to tell how far he was able to assume co-ordinated self-
control of a damaged nervous system.

Ultimately it mattered little, except to the royal physicians, whether
these injuries were the consequence of a pre-natal accident or of the
difficult delivery. It was, however, especially tragic that the victim of
such misfortune should be the offspring of families in which there was
already a high incidence of mental instability. The young prince's
great-uncle, Frederick William IV (still titular King of Prussia), was
recognized as prematurely senile in the autumn of 1858 and was now
playing out his last months of life at Potsdam, unaware of anything that
happened beyond his palace walls. Moreover Prince William was the
firstborn descendant both of Tsar Paul and of King George III, great-
great-grandfathers whose minds frequently wandered into twilight
worlds of suspicion and unreality. There were still living in German
princely courts those who could remember England in the years when
her sovereign was a Lear-like figure, hidden by the windows of
Windsor. The possibility of an alleged hereditary madness manifesting
itself within the family haunted the Prince Consort and, not surprisingly, his daughter in Berlin as well.

Yet, in those opening months of 1859, this particular fear lay dor-
mant. Vicky, as she told her mother a shade tactlessly, was pleased and
proud her first child should have been a son. The baby's baptism was
arranged for the eve of Lent, 7 March, which was far sooner than Queen
Victoria wished. She was angry because domestic political difficulties
prevented her going to Berlin: 'Oh! dearest Uncle, it almost breaks my
heart not to witness our first grandchild christened!', she wrote to King
Leopold of the Belgians. 'It is a stupid law in Prussia, I must say, to be
so particular about having the child christened so soon.' She was

represented at the ceremonies in Berlin by Lord Raglan, son of the much criticized commander in the Crimea. As Vicky recalled later, he was one of the few guests who did not comment on how small and delicate the child appeared to be. The princess remained extremely sensitive despite her hopes of a successful cure: 'It went to my heart to see him half covered up to hide his arm which dangled without use or power by his side', she wrote.[4]

Victoria and Albert were both godparents, but the Queen was disconcerted to find they shared this honour with no less than forty other royal and princely sponsors. Although she consoled herself with the thought that godparents who were also grandparents must be reckoned in a special category of divine guardianship, she remained vexed by what she considered the strange behaviour of the Prussian court; and until Vicky crossed to England in May – her first visit home since her marriage – letters from Windsor to Berlin showed affection, solicitude and asperity in almost equal parts. The Prince Consort, on the other hand, was positively light-hearted in his comments, notably on the decision that the baby should be known as William: 'What epitaph history will attach to his name is in the lap of the Gods', he wrote to his son-in-law two days after the christening, 'not Rufus . . . not the "Silent", not "the Conqueror", perhaps "the Great". There is none with this designation.'[5]

When Vicky returned to England in May she could not bring the delicate baby with her, and Victoria and Albert had to wait until September 1860 to see their grandson. By then William was twenty months old and had a sister of seven weeks, Charlotte, a healthy child born after an easy labour. The Queen and the Prince Consort, who were staying at Coburg, were delighted by William: 'He is a fine fat child, with a beautiful soft skin, very fine shoulders and limbs, and a very dear face', Victoria wrote, as though defying the comments of the Prussian doctors; and Albert is alleged to have perceived, even at this early stage, a high degree of intelligence in his grandson. Next August, Vicky and her husband – the royal families called him 'Fritz' – brought William and Charlotte to England and they were able to spend some gloriously hot days on the Isle of Wight. 'Osborne', wrote William sixty-five years later, 'is the scene of my earliest recollections', and he always claimed he could remember Grandpapa Albert, who 'used to like dandling me in a table napkin', a reminiscence which may have become embellished by family tales lovingly and frequently repeated.

Vicky, Fritz and the children left Osborne on Friday, 16 August, just seventeen weeks before the Prince Consort died. William therefore possessed an advantage over Victoria's seventeen other grandsons: he alone among them had been seen by Albert, and praised by Albert, and petted by Albert. To Victoria he remained, as she told uncle Leopold, 'a clever, dear, good little child, the great favourite of my beloved Angel'.[6]

By the time of his visit to Osborne the 'great favourite' had already advanced one stage nearer the Prussian throne. Frederick William IV died at Potsdam on 3 January 1861 and was succeeded by his brother, the former Prince-Regent, who was crowned King William I of Prussia at an impressive ceremony in Königsberg the following October. The new king had taken an affectionate interest in his grandson ever since those first salutes in the Lustgarten brought him hurrying back to the Oberwaldstrasse. At times King William was intensely irritated by the good advice which he used to receive from London, especially while the Prince Consort was alive, and he occasionally snubbed his daughter-in-law whose English ways alienated so many figures at his Court. But the King, if vexed, was at least straightforwardly hostile: his consort, Queen Augusta, was devious, mischievous and totally unsympathetic to Vicky or to anything which seemed to emanate from Coburg or Windsor, King William told his grandson tales of the war against the great Napoleon, of the battle of Leipzig and of how at seventeen he had entered Paris beside Tsar Alexander I in 1814; Queen Augusta, on the other hand, fed the child's growing mind with hints of neglect and of affronts to Prussian tradition on the part of his mother. If William came to believe his mother preferred her other children, the blame rests almost entirely with Augusta and her bitterly jealous tongue. On one occasion the Crown Princess – as Vicky had now become – complained to Queen Victoria that William was encouraging his grandson to have ideas which 'were neither wholesome nor good'; but psychologically they were far less damaging than the muddled resentments stirred up by Grandmama Augusta and her ladies at Court.

Ultimately it was the grandmother at Windsor and Osborne who made the greatest impression on young William, even though he saw her so rarely. By the 1860s Queen Victoria's ascendancy was complete in Europe, despite her prostration after Albert's death. Although only forty-two when she was widowed, the Queen had already reigned longer than any of her contemporaries; she was not inclined to conceal feelings or change an opinion over questions of principle, for it did not occur to her that she could be wrong. Often she looked on lesser mortals with amiable condescension: 'Poor dear soul', she wrote of Augusta, after Vicky reported one particularly mischievous outburst, 'her worries and annoyances make her quite cross.'[7] But the Queen herself was both obstinate and proud. Nothing could convince her that Prussian physicians equalled in skill of diagnosis or treatment the talents of her royal doctors, Sir James Clark and Sir William Jenner. Fortunately she had taken a liking to Fritz when he first visited London in 1851, a few months short of his twentieth birthday, and she continued to look for his qualities as well as those of Vicky in their eldest son. So long as William was a child she treated him indulgently, smiling happily at his naughtiness, commending his courage when he had a tooth out, allowing him to play at Osborne with the miniature cannons on the fort in the grounds which Albert had designed for his own sons. In March 1863 the four-year-old prince was brought from Berlin to Windsor for the wedding of his uncle Bertie, the Prince of Wales, later King Edward VII. William amused himself by throwing an aunt's muff out of a carriage window and a decorative stone from his dirk across the floor of St George's Chapel. When Prince Leopold – not yet ten, and also dressed in a kilt for the occasion – tried to restrain him, William caused a minor commotion by seeking to bite his uncle's leg. Yet whatever the younger generation may have felt about his behaviour, 'precious little William' was a delight to his grandmother, brightening momentarily the widow's gloom in which she enveloped herself. It is not until after William had twice stayed at Osborne without his parents that a warning note appears in the royal correspondence: on his sixth birthday the Queen told her daughter she hoped that 'our darling William', who 'is so dear and so good', would be brought up 'simply, plainly, not with that terrible Prussian pride and ambition, which grieved dear Papa so much'.[8]

There was, of course, also a specifically British pride, and it was around the young prince every time he went to Osborne. He found it exciting to look out from the windows of the house across the parkland to Spithead, where he could watch the warships sailing in and out of Portsmouth. But in Berlin, farther from the sea than anywhere in England, a different tradition predominated: the Prussian capital could not shake off the legacy of Frederick the Great. William I himself always behaved as though soldiering was the true vocation of the House of Hohenzollern and, though Frederick had died in 1786 disillusioned and far from popular, dynastic sentiment perpetuated his achievements and he was remembered as the victor of Rossbach and Leuthen. When Treitschke began his history of nineteenth-century Germany, he declared, 'The twelve campaigns of the Frederician Era have left their mark for ever on the martial spirit of the Prussian people and the Prussian army'; and William I insisted that the first presentation of colours to new regiments after his accession should take place at a ceremony beside Frederick's tomb in Potsdam. Nor was this romanticized past so very remote. 'Those that knew him are still alive', the Crown Princess reminded her mother early in 1863; and added that she herself was acquainted with two of them.[9]

An Englishman visiting Berlin in the 1860s declared that nowhere in Europe were so many uniforms to be seen in a street. Prussia was the supremely militaristic society of the post-Napoleonic era, and from earliest days the young prince was accustomed to the trappings of soldiery – dark blue service dress, white ceremonial tunics, epauletted shoulders, long leather boots, flat caps, spiked helmets, fur hats bearing the death's head emblem, iron crosses, the stars and pendants of military distinction, the ribbons and sashes of the great orders. He grew up to the sounds of an army at the ready: the rattle of scabbards and cavalry spurs down palace corridors; the sharp clicking of heels; hoof beats of carriage escorts; saluting cannon; fifes and drums; staccato commands on open squares; bugle calls and regimental bands. Each day at noon the prince could see from the palace windows an elaborate ceremony of changing the guard, sometimes with his grandfather taking the salute. There were garrison parades, church parades, and special parades for royal birthdays and national festivals. But it was not always mere masquerade. The impressionable years of William's boyhood coincided with the wars which enabled Bismarck to create his united Germany. He watched a regiment of Hungarian infantry march down the Linden in 1864 on its way to fight alongside the Prussians against the Danish army in Schleswig-Holstein and Jutland. Soon afterwards William saw his first victory parade, with captured flags borne in triumph past the Brandenburg Gate. Two years later there were even greater celebrations for the victory of his grandfather's armies over the Austrians and their allies among the smaller German states. It seemed in that autumn of 1866 as if Frederick the Great's mission was at last completed, with Habsburg Austria out of the reckoning as a Germanic power.

In these campaigns the Crown Prince won a reputation as the most successful general in the Hohenzollern family for four generations. Without his arrival on the battlefield the decisive encounter at König-grätz on 3 July 1866 would have been unresolved, or perhaps even a defeat for Prussia. William joyfully welcomed his father back from the war and on 20 September saw the King on horseback lead his armies through the centre of Berlin. The details of this occasion William remembered vividly throughout his life.[10] Princely cousins rode at the head of regiments they had taken into battle. Not all the relatives in the parade were Hohenzollerns: great-uncle Duke Ernest of Saxe-Coburg, brother of the Prince Consort, was there, commanding a battalion in the procession as he had done in the campaign itself. For William, however, there could be no question that the hero was Papa, the Crown Prince, gaunt and bearded at the head of the Second Army. Yet if the enthusiastic applause of the Berliners filled William's heart with pride, it also emphasized the bitterness of what his mother was already calling 'the cross' he bore. In the previous year he had for the first time become acutely conscious of his afflictions: he could not keep his balance so as to run like other boys of seven, nor could he hope to climb, let alone mount a saddle. How, then, was he ever to ride beside his father and grandfather at the head of Prussia's victorious troops? To a royal child in Berlin in that autumn of military triumph it seemed as though sitting a horse was the first essential of popularity.

2. Hinzpeter's Pupil

The pattern of William's education was settled soon after his seventh birthday; but not, perhaps, wisely. Both parents had convinced themselves of the need for stern discipline. Leisure hours were an exceptional privilege, not a natural condition for a growing child. His father wanted Willy to understand the army and its traditions, and to master several languages: his mother hoped he would acquire intellectual curiosity and aesthetic judgement. The Crown Prince had little difficulty in finding a suitable military governor, from whom his son could learn the rudiments of soldiering. Captain von Schotte was a veteran Guards officer, naturally compassionate towards a boy whose disabilities were so grave that they would have ruled out military service for any lesser person in the kingdom. But the dominant figure in the young prince's schoolroom was a civilian, Dr George Hinzpeter, the thirty-nine-year-old classicist who was given charge of William at the Neues Palais in Potsdam shortly before midsummer in 1866.

Hinzpeter's is a strange shadow across the margin of history. Few tutors have been less well-fitted for their task. His social background and manner – even his appearance – were against him. He was born into a Calvinist family who lived in the Westphalian textile centre of Bielefeld and he attended the local high school (*Gymnasium*), where his father taught classics. The austere tenets of Calvinism imposed a moral order on Hinzpeter's life. He was taught to find joy only in the virtuous satisfaction of duties fulfilled. Other students of his age were stirred by the lyricism of Heine and the Romantic poets, but their ecstasies kindled no flame in George Hinzpeter's soul. He gained his doctorate in philological studies and then returned to Westphalia as a schoolmaster, marked out for advancement by his diligence and moral rectitude. These qualities led him to tutorships in a succession of aristocratic families, and the Crown Prince first met him in the household of Count

Emil von Görtz. Hinzpeter had no great range of intellectual interests:
he would not have impressed Frederick the Great. His artistic sen-
sitivity was undeveloped, partly because his upbringing sternly repudi-
ated even the most harmless pleasures of social convention. Fritz
admired his quietly reserved air of dedication, but he was prepared to
leave the final word on William's schooling to Vicky, and she had three
other candidates in mind, apart from the Westphalian.

On first acquaintance, the Crown Princess found Hinzpeter puzzling.
She wrote subsequently to Queen Victoria, telling her that 'Willy's
tutor' was a trustworthy, good-natured man but 'not very bright', and
she complained of his irritating habits of eating with a knife and resting
his elbows on the table.[1] He had, however, two strong recommendations in her eyes. Sir Robert Morier, a British diplomat whom
she respected, had met Hinzpeter, talked political abstractions with
him and thought him a tutor of probity. And when Vicky herself began
to talk to Hinzpeter she found him a man of system and ideals. He
assured her that he believed the crowning virtue of an educational
method was its simplicity. To a mind moulded by the Prince Consort
and still chafing at the ceremonial in an alien court, this vague concept
of education was comfortingly reassuring. Hinzpeter was appointed
principal civilian tutor to William and to his brother Henry, who was
three and a half years his junior. By Christmas in 1866 Vicky was so
pleased with her appointment that she was praising Hinzpeter's 'sense,
tact and intelligence' and telling her mother how readily she would
follow the advice which he (and the children's French tutor,
Mademoiselle d'Harcourt) offered her.[2]

The Crown Prince told Hinzpeter to give his eldest son a mental
training fit to match the 'intellectual cream' of the kingdom. This was a
formidable assignment, but Hinzpeter did not lack self-confidence and
he set about his task without demur. Tuition began at six in the
morning, except in the winter months when it was moved back to seven.
It continued for twelve hours each day, with two breaks for food and for
physical exercise. Official duties were frowned on: they were as wasteful
as the extraneous non-academic studies originally prescribed by the
princes' military governor. Hinzpeter insisted that a tutor must have
prior claim on a pupil's time whatever the obligations of royalty. There
was nothing new in such a demand: it was as old as the education of
princes, and normally ignored. But there was a rare earnestness in
Hinzpeter; the more he fussed, the more Vicky, Fritz and the court

authorities respected him. Certainly he was intimidating. 'A dry and pedantic person with a gaunt, slim figure and a face of old parchment', William described him many years later. His classicism was inspired not by the serene grandeur of Athens and Rome, but by the discipline and frugality of Sparta. Praise, the princes learnt, would be given for perfection, never for sustained effort or improvement. William was taught that it was not sufficient to do as well as anyone else: he had to excel.

Hinzpeter found Willy strong-willed and obstinate, 'my much loved problem child', he called him. Nearly thirty years later he wrote, 'What especially impressed one in this good-looking but girlish boy, whose delicate softness was turned into almost complete frailty by the embarrassing uselessness of his left arm, was his resistance ... to every attempt which would have forced his inner self in one direction or the other.'[3] If there was an effeminate streak in the unfortunate prince it was soon suppressed. His tutor assumed responsibilities far beyond the narrowly academic. The prince was made to steel his mind in order to overcome physical clumsiness. By his tenth birthday he had acquired poise, self-assurance and independence. It was Hinzpeter, and not the riding master, who taught William the basic skill of horsemanship. At the age of eight William's riding lessons were a pathetic charade: a groom would lift him on to the back of a pony and lead it on the rein. It seemed to Hinzpeter that such an exercise was an abject surrender to his pupil's disability and therefore represented a challenge to his own principles of education. He browbeat a frightened and weeping prince into sitting on the pony without stirrups and taking the reins in his right hand. When the boy fell to the ground – as, at first, invariably happened – Hinzpeter picked him up without sympathy or encouragement and put him back on the pony 'despite his prayers and tears'. After several weeks William began to acquire a sense of balance. Gradually he learnt, again after weeks of bruises and tumbles, how to trot and canter across the parkland of Potsdam. By the early summer of 1868 he could sit a horse; and in July 1871 he was a sufficiently assured horseman to follow his father through the Brandenburg Gate in the procession celebrating victory over France. It was an astonishing personal achievement, though the cost in physical agony and nervous repression was enough to sear a boy's character.

These brutal methods of instruction were less effective in the schoolroom. A more imaginative tutor, not circumscribed by an established curriculum, might have given depth to his studies and suggested standards of critical judgement. As it was, William could not concentrate on anything academic. To the disappointment of both parents he became – and remained – an arch-dabbler, a dilettante who showed promise but never fulfilment. There was in him none of the scientific and mathematical curiosity which Vicky had admired in her father. Hinzpeter assigned a disproportionate number of hours to studying the linguistics and grammar of Latin and Greek, but he could not awaken any inner sympathy with the ancient world. At thirteen William considered Ovid a 'very childish' poet: he enjoyed the Gallic Wars – 'Rhine bridges, Germanic arms, crossing to Britain and Siege of Alesia' – but complained that Caesar was unfair to the barbarians. No doubt Hinzpeter's intentions were sound. He insisted on escorting William and Henry to museums and art galleries. Both young princes were bored by these dutiful visits and in their adolescence pained their mother by becoming self-assertively philistine: 'Willy . . . does not care to look at anything . . . would not look at a Guide Book, or any other book which would give him information about the places to be seen', she wrote to Victoria after a journey through Belgium and Holland. Yet William himself subsequently praised Hinzpeter for taking him to factories and mines where he saw the nation's growing industrial strength.[4] This early acquaintance with industry gave him an insight into the social problem; or so, at least, he claimed in later years.

It was in many ways a lonely childhood, with few companions of his own age. In 1870 Hinzpeter encouraged the Crown Princess to invite Poulteney Bigelow, the fifteen-year-old son of the American minister in Berlin, to visit Willy and Henry at Potsdam so that they might have some youthful company. Bigelow, who in Paris had been an occasional playmate to the Prince Imperial, found the two Prussian princes more fun, although overshadowed by their tutor, whom he later described as 'a dessicated schoolmasterly stripe of Prussian'. At the Neues Palais 'there was an empty attic, running the whole length of the palace roof, and here on rainy days we kicked footballs until the broken panes of glass attracted Dr Hinzpeter's attention', Bigelow wrote in 1915. No game interested William that did not, in some way, suggest war: and the two princes' chief delight was to sail a model frigate, about the size of a launch, which had been presented to their great-uncle by William IV of England. This vessel, so Bigelow suggested, was 'the parent ship' of Willy's later navy.[5] The young prince's friendship with Bigelow continued intermittently into manhood, and they corresponded with each other even in William's final years of exile; but William had no close contact with German boys until he was in his sixteenth year. Crown Prince Rudolph of Austria, Francis Joseph's only son, was a few months older than William; and when Fritz and Vicky went to Vienna for the 1873 Exhibition they took Willy with them. Unfortunately William's voice had just broken that spring, and to his mother he seemed loud and uncouth, 'a bear or a schoolboy beside Rudolph', she wrote to Queen Victoria. The two princes had little in common.[6]

Theoretically William was prepared for his responsibilities with greater care than any of his Prussian predecessors. In September 1874 he became a pupil at a public high school, the *Gymnasium* at Kassel, remaining there until a few days before his eighteenth birthday. It was an astonishing innovation for a future sovereign in Berlin to spend over two years beside boys whose fathers were not even officers in the reserve. William I thought the *Gymnasium* unsuitable for his grandson: Willy might be exposed to dangerous influences if some of the teachers held new-fangled beliefs. Yet the prince had little contact with the middle-class world of Kassel: Hinzpeter supervised his studies, staying in the town palace during the winter months and riding in with him each day in summer from the royal residence at Wilhelmshohe, three miles away. William had no opportunity to make friends among the other sixteen boys in his class, nor to follow his own academic tastes (such as they were). He enjoyed recent history, but history teaching at Kassel ceased abruptly in 1648, and the curriculum was overwhelmingly classical in structure. A few years later Willy met a group of Etonians of his own age and decided they 'had learned much less Latin and Greek' at school.[7] He neither especially liked nor disliked the *Gymnasium* experiment, but he did blame his parents for exposing him to the humiliation of lower class marks than mere commoners, and in this grievance he was warmly supported by his grandfather. The prince saw no merit in competition he could not win.

Already his character was beginning to cause anxiety. The Crown Princess regretted that Willy was 'selfish, domineering and proud', but consoled herself by the earnest manner in which he affirmed his faith during the protracted ceremonies of confirmation, in the Friedenskirche at Potsdam on 11 September 1874. The Prince of Wales was impressed by such pious fortitude. Other members of the family were less sure of William's sincerity. Queen Sophie of the Netherlands –

a distant cousin whom Willy called 'Aunt' – had inherited the sharp eyes and sharp tongue of her mother, Catherine Pavlovna, favourite sister of Tsar Alexander I. Sophie saw a lot of Vicky and her family during that summer of 1874; and she was puzzled to find William inventing total fantasies. 'His strange propensity for lying' alarmed her: 'In every sense', she reflected, 'he will be an odd specimen of a Sovereign, perhaps the more warlike because nature did not fit him for a soldier.'[8]

This need to appear every inch a soldier obsessed William's mind throughout his adolescence. He was nominally commissioned in the first infantry regiment of Guards on his tenth birthday and continued to receive military training, often against Hinzpeter's wishes, while at Kassel. The army, so his tutor wrote later, provided him with many hours of 'dreaming, thinking and acting', but he shared with his brother Henry an enthusiasm for warships and the sea. Here was an interest which marked off the two boys from earlier generations of Prussian princes, soldiers through and through, unable to tell port from starboard. The German fleet in the 1870s was small: control of the Admiralty in Berlin was entrusted to temporarily desk-bound generals who looked on the navy as an auxiliary arm, staffed by officers of inferior social status. For a future heir to the throne to become a naval cadet was unthinkable. Even in England Queen Victoria criticized the decision to send the two eldest sons of the Prince of Wales to HMS *Britannia*, and however much her German grandson may have envied his English cousins' good fortune he never seriously thought of avoiding his spell of service with a Guards regiment. Yet court conventions were changing in Berlin no less than in London. There seemed no reason why the crown prince's second son should not be trained as a naval officer; and William found it both exciting and frustrating when Henry left the Kassel *Gymnasium* for Kiel and the sailing frigate *Niobe*.[9]

Technically William came of age on his eighteenth birthday, an occasion of great celebration.[10] Emperor William I invested his grandson with the Order of the Black Eagle and Queen Victoria wished the British ambassador to confer the Order of the Bath on him that day. But there was a problem. Discreet messages passed from Potsdam to Windsor: 'Willy would be satisfied with the Bath, but the nation would not', Vicky told her mother; and the Queen, with an indulgence reserved for this most favoured grandchild, agreed that William should be created a Knight of the Garter. Once again he was receiving special treatment from his English relatives: no foreign prince had ever before been created a Knight of the Garter so young, nor had three generations of the same foreign dynasty ever held the dignity at the same time. He was delighted and for several years signed letters in English, 'William, Pr. v Pr., K.G.', a practice his grandmother considered unnecessarily affected. The honour had long been prized in Berlin. When the German Empire was proclaimed at Versailles in 1871, Fritz had taken care to wear the Garter, 'an omen of intimate union between the Reich and England', as he wrote in his journal; but he regarded conferment of the distinction on his eldest son with mixed feelings. 'That boy will never mature, never come of age', he complained to a distinguished professor who offered congratulations after the eighteenth birthday celebrations were completed.

Both parents were disappointed in William. 'It has been the dream of my life to have a son who in soul and mind would be like beloved Papa', Vicky told her mother;[11] and Willy fell short of this ideal. Fritz, while not seeking a reincarnation of Albert the Good, at least hoped for a balanced, rational and kindly young man with whom to discuss his hopes and fears for Germany. Instead, he was confronted with an emotional adolescent, starry-eyed with admiration for the creator of the unified German Empire, Chancellor Otto von Bismarck. The Crown Prince's sentiments were liberal rather than authoritarian: he had long opposed Bismarck although at times the two men co-operated for a particular objective. But there had never been any lessening of tension between the chancellor and the Crown Princess: she loathed 'blood and iron'; he distrusted her English loyalties. It was galling to find the emperor and Bismarck encouraging her eldest son in his deplorable attitudes. But Willy had no reservations: Bismarck was for him the genius who raised his grandfather 'to the pinnacle of the German Empire'. If Papa and Mama failed to admire his statesmanship then this was a reflection upon them rather than on the chancellor: William despised those whose natures did not warm to his own intensity of hero worship.

The prince's eighteenth birthday marked the end of Hinzpeter's direct responsibilities. Although only fifty he looked older, and retired to Bielefeld with the former Mademoiselle d'Harcourt, whom he had married two years before. The emperor insisted that William should spend six months in the army. There he acquired the highly affected Potsdam accent (*Potsdamer Ton*), a nasal bark which ruined the civilities of normal conversation by its arrogance and coarseness. It was a style which ill-suited his priggish attitude to moral questions, and it did not make him a more attractive or sympathetic person. The Crown Princess cherished a plan, which she discussed with Sir Robert Morier and with Hinzpeter, for William to spend a few terms at Oxford. She hoped he might sharpen his mind at Balliol, where Jowett was in his prime as Master and would have welcomed the prince as an undergraduate. No one else at the Prussian court favoured the idea, and it is of course probable that William's academic attainments would have fallen short of Balliol's standards.[12] Clearly it was far more convenient for a German prince to spend two and a half years at Bonn, and in the autumn of 1877 he matriculated at the university where his father had been a student in the restless days following the 1848 revolutions. Yet William gained less than his father from the university: he picked up a smattering of law, history and science; and he joined one of the student societies, the Borussia Corps, although he never became a full member and frowned on duelling, gambling and excessive drinking. Occasionally he would play croquet with the daughters of a local magistrate; but in general he cut himself off from his fellow students, living in even greater isolation than Hinzpeter permitted at Kassel. Lecturers and tutors came to his residence, the Villa Frank in the Koblenzstrasse, unless they wished him to observe a scientific experiment, when he would honour one of the demonstration theatres with his presence. He was *at* the university but not *of* the university, any more than his uncle, the Prince of Wales, had been as a Cambridge undergraduate in 1861.[13]

During his vacations William travelled. A visit to Paris, where he made a balloon ascent, was not a success: he gave the impression that he was shocked by the lax standards of life in the city, but it is probable he chiefly resented the coolness with which he was received, for it was only seven years since the Franco-Prussian War. 'I never wanted to see the French capital again', he wrote in his memoirs; and he never did. Venice, Monza and Genoa were more to his taste, but much of his time was spent in the British Isles, trying to understand a people towards whom he constantly felt both admiration and resentment. He visited his grandmother again at Osborne, Windsor, and Balmoral; and he met Disraeli, whose 'cleverness and cold calculation' together with 'a submissiveness to his sovereign' failed to make 'an agreeable impression'. ('How jolly!', Willy had written to his mother on hearing that Disraeli had secured for Britain the largest single holding of Suez Canal shares.) Rather unexpectedly he stayed for some weeks at Ilfracombe in north Devon for the good of his health, and once spent a puzzled day at Lords' seeking to make sense of the Eton and Harrow cricket match. There was, as he noted, nothing in Germany comparable to the enthusiasm with which the English people followed competitive games.[14] Sporting metaphors were duly absorbed into his English vocabulary, whence eventually they emerged – heartily inapt – to confound crises in later years.

On most weekends in his first summer at the university William liked to escape from Bonn and travel down through Hesse to Darmstadt, where his mother's sister, Alice, was married to the Grand Duke. The Hessian court was pleasantly unpretentious and the prince enjoyed showing off to his six cousins. In that summer of 1878 the eldest, Victoria, was fifteen, while her constant companion, the second daughter, Elizabeth ('Ella'), would be fourteen in the following November. They were not impressed by Willy's behaviour: it was disconcerting to lob a tennis-ball over the net one moment, and find him wishing to read aloud a favourite passage from the Bible the next. Victoria was too much a tomboy to win William's admiration, but he was increasingly attracted by Ella. That winter, tragedy hit the Hessian royal family: the youngest child, four-year old May, died from diphtheria, and Princess Alice succumbed to the same virus four weeks later. William was deeply moved by his aunt's death and filled with sentimental compassion for Victoria and Ella. He spent leisure hours writing verses for Ella – though none have survived – and, in the following summer, sought always to be near her when he visited Darmstadt or the wooded Schloss Wolfsgarten, a mere ten miles from the Rhine. By now he was smoking heavily, a habit which his cousin Victoria secretly picked up from him, and he seemed even more erratic and restless.[15] His mother thought it undesirable for her eldest son to marry her niece (although nine years later Henry was allowed to marry Ella's younger sister, Irene) and no one, apart from William, took his infatuation with Ella seriously. He was too egocentric for either of his Hessian cousins; Victoria was to marry Prince Louis of Battenberg and settle in England, while Ella married the Grand Duke Serge of Russia. William needed a more placid and less intelligent creature than Ella for his wife.

He had, in fact, already found such a person in Princess Augusta Victoria of Schleswig-Holstein-Sonderburg-Augustenburg. 'Dona' (as she was called in her family) possessed a pretty face, a dignified manner and an even temper. She was Willy's senior in age by a mere fourteen weeks. Her father, Duke Frederick of Augustenburg, had long been a friend of the Crown Prince, who unsuccessfully championed his claims to Schleswig-Holstein against Bismarck's policy in 1864–5, and William first met Dona on holiday in Thuringia during the spring of 1868, when they were both nine. Ten years later William began to pay her more attention, visiting the family at Gotha and in return escorting her around Potsdam. She did not inspire love poems, but there is no doubt he found her physically attractive and she idolized him, although she had few illusions about his temperamental immaturity. Unfortunately the Augustenburgs were considered of lowly rank among German princely families and William knew that a projected marriage with Dona would be unpopular at court. His parents, however, agreed with him and by Christmas 1879 he had almost made up his mind.

Early in January 1880 Dona's father died. Once again, as with Ella, bereavement brought out a protective instinct in William; and the death of 'that idiot from Holstein' – as Bismarck called the duke – improved the prospect of securing the emperor's consent for the marriage. The young couple became secretly engaged on St Valentine's Day, 1880, for both were romantics at heart. The emperor showed some reluctance to make the betrothal public, no doubt because he would personally have preferred a Russian dynastic connection. But in the end he agreed to 'proclaim the event' at Babelsberg on 2 June. The marriage was arranged for the following February.[16]

Everyone liked Dona personally. 'Her smile and her manners and expression must disarm even the bristly, thorny people of Berlin with their sharp tongues, their cutting sarcasms about everybody and everything', Vicky wrote to Windsor. And the Queen herself, who welcomed Dona to England for the first time in March 1880, thought her 'gentle and amiable and sweet'. Bismarck, lapsing into a coarser style, remarked that the 'Holstein cow' would introduce a fresh strain to the Hohenzollern breed; he was thankful Dona was not English, nor endowed with such spirit as Vicky or the Empress Augusta. 'An excellent woman', wrote Waldersee, one of the rising stars on the General Staff, in his journal; and Hinzpeter, who had been with William at that first meeting in 1868, told Dona he was glad that 'my dearly beloved problem child' would be united 'for life with someone who understands him and sympathizes with him in his weaknesses'.[17] There was a general impression that, in some undefined way, Dona would do him good.

The wedding festivities lasted three days. On Saturday, 26 February, the bridegroom – newly promoted to the rank of captain – led a detachment of Guards through the Brandenburg Gate and along the Linden to the royal palace, where they formed a guard of honour to welcome the bride on her formal arrival at the capital. A flock of white doves was released as her carriage reached the Brandenburg Gate and passed, in fine state, between crowds lining the Linden. The inexplicable intrusion into the procession of an advertising float recommending, for all newly-weds, the merits of Singer's sewing machine did not please Dona and, to at least one of her attendants, William seemed more concerned with the appearance of the Guard than of the bride; but the Berliners were delighted, and remained in holiday mood the whole weekend. The festivities within the palace that evening lasted for six and a half hours, and the ceremonies on the Sunday (the actual wedding day) were no less protracted. The formal banquet was held on the Monday, followed that night by a gala performance of *Armide* at the Opera House.[18] There was no honeymoon: the couple left for Potsdam, where William was enjoying regimental life with the Foot Guards. It was fortunate that Dona was too docile, dutiful and conventional to resent the 'army mania' hereditary among Prussia's royal princes.

3. Prince of the Marble Palace

William and Dona spent their early married life at Potsdam. At first they occupied a wing of the old *Stadtschloss*, in which Frederick the Great lived before the completion of Sans Souci, but by the spring of 1882 the Marble Palace was ready for the young couple. It was a pleasant, late-eighteenth-century building set in parkland above the Heiligersee and about a couple of miles north of the town. Terraces led down to the lakeside so that, although the palace was compact, it asserted a natural self-assurance over the landscape, like an Italian villa. In later years Dona maintained she had never been so happy as in those summers at the Marble Palace, and her four eldest sons were born there. William fulfilled the duties of a regimental officer with enthusiasm, recalling long afterwards not merely parades and field exercises but the eccentricities of battalion commanders and the jaunty small talk of mess dinners. Once again, as in his boyhood, he steeled himself to achieve what seemed impossible to most observers. He handled the cavalry faultlessly on manoeuvres despite his disabilities, and he varied his military experience, spending some months with the artillery and also receiving training for the General Staff. He rose rapidly in rank: major in September 1881, colonel in October 1883, general in January 1888. No doubt princely birth steadied the ladder of advancement, but this speedy promotion was well merited. William I was impressed by his grandson's persistence, and so were other veterans in the officer corps. 'Never had there been enrolled in the Prussian army a young man who seemed physically so unfitted to shine as a cavalry officer', Hinzpeter wrote. 'Those few who understood the meaning of this triumph of moral force over bodily weakness felt their proud hopes for him as an exemplar of royalty fully justified.'

Vicky could not share these feelings.[1] She was glad her eldest son had conquered his infirmities, but it saddened her he should be using his brains and his privileged position to ingratiate himself at court with those who opposed her. He was headstrong and tactless, as indeed she was herself, but he was also given to dramatic poses and cheap jibes, his tongue readily sarcastic. At times it seemed as if he approved of nothing she said or did. 'This son has never really been mine,' she sighed shortly before his marriage. Nor was her husband pleased with William's progress. 'Look at my son – the complete Guards officer', Fritz was once heard to remark in a tone of bitter contempt. Yet what should William have done? Had he been 'sharp enough to see through the system' (as his mother wrote) and accept his parents' criticism of Bismarck, he would have been written off as a weakling who lacked a character of his own. As it was, he stood by his principles. His brother officers complained to one another of his prurience, resenting attempts to impose a puritanical code of behaviour on men under his command. He was far from popular with the officer corps, not least because he criticized the excessively high proportion of aristocrats among the cavalry cadets. His round condemnation of gambling and casino life brought him into conflict with an influential 'establishment' figure, General von Albedyll, the head of the emperor's military secretariat. For several months in 1886 they were not on speaking terms. He could only afford the luxury of a dispute with Albedyll if he was sure of his good standing with the chancellor.

At first, when William and Dona moved into the Marble Palace, Bismarck assumed his son, Herbert, would cultivate the young couple; and within a few months Herbert – whom his father was grooming in the foreign service as a future minister – was behaving as though he were William's boon companion. This, however, he never became. 'Beyond a certain comradeship such as readily arises between young men', wrote William later, 'we were never united by sentiments of real friendship.'[2] He found Herbert rude and lacking in consideration for other people, criticisms often levelled against William himself. On the other hand, his admiration for the chancellor deepened in the first years of his married life, not least because Bismarck personally began to flatter him, seeing him as a useful auxiliary in the long struggle against the Crown Prince and his liberal friends. In May 1884 the chancellor persuaded Emperor William I to send the prince to St Petersburg as Germany's representative at the sixteenth birthday celebrations of the Tsarevitch, when the future Nicholas II came of age. Although the Crown Prince felt aggrieved at these favours shown to his son, Bismarck's proposal made good sense; eventually 'Willy' and 'Nicky' would reign as sovereigns, and William I was glad to strengthen the bonds between Russia and Prussia since he had always felt the Hohenzollern and Romanov autocracies linked in destiny. Eighteen months later Bismarck suggested that Prince William should be attached to the Foreign Ministry, where Herbert would teach him the mechanics of diplomacy. This time the Crown Prince was indignant: he had never been permitted to see how foreign policy was shaped. 'In view of the unripeness and inexperience of my eldest son', he wrote to Bismarck, 'together with his tendency to brag and his overweening conceit, I consider it a positive danger for him to be allowed to come into contact with foreign affairs.'[3] Bismarck ignored Fritz's complaint, although he kept the letter and made use of it in his memoirs after his relations with William turned sour. The prince was introduced to the work of the Foreign Ministry in September 1886, and he continued to visit the Wilhelmstrasse intermittently throughout that winter and the next.

The Crown Prince's strictures were harsh, but not unmerited. Already on his journeys abroad William had shown he was no diplomat. There was, for example, a disastrous private visit to England in November 1880 when the prince abruptly left Sandringham on the eve of the Prince of Wales's birthday and stayed, for another fortnight, at Cumberland Lodge, Windsor, the home of Dona's uncle. From Cumberland Lodge he was taken one day to Portsmouth where his interest in the fortifications astounded his hosts: a detailed report on 'the forts and docks of Portsmouth', with sketches, was duly sent to William I by his grandson from Windsor, and would have been a credit to any spy.[4] The prince's visit to St Petersburg (which gave him the opportunity of sending the Emperor a similar survey of Kronstadt) was hailed at the time as a personal success, even by Herbert Bismarck who grudged generous words. But after his return to Berlin William made the mistake of attempting to establish a regular correspondence with Tsar Alexander III and his son. The Tsar, who had thought highly of his visitor's intelligence so long as he was in Russia, soon revised his opinion; for William clumsily attempted to prejudice him against the Prince of Wales, a brother-in-law towards whom Alexander felt genuine affection. When, during a visit of the Prince of Wales to Berlin, William complained to Alexander that 'These English have forgotten *I* exist', it was difficult to take him seriously. Nor was the Tsar impressed by William's unsolicited advice that he should pay no attention to 'anything you may hear from my father' who 'is under my mother's thumb and she, in turn, is guided by the Queen of England and makes him see everything through English eyes'.[5] When next Alexander III and Prince William met – at Brest-Litovsk in September 1886 – the Tsar was barely cordial, and he continued to treat the prince coldly for the remainder of his life. Alexander III looked on the family as a sacred unit, and he could not respect a son so ready to abuse his own parents.

By the spring of 1885 William had given up all outward pretence of filial loyalty. He was at pains to show Herbert Bismarck and his brother Hussars of the Guard that, though a grandson of Queen Victoria, he was in temperament as sound an Anglophobe as any solidly Prussian member of the officer corps. For by now he had convinced himself that his mother, and her English relations, were scheming against Germany's interests. His second sister, Victoria ('Moretta' to the family), wished to marry Alexander of Battenberg, who was at that time the reigning Prince of Bulgaria. Bismarck opposed any such union: he distrusted the ambitions of the Battenbergs, who were popular in southern Germany; and he was afraid a Hohenzollern princess in Sofia might provoke friction with the Russians, who were always suspicious of political intrusions into the eastern Balkans. William sided demonstratively with Bismarck, even though he knew that Moretta was in love with her 'Sandro'; and the chancellor, in his turn, was supported by the aged Emperor. So long as William I lived, there could be no prospect of such a marriage, but neither the Crown Princess nor her daughter gave up hope. The chief consequence of William's vigorous opposition to the marriage was bitterness within the family circle.[6]

Vicky blamed the Bismarcks for her son's behaviour. 'It is quite useless to attempt to enlighten him', she wrote to Queen Victoria. 'The malady must take its course and we must trust to later years and changed circumstances to cure him.'[7] She thought William a blind admirer of the Bismarcks, choosing friends from their acquaintances and ill-disposed towards anyone rash enough to criticize the chancellor. This, however, was an over-simplification. Ever since he moved into the Marble Palace, William had looked for companionship to the Guards regiments with whom he was closely associated, and he enjoyed 'beer and tobacco evenings' with them, much as had his eccentric ancestor, Frederick William I, in the early years of the previous century. Most of William's guests and hosts at Potsdam belonged to his parents' generation rather than his own, and few approved of Bismarck. General

Max von Versen and General Wilhelm von Hahnke were distinguished veterans of the Franco-Prussian War, highly critical of the chancellor's attitude to the General Staff and its problems. The most influential of William's friends, General Count von Waldersee, was devious, ambitious and conspiratorial by nature. Although he used Herbert Bismarck as a link with the chancellor he was convinced Germany and Prussia no longer needed the Bismarck family at the head of affairs. For some months he hoped to reconcile William with the Crown Prince. During these years at the Marble Palace, William does not seem to have been aware of Waldersee's ambitions or of his dubious personal loyalty. Moreover, Waldersee's wife – born Mary Lee of New York City – fascinated William, not so much by her charm as by her sympathetic approval of everything he said and did; and she also befriended Dona, treating her lightweight opinions with a respect she never received from the Crown Princess (who was, in fact, two years younger than Countess von Waldersee). By 1887 William was far from being 'Bismarck's willing tool and follower', as his mother complained. Even his friend, Colonel von Kessel, who was related to Bismarck, criticized the chancellor's attitude towards Russia.

It was difficult for William to become intimately friendly with any-one of his own age.[8] In a happy mood his geniality never quite freed itself from inhibitions of rank, and he would tease an acquaintance with a hearty jocularity no one dared reciprocate. The only junior officer and exact contemporary to become a close friend of William and Dona during their years at Potsdam was a man whose outlook and interests seemed alien to the prevailing mood in the Prussian Hussar regiments. Captain Oskar von Chelius, who became in due course a major-general and principal aide-de-camp to his emperor, was an aesthete and an amateur musician: it was said of him that he knew more about the world of Grand Opera than did the critics of the Berlin newspapers. He was a fanatical Wagnerian and, at the same time, a devotee of every-thing which concerned Italian life and literature. Dona, with her nar-row Protestant prejudices, was so enchanted by Chelius's talents that she tolerated his Roman Catholicism. He first delighted William and Dona with his skill on the piano in their earliest weeks at the Marble Palace. Over thirty years later he was still playing Schumann and Beethoven for them during the war, in which both his sons perished.

There were some aspects of William's character – they were as much

25

Coburg traits as Hohenzollern – which reacted excessively against the brutalizing discipline of Prussian tradition. An assumed toughness, repressing natural sympathies and affection, led in moments of relaxation to over-emotional sentimentality. On such occasions Chelius at the piano or reading translations of Italian verse satisfied the prince's romantic imagination, widening horizons limited for most of the time to the parade ground and field manoeuvres. William, impatient with routine and restless in temperament, needed a Chelius to rescue him from the constraining effects of regimental stagnation. But so retarded was William's adolescence that he required more than Chelius's musical gifts could offer: he wished for a counsellor, abler and more experienced than himself, who would take equally seriously his soldiering and his dilettante dabbling in music and the arts, someone who would accord him the adulation for which he craved rather than dismiss him inconsequentially as 'the complete Guards officer'. Early in 1886 William found such a friend and confidant in Count Philipp zu Eulenburg-Hertefeld, a thirty-nine-year-old junior diplomat, serving as First Secretary of the Prussian legation in Munich.[9]

William met Philipp Eulenburg on a shoot at Count Richard Dohna's estate in East Prussia. Eulenburg, who was twelve years older than the prince, was the son of a typical Junker officer and of an artistic mother to whom he was excessively devoted. He served with the Guards from 1886 to 1871 and won the Iron Cross for bravery in the Franco-Prussian War, but he had never liked garrison life and, with a doctorate in jurisprudence to his credit, he transferred to the diplomatic corps. When William first knew him he was a father to three sons and three daughters, two other children having died in infancy. His character was less conventional than his career and family background would suggest. He was a sensitive and perceptive representative of a largely make-believe society, a mock-Gothic figure who despised the brash vulgarity of an industrialized Prussia and questioned the accepted standards of Potsdam. A satirical novel brought him into conflict with Waldersee and the demigods of the General Staff several years before he was introduced to William. By then he had acquired a specialist knowledge of Nordic ballads, composed a collection of *Lieder*, and written several lightly amusing short stories. An Englishwoman who spent many years at the Prussian court remembered him as a first-rate conversationalist who 'told his tales in a quiet, soft subtle voice with a grave smile and a certain fascinating charm of manner'. He possessed a quizzical mind, capable of making William see the haziness of his preconceived ideas and values.

'Prince William', wrote Herbert Bismarck to Eulenburg in August 1886, 'thinks a great deal of you, and has sung your praises to me in every kind of way. You must make use of this . . . and get an influence over him. For the heaven-storming strain in most of his opinions must be more and more toned down, so that the Potsdam Lieutenant's outlook may gradually give way to statesmanlike reflections.'[10] Family connections had long given Eulenburg free access to the Bismarck circle, but hitherto neither the chancellor nor his son had taken him seriously. Now it was accepted in Berlin that Eulenburg had the makings of a court favourite, and he was treated with respect both by the Bismarcks and by the all-important head of the political department of the Foreign Ministry, Friedrich von Holstein, who consulted him over the troubled dynastic problems of Bavaria. Not surprisingly Eulenburg hoped for advancement in his diplomatic career, and on occasions he presented unpopular views to William with tact and ingenuity. But he was not prepared to be a mouthpiece either for Herbert Bismarck or Holstein, and in these first years of friendship with the prince he saw to it that their letters and conversation were concerned more with music and the arts than with questions of government.

In 'Phili's' letters to William there was a lush sentimentality which, though relieved by shafts of sardonic humour, remains unattractive to the reader. His memoirs, too, conjure up a strange atmosphere of extravagant amiability. During musical evenings, we are told, William would sit beside Eulenburg on the stool, turning the pages as he played the piano and sang his own compositions with such feeling that the prince would be driven 'into almost feverish raptures'. We learn, from Eulenburg's recollections, how 'when we met in the forest on morning shoots' the prince 'would delight in greeting me with words and phrases from my verses'. Clearly the talents of poor Captain von Chelius were soon outclassed. 'You must meet my bosom friend – the only one I have', William said to Hinzpeter when he introduced him to Eulenburg early in 1887. By then it was clear that William felt a deeper affection for Phili Eulenburg 'than for any other living person', and this heady emotionalism was reciprocated. They had been able to slip away for a carefree holiday in Bavaria during August 1886, 'our excursion' as it became in their correspondence. Bismarck himself subsequently

27

commented that when Eulenburg was in William's presence he adopted 'an attitude of adoration which I believe to be sincere'. Every time the prince looked up, Bismarck added, he 'could be certain of seeing those worshipping eyes fixed upon him'.[11]

Ardent friendships between raging egotists were by no means rare in the Prussian officer corps. The sense of superiority within a military caste made it appear sophisticated to despise conventions which regulated commonplace lives. These relationships, though often striking a ludicrously high romantic note, were not necessarily homosexual in any physical sense. It is unlikely that, when together, the prince and Eulenburg indulged in practices which ran counter to the strict moral code of the day: each of them was so conscious of self that the gratification of mutual flattery outweighed any purely sensual pleasure. Eulenburg was delighted his future sovereign should address him by the familiar 'Du' and admire his musical and artistic talents; and William, who had been starved of praise in his boyhood, was so childishly pleased with Eulenburg's approbation that he willingly accepted from him criticism he would have resented from his mother and father, or indeed from Dona had she possessed the courage or the intelligence to offer it.

To the Bismarcks the significance of Eulenburg's favoured position with the prince was always political rather than moral. For, despite 'dear Phili's' avowed enthusiasm for music and the arts, they knew he held strong opinions on the conduct of government, and had the ability to impart them to William. The chancellor might question Eulenburg's judgement on matters of high policy and complain that he gave too much attention to 'gossip and scandal', but he could not dismiss Eulenburg as a fawning poseur. It was improbable he would seek high political office himself, but, with both an uncle and a cousin who served as ministers, he had strong family links with the Junker heartland of Prussia; and by now Bismarck had come to take him seriously.

These considerations assumed an immediate importance in the spring of 1887. Emperor William I, who celebrated his ninetieth birthday that March, was subject to fainting fits and it was clear he could not survive for long. The Bismarckian coalition of national liberal and conservative parties – the so-called 'Cartel' – had triumphed at the polls in February and thereby ensured that, should Fritz come to the throne in the near future, the chancellor had a comfortable parliamentary majority with which to combat the alleged 'Gladstonian' principles of his new sovereign. The Crown Prince, however, had been unwell since soon after the beginning of the year and by the middle of May it was suspected he was suffering from cancer of the throat. There was now a prospect that William's accession to the imperial throne would take place within a matter of months. 'The relentless course of world history is unexpectedly altered. Prince Wilhelm may be Kaiser at thirty. What will happen then?', wrote Friedrich von Holstein in his diary. 'God moves in a mysterious way.'[12]

William was deeply moved by the tragedy threatening his father, but he could not hide his excitement at the prospect of succeeding to the throne as a young man, and in consequence his behaviour was frequently in bad taste. Even before the end of May 1887 Herbert Bismarck was complaining that the prince, whom he had praised to his cronies in earlier years, was 'heartless, superficial, vain' and so lacking in human feelings that he seemed as cold as a block of ice. The elder Bismarck, on the other hand, was troubled, not so much over William's attitude to his father's illness as over his political impetuosity. In particular the chancellor distrusted the influence of Waldersee, now deputy chief of the General Staff. Waldersee, whom Bismarck knew to be establishing contact with army leaders in Austria-Hungary, did not bother to conceal his belief in an inevitable conflict between Germany and Russia; and it was disturbing that William, with his Potsdam subaltern mentality, should so often be his guest. Already Bismarck had been surprised by Willy's wild talk of military expeditions during visits to the Foreign Ministry. To have on the throne a young emperor, giving free rein to Waldersee and the unpredictable Eulenburg, was an alarming prospect for the seventy-two year old chancellor. A carefully worded article was inserted in the *Norddeutsche Rundschau*, one of the newspapers under Bismarck's control: it deplored Prince William's attendance at a luncheon in the Waldersees' Berlin apartments where speeches were made in support of a new militantly Protestant and anti-semitic popular movement. Never before had William been criticized in the 'respectable' press: he now accepted that the Waldersee circle represented a minority style in Berlin politics, and began to treat them with greater caution; but he resented the implied snub in the *Norddeutsche Rundschau*, and knew that Bismarck had inspired it.[13]

At first the Crown Prince received treatment from a team of German doctors and the British laryngologist, Morell Mackenzie, at his favourite residence in Potsdam, the Neues Palais, a mere two and a half miles from William and Dona at the Marble Palace. Mackenzie held out hopes of recovery, but was soon at loggerheads with the German specialists, who let William know of their disputes. By early June there were disturbing rumours in the capital. It was said – and vigorously denied by Bismarck – that the Crown Prince would renounce his right of succession in favour of his eldest son, since the German Empire could never be ruled by a sovereign whose verbal power of command was impaired. William himself put forward this thesis in conversation with Eulenburg, who did not however encourage him. Already William was thinking of his form of government: one of the chancellor's loyalest ministers was astonished when the prince, ignoring the fact that his grandfather and father still lived, blandly remarked that 'one would need Prince Bismarck desperately for some years to come, but then it would be possible to divide his functions up and the sovereign himself would take over more of them'. Berlin and Potsdam seemed full of would-be gravediggers eager to dispose of two generations of Hohenzollerns, men of tomorrow trying to calculate to a nicety the likely date of succession. William's maladroit tactlessness upset his mother and could not be kept from his father who, Vicky wrote in a letter to Windsor, was 'terribly annoyed at William wishing to come forward so much and take his place without asking him, etc.'.[14]

Despite his illness, Fritz planned to attend Victoria's Golden Jubilee celebrations on 21–22 June 1887; and he hoped, at the same time, to receive treatment for his diseased larynx from Mackenzie. There was an unpleasant scene at the Neues Palais when William told Vicky he had himself written to the Queen and informed her that he, rather than his father, would represent the German Emperor at the Jubilee. When Vicky insisted she and Fritz would make the journey, William thoughtlessly and angrily remarked that if Mackenzie was encouraging her to believe in his father's recovery, he was 'merely holding out false hopes'. Everything was done to dissuade the royal couple from crossing to England.

Vicky had her way. They left Berlin on 12 June, and Fritz was able to ride in the procession which escorted his mother-in-law from Buckingham Palace to Westminster Abbey. William and Dona were also present, having taken their five year old son 'little Willy' to meet his great-grandmother ('a dear little boy', she wrote in her journal). William found the service in the Abbey 'profoundly touching': 'That day gave us all an overwhelming impression of the power and extent of the British Empire', he recalled nearly forty years later. At the time, however, he was irritated by his lowly status on the seating plan of the Jubilee dinner, and he remained disagreeable for much of the visit.[15] His mother and father stayed another two months, mostly at Osborne and Balmoral, but the weather was damp and cold. In August they travelled to the Tyrol and on to Venice before wintering, first at Baveno on Lake Maggiore and, when the cold weather set in, at San Remo. Vicky was determined to keep Fritz away from Berlin until he recovered his strength. She did not attempt to understand the problems of an autocratic state in which the sovereign was old and frail while his sick heir was an absentee claimant. Inevitably, under these conditions, there were political intrigues which thrust William more and more to the centre of affairs. It was rumoured he had already drafted an Imperial Edict for despatch to the German princes on his accession.

Tales of her son's alleged machinations angered the Crown Princess. 'We wished William . . . out of the Berlin and Potsdam atmosphere, both socially and politically so bad for him, where he is flattered and spoilt, and makes the Emperor do everything he likes', she wrote to Victoria on 14 September.[16] He visited his parents at Baveno in October and at San Remo three weeks later. On the first occasion his consideration for the sick man pleased his mother, who was comforted by his presence; but at San Remo his mood was totally different, haughty, unapproachable and resentful. He had, so he announced, 'come to take matters into my own hands', with orders from the Emperor to make certain 'the right thing' was done. Subsequently the Crown Princess complained of his rudeness and impertinence, adding in a letter to Victoria that, 'I pitched into him with, I am afraid, considerable violence, and he became quite nice and gentle and amiable (for him)'. Yet, although William often lacked filial respect, not all the blame for family tension rested with him. In the third week of November the condition of William I was so bad that Bismarck arranged for William, as ultimate heir presumptive, to have the authority to sign state papers if the Emperor was incapacitated. The Imperial Order was sent to San Remo but withheld from the Crown Prince by his wife, who feared the decision might worsen his condition. This was an error: Fritz learnt of his eldest son's new responsibilities in a letter from William himself, handed to him by his son Henry. 'Fritz', wrote Vicky, 'was much upset, very angry and much excited . . . and said he would go instantly to Berlin.' But Christmas and the New Year passed, with the sad couple still at San Remo. Meanwhile, in Berlin, William was telling the British military attaché how much he admired England, and hoped Britain and Germany would together uphold the peace of Europe – 'You with a good fleet and we with our great army can do this', he declared. Lord Salisbury, the British prime minister, noted that already he was behaving as though he shaped German policy: it was not, Salisbury thought, an encouraging prospect.[17]

William I died on the morning of 9 March 1888. Emperor Frederick III left San Remo within twenty-four hours of his accession and travelled back to Berlin, thus setting foot in Germany for the first time in nine months. He was to reign a mere ninety-nine days. William – now, of course, Crown Prince – shed tears as he took his military oath to the new sovereign, and greeted him with deep emotion when the train from San Remo reached the capital. But his behaviour continued to shock many observers. He showed neither sympathy nor under-standing for his mother's constant distress. 'William fancies himself completely the Emperor – and an absolute and autocratic one', she wrote to Victoria in the second week of May; no one at court respected her wishes or looked upon her husband as more than 'a mere passing shadow, soon to be replaced by reality in the shape of William'. In her sorrow it is possible she exaggerated. Military details were handled by William with fussy efficiency: Queen Victoria herself was impressed by the guard of honour which he paraded before her when she came on a last visit to her beloved son-in-law; and William thought to please his father by arranging for the Guards to march past their Emperor at Charlottenburg, the poor man sitting upright in his carriage to take the salute. It was William, too, who arranged the transference of his father by canal and river from Charlottenburg to his favourite home, the Neues Palais in Potsdam.[18] But over non-military matters William remained boorish and obstinate. When, for example, it seemed as if Frederick was going to give his blessing at last to the marriage of his daughter 'Moretta' and Alexander of Battenberg, William vehemently opposed his father, throwing his support behind Bismarck, who was still hostile to the marriage project. On Bismarck's birthday William invited himself to dine in the chancellery and proposed a flamboyant toast to the chancellor, a 'standard bearer to whom forty-six million loyal German hearts turn with solicitude'.[19] No word was said of the special loyalty due to a stricken sovereign.

Emperor Frederick's strength began to decline rapidly in the second week of June. Even Vicky gave up hope of recovery. Exactly a year before, when they had visited London for the Jubilee, some private papers were brought for safety to Windsor. Now she was afraid others would fall into the hands of personal enemies. On Thursday, 14 June, when it was clear her husband could not live for many more hours, she received the British ambassador and entrusted him with confidential documents. The British military attaché left almost immediately for home and on the following Sunday duly handed over to Queen Victoria in Balmoral 'some papers, which Fritz had desired should be placed in my care'.* Among these documents were a personal journal and a will, ensuring his widow's financial independence of any settlement made by his successor.

These precautions were justified. William arrived from the Marble Palace between eleven o'clock and noon that Thursday, and joined the vigil around his father's bed. But while William remained in the palace his Guard regiment was preparing to seal off the park and its approaches. The Emperor Frederick died at a quarter past eleven on Friday morning, 15 June. By noon park and palace were under the control of William's officers. No one – not even a member of the royal family – was allowed in or out unless authorized by a signed permit. Every letter and parcel was examined by the military authorities, who also took charge of the telegraph office. William himself, in the red full-dress uniform of the Hussars, searched his parents' rooms with his sabre at the ready. It was more like a military *coup* than the succession of a son whose father's life had been cut short by such a tragic illness. Yet if, as the widowed Empress later maintained, William sought 'proof' of liberal plots against the constitution, he was disappointed. 'There is', he complained to Waldersee, 'nothing in writing to be seen, everything has been done away with.'[20] But, though he did not mention it to Waldersee, he found in a ransacked drawer the faded telegram sent from Windsor on that anxious January night twenty-nine years before: 'Is it a fine boy?.' It was a question to which there seemed no easy answer.

* It has sometimes been stated that the papers were entrusted to an American journalist, Inman Bernard, who was a friend of Mackenzie and who claimed to have received a parcel from the doctor in the Empress's presence. But it is far more probable that valuable papers would have been handed to the ambassador, who was fully entitled to convey documents between the sovereign to whom he was accredited and the sovereign whom he represented. The timing of the ambassador's visit – he was received by the Empress on the Thursday morning, *before* the arrival of William – and the subsequent movements of the military attaché suggest that this is what occurred. If Inman Bernard received a package from Mackenzie, it was possibly of less importance. Significantly William treated the British diplomats coolly for some weeks after his accession.

4. Chancellor and Kaiser

The reign of the new Kaiser began as it was to continue, with swagger and bombast. 'We are bound to each other – I and the army – we are born for each other, and we shall hold together indissolubly whether it be God's will to send us calm or storm', William declared in an accession proclamation of which he was himself the author. He promised to remember how 'from the world above the eyes of my forefathers are looking down on me' and how 'one day I shall stand accountable to them for the glory and honour of the army'. In London and Paris there was uneasiness that the Kaiser should have addressed himself, in the first instance, to the army rather than the people, but his choice of words caused no surprise in Berlin. A mood of militant camaraderie and Providential mission was characteristic of the Germany which Bismarck had made, though not of the chancellor himself. Young officers grown to manhood in the shadow of a unified Germany's limitless might were gratified at pledging loyalty to a sovereign who acknowledged God and the army as the source of authority. 'Everyone in the army is rejoicing over our new ruler', Waldersee noted in his journal. 'It is as if we had recovered from a serious malady and are now heading for happier days.'[1]

There was no long period of respectful mourning. When Queen Victoria commented, in pained surprise, on the excessive number of state functions undertaken by her grandson in the first weeks of his reign, she was told that 'State interest goes before personal feelings', an unaccustomed snub which angered her. At the accession ceremonies in the Berlin *Schloss*, during the last week of June, court pages wore bows of black crape around their knees, but there was otherwise no public reminder that Germany had lost two emperors in fifteen weeks. The most impressive occasion was a ceremony in the *Weisser Saal* when the Kaiser made his first appearance before representatives of the states which comprised the empire. The Knights of the Black Eagle were richly accoutred, the palace guard fitted out in the fashion of Frederick the Great's reign. William himself was resplendent in a newly designed crimson mantle, which he threw back dramatically before beginning his speech, a Siegfried *manqué*. Colonel von Moltke, forty-year-old nephew of the legendary Field-Marshal (who, at eighty-eight, himself took part in the ceremony), claimed in his memoirs that there had never been such a show of splendour in the *Weisser Saal*, and he may well have been right. Only Bismarck, who had been content with active service uniform when the Empire was proclaimed at Versailles in 1871, declined to dress up for this third scene in the imperial pageant.

To many observers the props and settings for William's star performances seemed excessively ostentatious. Emperor Frederick had been a sensitive critic of vulgarity, and his father austere and parsimonious – but not William II. He wished Berlin to reflect the glories of a German Reich fortunate enough to be ruled by the hereditary sovereign of Prussia. There was a purpose behind the bad theatricality. 'Our new young Kaiser', as veterans in government service patronizingly called him, had no accumulation of personal legend upon which to draw. Each of those Hohenzollern forefathers whose memory he readily invoked had seen the vicissitudes of a military campaign before ascending the throne. His two immediate predecessors were heroes in their own right: William I entered Paris on the heels of the great Napoleon in 1814 and received the surrender of the lesser Napoleon in 1870: Frederick made certain of victory at Königgrätz-Sadowa in 1866 and at Wörth four years later. By contrast war for William II was a matter of bulletins and triumphal processions. Everyone of the kings, grand dukes and princes within imperial Germany had more knowledge of war and high politics than had their Kaiser. Small wonder he stressed his importance by extravagant words and actions, nor that he asserted a possessive quality over 'my cavalry', 'my new gun', 'my Guards regiments' and, above all, 'my navy'. No doubt inner contradictions of personality, the egotism his will imposed upon an insecure diffidence, inclined him easily to strut and swagger, but that was also the mood of the militaristic society in which he flourished. By emphasizing a bond between his subjects and himself in the common, all-German experience of service in the armed forces, he was associating his person with the most revered institution in the Reich. So long as the German people were sensitive over national status and consciously

35

proud of the empire's strength, the bravado of a Supreme War Lord appealed to them more than cautious statesmanship. Had the young Kaiser required a vote of confidence in the months following his accession, there is little doubt the mass of his subjects would have given it to him decisively. Throughout the first half of his reign he continued to express – and, indeed, to amplify – the sentiments and prejudices with which they looked out upon the world.

There was, of course, no constitutional provision for any such reference back to the people. The German constitution of 1871 was a cumbersome document, an expedient designed by Bismarck to perpetuate the partnership he had achieved with William I in the eight years since he became Prussia's chief minister. The constitutional position of both the Kaiser and his chancellor was extremely peculiar and ill-defined. Basically the empire was a federal union of allied states, with representative assemblies of their own but sending delegates to a federal council (*Bundesrat*) and deputies elected by universal male suffrage to a parliament (*Reichstag*) in Berlin. Article XI of the constitution declared that 'the presidency of the union belongs to the King of Prussia who shall, in this capacity, be termed German Emperor' (*deutscher Kaiser*). There could be no sacred ritual of coronation for the Kaiser as there was for a Tsar of All the Russias, if only because there was no imperial crown. Once at least, in March 1897, William II complained petulantly to his chancellor, 'The Kaiser has no rights'. Strictly speaking, this was nonsense: he was a quasi-autocrat; the only limitations on his sovereign authority were the need for imperial decrees to carry, beside his signature, the signature of the chancellor (who, so the constitution declared ambiguously, 'thereby undertakes responsibility'), and the obligation to respect the rights of the lesser monarchs and princes within the federalized empire. Otherwise the Kaiser enjoyed all the powers normally assigned to a head of state, together with the right to summon and dissolve the Bundesrat and the Reichstag, the right to propose legislation, and – most important of all – the right to appoint or dismiss every minister, from the chancellor downwards. Moreover, William enjoyed additional authority as king of the largest state within the imperial federation, for in Prussia the supremacy of the crown had never been effectively challenged and the Prussian representative assembly (*Landtag*) was elected on a three-tier voting system which favoured the Junker landowning minority. The Prussian kings traditionally looked for advice to military secretariats and civil secretariats, which were not part of the government, but whose nominated chiefs considerably influenced policy, independent of ministerial decisions. These two secretariats, though never recognized by any constitution, continued to tender advice to the sovereign in his imperial capacity as well as in his role as King of Prussia. William II appointed his friend General von Hahnke as chief of the military secretariat at his accession, and a year later he created a naval secretariat whose chief would enjoy equal status with General Hahnke and his successors. Technically, the Kaiser thus had ready to hand the structure of an autocracy if, as seemed probable, the constitution of 1871 proved unworkable for a new generation. 'In Prussia', Bismarck had long ago told Napoleon III, 'it is only the kings who make revolution.' Since the sovereign was left to create and define the imperial role himself, there was no reason why a kaiser should not continue the revolutions from above which the kings began before them.

At first Bismarck saw no threat from William's autocratic tendencies, although he was irritated and alarmed by the Kaiser's public style. The 1871 Constitution ensured that the chancellor's powers over foreign policy and domestic legislation were left independent of control so long as he retained the confidence of the emperor. He could initiate debates in the Bundesrat and the Reichstag, address either assembly whenever he chose, propose laws, and ignore any votes that went against him. Every imperial institution in government was an offshoot of the chancellor's office, rather than, as in most countries, a 'ministry' in its own right. His privileges as Prussian chief minister were no less extensive, although geographically limited by the boundaries of the kingdom. For seventeen years he had enjoyed an authority vested in no other statesman of Europe. It seemed inconceivable that the inexperienced William II would wish to rule rather than strike heroic attitudes. The constitution Bismarck had given Germany made no allowance for an emperor who asserted himself.

A warning note was sounded within three weeks of William's accession.[2] At the beginning of July the Kaiser consulted the director of naval construction over shipbuilding plans without first informing the Chief of the Admiralty, General von Caprivi. When Caprivi, in protest, tendered his resignation, it was accepted: ministers had to learn their new master was a man of such talents that he would probe into any aspect of government which happened to interest him. But Bismarck was not troubled by the Caprivi episode. It was obvious William had an obsession about the navy: neither his grandfather nor his father had ever bothered to wear naval uniform; but on 14 July – a month after his accession and a mere nine days after Caprivi's dismissal – the Kaiser, in his capacity as Admiral of the German Fleet, was at Kiel where twenty-four vessels sailed past the imperial yacht in the first of many naval reviews. Playing with warships, however, seemed to Bismarck a harmless diversion for the young man. While the Kaiser led his squadron to St Petersburg, Stockholm and Copenhagen, the chancellor retired to his estate at Friedrichsruh. Government officials, businessmen, German diplomats, foreign ambassadors could visit him when they wished: the main railway from Berlin to Hamburg went by the borders of the estate. Even the Kaiser broke his journey there when the fleet was safely back at Kiel: so considerate and generous, commented Bismarck to his family with serene satisfaction.

'I shall give the old man six months to get his breath back and then I shall reign myself', William remarked on returning to Berlin. Yet, as often in these early years, his imagination sought to speed the passage of events. Six months later the political scene was much the same: firm government by Bismarck, exercised mostly through remote control; restless activity by his imperial and royal master, who was delighted by star-billing not only in the German cities but in Vienna and Rome as well. William greeted the New Year of 1889 with a telegram to the chancellor rejoicing that 'you are still at my right hand' and hoping 'it will long be permitted for me to work with you'. A new imperial train – twelve pullman coaches, glistening with gold, blue and cream paint – was constructed in order to convey William and Dona in the style to which he believed they should be accustomed; William I had been content with ordinary first-class carriages. The Kaiser informed his entourage that henceforth cruises in the imperial yacht *Hohenzollern* would find a regular place in the court calendar, despite the fact that he personally was a poor sailor. 'If he were never sea-sick', sighed one land-lubber in his suite, 'we would *always* be on the water.'[3] The wits in Berlin began to call him '*der reise Kaiser*' ('the travelling emperor'), an appellation he enjoyed.

There was, however, one cloud over these 'honeymoon days' of the reign. Relations between the Kaiser and his English relatives began to deteriorate at the Emperor Frederick's funeral. They were worsened by a strange incident in Vienna, where William insisted he should be spared the embarrassment of meeting his uncle, the Prince of Wales, who was on a private visit to Austria at the time. Some of the blame for this coolness undoubtedly rested with the Prince, who had spoken indiscreetly to Herbert Bismarck and who, while on holiday in Hungary, barely troubled to conceal his contempt for the pretensions of 'William the Great'. Yet the Germans too, bore responsibility: the Kaiser's treatment of his mother and his scant regard for the conventions of court mourning rankled in London; and there were several members of his foreign service who mischievously fanned old grievances and suspicion. Queen Victoria – by no means uncritical of the Prince of Wales – was nevertheless indignant with William, whom she described to her prime minister (Lord Salisbury) as 'a hot-headed, conceited, and wrong-headed young man, devoid of all feeling'.[4] Salisbury had no liking for the Kaiser, nor indeed for the Bismarcks. Privately he told the Prince of Wales, after careful reflection, that he thought William 'a little off his head', but he hoped his excitable behaviour would not affect Anglo-German relations. If he wished to pay a state visit to his grandmother in the summer of 1889, Salisbury argued that every effort should be made to smother his resentment with courtesies. It was agreed, in June, that the Queen should confer on her eldest grandson the rank of Admiral of the Fleet in the Royal Navy.

This honour delighted William. Pleasure and excitement ran away with his pen. 'Fancy wearing the same uniform as St Vincent and Nelson; it is enough to make one quite giddy', he wrote in a letter to the British ambassador, which was forwarded to Balmoral; and he continued – less happily, perhaps – 'I feel something like Macbeth must have felt when he was suddenly received by the witches with the cry of "All hail, who art Thane of Glamis and of Cawdor too"'.[5] He arrived in the *Hohenzollern* off Cowes on 2 August, with an escort of twelve German warships, and spent five days making himself agreeable to his grandmother, who easily succumbed once more to his charm. The visit coincided with Cowes Regatta, which greatly interested William, who was proposed as a member of the Royal Yacht Squadron by the Prince of Wales. The combination of his new naval rank, the delights of 'that dear old home at Osborne', and the whole ritual of the regatta fascinated him: to the Prince of Wales's dismay, he made a practice of keeping his engagements in early August free for the next six years, so that he could race at Cowes and wear, for a few evenings, the uniform of St Vincent and Nelson.

Lord Salisbury believed the Kaiser's visit had restored good relations between the two countries. Nobody expected he would take his honorific rank in the Royal Navy seriously, but within a few days of his return to Germany he was writing to the Queen of his pleasure at being 'able to feel and take interest in your fleet as if it were my own'. 'Should the Will of Providence', he added, 'lay the heavy burden on us of fighting for our homes and destinies, then may the British fleet be seen forging ahead side by side with the German, and the "Red Coat" marching to victory with the "Pomeranian Grenadier"!' Such sentiments were no doubt excusable as he was writing from Bayreuth, where apocalyptic visions lay readily to hand: more surprising were two telegrams, sent within three weeks of each other, informing the Queen that he had inspected her Channel Squadron at Kiel ('ships in perfect order and trim') and her Mediterranean Squadron in Phaleron Bay 1300 miles away ('ships in excellent order'). In a conversation with the Prince of Wales in Athens William commented on the 'dangerously low' strength of the Royal Navy in the Mediterranean, and he offered to send the commander-in-chief a plan which would enable the fleet to be concentrated more effectively against any threat from the French. He was courteously thanked for his solicitude: the fleet remained, for the present, where it was.[6]

William's energy that year was remarkable. In the last six months of 1889 he received in Berlin the Shah of Persia and the Tsar of Russia, visited Queen Victoria, King Umberto of Italy (twice), the Sultan of Turkey at Constantinople, and attended the wedding of his sister, Sophie, to Crown Prince Constantine in Athens. He cruised off the Norwegian coast, spent some days in Venice and Corfu, hunted in East Prussia and Bavaria, shot pheasants in Silesia, attended the autumn manoeuvres, inspected the cavalry at Hanover and the German navy on at least four occasions, paid state visits to Dresden, Stuttgart, Darmstadt, Wörms and Frankfurt-am-Main, delivered six jaunty Sunday sermons on the imperial yacht, and found time to select half a dozen hats as a present for Dona, whose dress sense he considered inferior to his own. Some government officials complained he did not trouble to read the detailed reports they drew up for him: and Baron Holstein was intrigued to find it was the Kaiser's practice to have thirty to forty newspaper cuttings submitted to him which he would then read and annotate rather than study the press himself. He liked to reign at the double. To the irritation of his suite, he seemed never to relax. Each morning before breakfast he conducted a vigorous session of physical training whenever the imperial yacht was at sea; and he was constantly chivvying his wife and children – no lingering over meals for them. On the day after his departure from Cowes, Queen Victoria wrote thankfully in her journal of the delights of a quiet breakfast with only a daughter and son-in-law at table: 'All such a contrast to the great crowd of people and bustle.'[7]

One at least of the Kaiser's friends recognized that this endless desire for action and movement reflected an inner nervous uncertainty. 'I beseech your Majesty', wrote Eulenburg at the end of September, 'not to work beyond all reason and live so restless a life. My nerves were once what Your Majesty's are now. . . . Prohibitive measures are the only right ones – the pace of your life must be reduced as far as is possible.' The advice was sound but it was not heeded. William could no more control his restlessness than hold in check his verbal indiscretions. Yet, provided Eulenburg chose his words so as to flatter his master, he might offer criticism which no minister or court functionary dared make. Only Eulenburg could have praised the Kaiser's eloquence and then suggested that were he 'more economical of such a gift, it would be a hundredfold more efficacious'. To speak on every occasion, Eulenburg added, was to squander 'so fine a talent'.[8]

Bismarck did not wrap criticism so felicitously. Relations between the chancellor and his sovereign became strained in the spring of 1889. Subsequently there was never any genuine reconciliation. At first they differed mainly over foreign affairs. The Kaiser accepted the view of his chief of the General Staff, Waldersee, and the younger officers that Russia was a potential menace to the security of the Prussian heartland. He was alarmed by military intelligence reports of railway construction in Russian Poland and of revised plans for the disposition of the Tsar's army along the Russo-German frontier. Bismarck refused to believe in this particular bogey: for nearly thirty years he had made friendship with Russia a cornerstone of his policy. In June 1887, just twelve months before William's accession, he signed the secret three-year agreement known as the Reinsurance Treaty, an improvised understanding by which Russia and Germany pledged themselves to remain neutral in any major war unless Russia attacked Austria-Hungary or Germany attacked France. It was basically a negative safeguard, but at least it ensured peaceful continuity in Russo-German relations. The chancellor had no intention of allowing Waldersee to undo the work of thirty years by stampeding William into hostility to Russia as a means of bolstering his dependence on the army chiefs. Throughout the summer of 1889 Bismarck encouraged a press campaign to weaken public confidence in the chief of the General Staff and to discredit his judgement in the eyes of the Kaiser. This campaign was only partially successful; Bismarck did not appreciate that Baron Holstein and other senior diplomats thought he was by now out of touch. They, like Waldersee, believed it was in Germany's interest to fight a preventive war in the east rather than risk a later and longer conflict timed to begin at Russia's convenience. Bismarck did not destroy Waldersee's influence, nor dispel the Kaiser's suspicion of Russia. There were two further disputes later that summer, linked to the central problem of Russo-German relations: and on both occasions the Kaiser, reflecting the views of Waldersee and Holstein, opposed Bismarck and the so-called 'pro-Russians'. 'If Bismarck won't go along with us against the Russians', William remarked to his ambassador to Turkey, 'then our ways must part.'[9] For the moment it suited Bismarck to 'go along' at least part of the way; and German investors were dissuaded from purchasing Russian bonds. But it was clear to the chancellor that, if he was to curb the impetuosity of the younger generation, he needed to make certain that William II was dependent on the Bismarck family as William I had been in the early years of his reign. A nice little crisis, in which the old illusionist could display his political skills, would help.

Not, however, a crisis which threatened foreign war. That device he had tried several times, most recently on the eve of the Reichstag election in February 1887 when a sensational newspaper article on the possibility of a surprise attack by the French duly rallied the electorate behind the Cartel (*Kartell*), the pro-Bismarckian coalition. Unfortunately this particular war scare had helped the army leaders, especially Waldersee, to strengthen their hold on policy making. The chancellor had no wish to play again into Waldersee's hands. Moreover William II's mercurial temperament might well inflate an artificial emergency until it burst into open conflict. It was safer to propel the Kaiser into a dispute over internal affairs, a confrontation with the Reichstag in which the sovereign would need all his chancellor's experience to save him from disaster.

Yet over home policy, too, there was a generation gap between the two men. Bismarck was a countryman, a landowner: he accepted a degree of social responsibility for the industrial workers, as he did for peasants on his estate, and he proposed insurance schemes and old age pensions which were far ahead of state welfare programmes in the other industrialized nations. But he did not believe in limiting hours of work on humanitarian grounds, for men, women or children. If a family wished to earn more money they were entitled to work more hours in order to acquire it, and he would not support legislation intended to restrain the employers' right to determine the length of a working day: German industrial workers in 1888 had, on average, a sixty-three-hour week compared with the fifty-two-hour week of the British industrial worker. Kaiser William II reached manhood during the years of Germany's most rapid industrialization: industrial production doubled between his thirteenth and twenty-third birthdays, and was still accelerating at his accession. He had little idea of living conditions in the slums and tenements of Berlin, north and east of the Alexanderplatz, but he had at least visited factories and mines as part of Hinzpeter's programme of education, and he was more sympathetic than Bismarck to a limitation in hours of work.

There was a significant incident on Tuesday, 14 May 1889: the Kaiser, brushing aside all constitutional convention, came in person to impose his wishes on a Prussian ministerial council meeting under Bismarck's presidency. That spring the Ruhr coalfields were paralysed by a strike which threatened industry throughout Westphalia. Bismarck did not plan to intervene on one side or the other. He was convinced misery and hunger would soon force the miners to accept the conditions of work which the mineowners laid down. But there was in William's character a lingering humanitarian sentiment, a sympathy with the working-class millions, which owed more than he admitted to his mother's social conscience. As usual, he cloaked his feelings with a clumsy display of militarism, bursting into the ministerial council wearing his Hussar's uniform with spurs and sword and ordering the ministers to settle the Ruhr dispute, speedily and fairly. By the end of the week the miners had won and the strike was over. To the workers it seemed a notable success in a country where trade unions were still in their infancy. Bismarck was left doubly uneasy: industrial bargaining was, to him, an alien and dangerous concept; and he regarded the Kaiser's intervention as an ominous precedent. Privately to his family he admitted that he feared the young emperor was resolved to rule as well as reign.[10]

The conflict between chancellor and Kaiser was postponed until after the end of the year. Bismarck was content to play for time:

elections for the Reichstag were due early in 1890 and could give him the opportunity to appear indispensable to an inexperienced ruler. During the summer and autumn of 1889 an anti-Bismarck faction became clearly defined at court and in Berlin. It included Holstein, Eulenburg and Waldersee and it received support from the most influential of the German princes, Grand Duke Frederick of Baden, who was the Kaiser's uncle by marriage. The Grand Duke's envoy in Berlin, Adolf Marschall von Bieberstein, had regular access to the Kaiser's presence and soon became a friend and political intimate of the other members of the faction. Their fear was that the Kaiser would act rashly and oust Bismarck prematurely. Popular sympathy would then be on the side of the fallen chancellor. The 'Kaiser's Friends' – as the faction might well be termed – sought to hold their ruler in check. They were eager for Bismarck to become politically isolated from other members of the government: a mass resignation of chancellor, imperial state-secretaries and Prussian ministers would alarm the nation as a whole and make foreign capitals uneasy. Ideally, Bismarck should be seen to slide from office, not fall dramatically.[11]

He remained on his estates at Friedrichsruh and Varzin for most of the seven months which followed settlement of the miners' strike. A combination of absentee chancellor and travelling emperor did not make for firm or consistent government and placed a heavy strain on ministers and officials. The two were together in Berlin for a mere ten days during these seven months, and much of that brief period – in October – was occupied with Tsar Alexander III's state visit. Back at Friedrichsruh, Bismarck gave most of his attention to foreign affairs, but he also began to prepare for the Reichstag election. He wished to appear as a defender of home and family against red revolution: he proposed, even before the election, to introduce an anti-socialist law which would have permitted the authorities to send dangerous agitators into exile. If such a measure was unacceptable to the more liberal members of the pro-government 'Cartel', so much the worse for them: he would collaborate with the right-wing parties, notably the Roman Catholic Centre Party, and let the old Cartel die a natural death.

The Kaiser too was giving thought to the coming election and to the social question. In October, before he left Berlin for the Mediterranean, the official gazette published a statement that 'His Imperial Majesty' gave unreserved support to the Cartel coalition. In private conversation he made it clear he wished the government to propose factory reforms. After his return from the east, in the third week of November, he began to sound out his old tutor, Hinzpeter, on the type of labour legislation which would best safeguard women and children against the more blatant forms of exploitation. There seems, at this stage, to have been a curious muddle in Berlin, or possibly at Friedrichsruh. Heinrich von Bötticher, who was Reich State-Secretary for the Interior and technically deputy chancellor, prepared a memorandum for Bismarck which never reached the old man's desk. At all events, the chancellor knew nothing of the Kaiser's enthusiasm for labour legislation until the end of the first week in January, when Bötticher travelled to Friedrichsruh to bring him up to date with events in the capital. Bismarck should have been put on the alert by a passage inserted by the Kaiser in his customary New Year's message of greeting. For, while rejoicing at 'our success' in preserving peace in Europe, William went out of his way to mention 'the welfare of the working population' as a topic 'particularly close to my heart'. But Bismarck no longer studied imperial messages as though they were holy script, and he missed the significance of the Kaiser's remark, if he bothered to read it at all.[12]

Bötticher's news irritated him. Labour concessions of this kind would lead to more and more demands from the workers and increase the vote of the Social Democrats rather than diminish it. 'Humanitarian humbug', he growled; and complained that the Kaiser listened too readily to irresponsible idealists, like old Hinzpeter. Bismarck refused to leave Friedrichsruh, he refused to identify himself with the Cartel in the coming election campaign, he refused to offer unsolicited advice to his headstrong sovereign. Not until 23 January, when he received a telegram summoning him to a Crown Council convened by the Kaiser for the following evening, did Bismarck decide to return to the capital.

William, on the other hand, used the first three weeks of the year sensibly. A close friend of Baron Holstein, Franz Fischer, was commissioned to prepare a memorandum on labour problems, making use of his specialist knowledge of the mining industry. At the same time Holstein appointed Paul Kayser, a legal expert working in the Foreign Ministry, to draft a report on the social question in general. Both these documents were ready by the middle of January: they were read by Holstein, by Eulenburg (who had long known Kayser and been

45

'crammed' by him for the diplomatic service) and almost certainly by Marschall, who records in his diary that he discussed labour relations with Holstein and Kayser at the Foreign Ministry. This specialist knowledge was therefore available to William before he summoned the Crown Council of 24 January: and he was able to confront Bismarck and the Prussian ministers with a detailed mastery of the subject which gave the lie to the chancellor's jibes at the amateur enthusiasm he had picked up from 'that dilettante muddler', Hinzpeter.

The Crown Council marked the opening of eight weeks of political drama, most of it performed away from the public eye.[13] The Kaiser informed the Council he wished to celebrate his thirty-first birthday, on 27 January, with the publication of two proclamations: one would promise new laws to protect working men and women and limit their hours of labour; the other would summon an international conference to Berlin where delegates could discuss methods of improving labour conditions throughout the continent. William spoke movingly of the exploitation of workers by thoughtless industrialists; he was convinced the omissions of the bosses rather than the will of good, loyal, German workers were responsible for the dangerous growth of socialism in the Reich, and he asked Bismarck to drop the clause in the proposed anti-socialist bill which would have expelled agitators from the country. The chancellor was unimpressed. He did not object to the proclamations, although he wished to rephrase certain passages, but he would not amend the anti-socialist bill. If, as seemed certain, it was rejected in the Reichstag, then he would introduce tougher measures after the election. It was folly to attempt to conciliate the workers: the Kaiser should risk social unrest now, rather than in a few years time, when it would pose a greater threat to the stability of the Reich. Should his fellow ministers accept the Kaiser's views over the anti-socialist bill, Bismarck concluded, he would resign as chancellor and as head of the Prussian government. He was safe. Each minister dutifully supported him. William, it seemed, had lost the first round.

'These ministers are not *my* ministers', he complained after the Crown Council, 'they are Prince Bismarck's ministers.' But Holstein was ready with advice: 'the Kaiser ... was right not to let the Chancellor go yet', he told Eulenburg, and he thought it would be beneficial if the Kaiser began to cultivate the Prussian ministers individually, receiving them in audience once a week or once a fortnight in order to hear their views and encouraging them to send written reports directly to him rather than to Bismarck as chancellor.[14] The great problem, however, for all the 'Kaiser's Friends' was to find a successor to head the government, if William again provoked an offer of resignation from the old man. The obvious candidate for the chancellorship was Waldersee, whose ambitions Bismarck had long distrusted. But politically Waldersee was short-sighted. He did not, at heart, sympathize with the Kaiser's interest in social reform, and he told Holstein that he thought Germany's future was prejudiced by schemes which promised the worker worldly pleasure rather than calling him to religion – 'Why are there no social democrats among the Moslems? It is because those people believe in a hereafter', he remarked. 'I don't think he has a good mind after all', Holstein confessed in a letter to Eulenburg, 'I wouldn't be surprised if he did not soon lose credit with the sharp-witted Kaiser. ... Then who?'[15]

The answer seems to have come first from another of the 'Kaiser's Friends'. On 29 January Marschall informed the Grand Duke of Baden that the next chancellor would be General Caprivi. Three days later the Kaiser summoned Caprivi, who was on garrison duty in Hanover, to the palace and told him confidentially that he was considering him as a possible successor to Bismarck. Caprivi's resignation from the Admiralty had convinced William he was a man of principle who respected constitutional form as well as being a sensible soldier, dutiful and loyal. He was genuinely unwilling to regard himself as a candidate for the succession, but was ready, as ever, to carry out his sovereign's commission. William could now, if he wished, call Bismarck's resignation bluff. The chancellor did not realize that he was no longer indispensable.

Throughout February there was an air of political uncertainty in the capital. The anti-socialist bill was defeated in the Reichstag, and difficulties in drafting the labour proclamations made it impossible for them to be published until a week after the Kaiser's birthday. Outwardly William made himself agreeable to the Bismarcks, father and son. It began to look as if the storm might blow over, as in April. But any chance of reconciliation was ruined by the Reichstag election on 20 February. The Roman Catholic Centre, led by the redoubtable Windthorst, emerged as the largest single party, with more than a quarter of the total seats in the chamber. The Bismarckian Conservatives had thirteen less seats than the Centre; and the National Liberals, who had backed the Cartel until the introduction of the latest anti-socialist bill, lost heavily. Only a skilled and experienced politician could secure the passage of legislation through a Reichstag in which supporters of the government were technically in a minority; and Bismarck accordingly believed the results of the election strengthened his position. In fact, they weakened it. The Kaiser was easily persuaded that the chancellor wished to govern by means of a compromise worked out with the Centre Party. To Eulenburg, to Waldersee, even to the unpolitical Dona, this implied Rome rule. The prospect stirred William's latent Protestant prejudices. News that Bismarck's banker had arranged for Windthorst to call at the chancellery convinced William the old man was ready to sell out to 'Jews and Jesuits'.[16]

On the eve of the election Bismarck discovered that the ministers were in contact with William directly. He resented this innovation in procedure: it was to him akin to treachery, and on 21 February he ordered a detailed search to be made through the government departments for a Prussian royal edict of 1852 which denied ministers individual and direct access to their sovereign. No one remembered the regulation, and it took more than forty-eight hours to find it. At first Bismarck hesitated over invoking its terms, but a week later (on 2 March) he formally read the Cabinet Order of 1852 to the ministers gathered in Council. He demanded that henceforth they should only discuss political business with William in his presence. It was now the Kaiser's turn to be incensed. He was already suspicious of Bismarck, for the chancellor had failed to co-operate in the arrangements for the international conference over labour conditions. In audience on 5 March Bismarck found the Kaiser so angry that he offered to drop the anti-socialist bill: it was the first clear sign the chancellor was slipping from power. Had he offered to resign that day, it would have been accepted; but still he held on.

It was, indirectly, Grand Duke Frederick of Baden who gave the final push.[17] On Monday, 11 March, the Grand Duke came to Berlin and visited the War Ministry. There he learnt from Waldersee, and from the minister himself, there was a possibility Bismarck might seek help from the army in a lightning move against socialist agitators throughout the Reich. This tale of a military *coup d'état* was passed on to Marschall, to Holstein and eventually to Eulenburg. Inevitably it became magnified, as were so many reports and rumours in Berlin during these days. Ultimately the Kaiser learnt of the possible *coup* from Eulenburg on the evening of 14 March, only a few hours after he had been informed of the political talks between Bismarck and Windthorst. He determined to provoke Bismarck into resignation as soon as possible.

There followed, on the morning of Saturday, 15 March, the famous melodramatic interview between Kaiser and chancellor. William began by asking Bismarck why he had seen Windthorst without his permission and he demanded cancellation of the 1852 Cabinet Order. The chancellor explained how difficult it would be to control an administration in which ministers regularly had direct access to their sovereign, who could discuss policy with him independent of the responsible head of government. But William was not to be placated. He believed Bismarck was trying to conceal some documents from him. Picking one up, he noticed on it a remark by the Tsar about himself – 'an ill-bred and dishonest boy'. William abruptly returned to the palace, having once more asked for the Cabinet Order to be withdrawn. No formal demand was made for Bismarck's resignation.

That afternoon Waldersee was received in audience. His journal makes it clear he believed he was giving the final blow to Bismarck's tenure of office: after listing the alleged weaknesses in the chancellor's attitude towards Russia, he formally recommended the Kaiser to dismiss him. On Sunday, as though following up Waldersee's remarks, detailed reports arrived from the Foreign Ministry which proved that the Russians were completing elaborate military preparations along their frontier. Now William could convince himself he was getting rid of Bismarck not simply over home affairs, but because his statesmanship no longer showed that masterful grip which had made Germany the leading power in Europe. 'You should have drawn my attention long ago to this terrible danger', the Kaiser wrote in one last hurried note to his veteran chancellor that evening.

William assumed he would have a letter of resignation from Bismarck during Monday. Twice General Hahnke was sent to see what was happening in the chancellery. There was no response. The inactivity worried William. He dined that evening with Eulenburg, his nerves on edge. 'Now you must sing so that we may clear our heads and think of other things', he told Phili. They crossed to the piano: Eulenburg sang, accompanying himself as William turned the sheets of music. Suddenly he was interrupted by the arrival of an adjutant. Hahnke reported that the letter of resignation was on its way: 'The Kaiser', Eulenburg recalled twenty years later, 'sat down again by the piano, whispered to me "It is all right" – and we went on singing.'[18]

5. Officer of the Watch

News of the change of chancellor was made public in Berlin on the evening of Thursday, 20 March 1890. William feared that Bismarck's resignation would cause widespread alarm in Germany and he was eager to stress a continuity in government and policy. On Saturday morning the principal newspaper in Weimar printed a reassuring message from the Kaiser to his subjects: 'The position of officer of the watch on the ship of state has fallen to me. The course remains the same. Full steam ahead.' These words were taken up by the press at home and abroad. A week later they inspired *Punch*'s famous visual comment on Bismarck's fall, 'Dropping the Pilot', and the salty tang of the Kaiser's metaphor went faithfully into the history books.

Another London periodical, *The Spectator*, was gloomier than *Punch*: the chief flywheel had been removed from the machinery of European diplomacy, it declared on 29 March, and added that if there was no crash, thanks should be offered to Providence rather than to the engineers.[1] Yet comment within Germany was less portentous, partly because the change in chancellor was seen primarily as an episode in domestic politics. There was little excitement. The German people were content with the order to 'steam ahead': they had been so doing for two generations. But should the course remain the same? The great commercial centres wanted tariffs eased in order to stimulate exports: they resented the care which Bismarck in his later years lavished on protecting Prussian agrarian interests. The workers, too, were puzzled. Was the unpopular anti-socialist law dropped with the pilot? Many had welcomed William's claim to defend labour from exploitation: it remained to be seen if a new chancellor could convert expressions of imperial grace into genuine and effective reforms. No doubt it was encouraging for forty-nine million Germans to think of their young emperor as officer of the watch, but some might well wonder who was in the chartroom.

The Kaiser sensed this mood when he visited Bremen on 21 April. That evening he dined as a guest of the *Nord-Deutscher Lloyd* Line in the pride of their passenger fleet, the *Fulda*, at Bremerhaven. It was a big occasion and inevitably his fellow guests (who included the fallen chancellor's second son) were treated to a speech filled with seafaring reminiscence. He recalled his first naval exercises in the Baltic. The imperial yacht, *Hohenzollern*, was leading the squadron through dense fog when it became necessary to alter course. Although doubts arose over the wisdom of this manoeuvre, the change was made: an hour later 'we were sailing with a fresh wind, a calm sea and a blue sky'. Then, he continued, 'we turned our eyes back to the fog bank and suddenly, high in the sky, as though borne by the hands of a cherubim, the German ensign floated onwards through the clouds'. It was, he explained, the admiral's flag on the main mast of the foremost warship still wrapt in mist below, but the sight was so impressive that all on the bridge 'involuntarily clicked their heels'. Soon the 'entire squadron emerged from the fog in perfect order, sailing upon the new course'.[2] The moral was clear: the German people could be certain of leaving in their wake all the fogs of the moment and, 'pressing onward, succeed in reaching our goal' – a haven which, it is interesting to note, invariably remained unspecified in these flights of nautical rhetoric.

Although his imagery seems jaded, the Kaiser's speech was well received. It now became fashionable to refer to the 'new course' set for Germany when Bismarck was dismissed. Nothing more was heard of the anti-socialist law, and in the late spring two measures designed to protect labour were placed before the Reichstag. William, however, was not a reforming emperor: he preferred stability to change. When he received Bismarck's letter of resignation, he still hoped to retain every other minister in the government. He made several attempts to dissuade Herbert von Bismarck from accompanying his father into the political wilderness. But Herbert had too much pride of family – and too many enemies – to welcome a prospect of serving under his father's successor. He, too, left Berlin and a non-Prussian, Marschall von Bieberstein, took his place at the Foreign Ministry. Otherwise the ministers remained in the posts which they had held under the old administration.

General von Caprivi, the new chancellor and chief minister in

Prussia, was a fifty-nine year old bachelor. He lacked political experience but possessed qualities which, in a parliamentary monarchy, would have made him a sound and reliable premier. From his father, a much-respected judge, he inherited a lawyer's gift of rapidly grasping the essentials of an unfamiliar problem. Politically he was a moderate, a neutral who was on amicable terms with the various party leaders. He did not come from a Prussian Junker family: the Caprivis originated in Carniola and exchanged Habsburg for Hohenzollern service when Frederick the Great annexed Silesia, where they had long held land. The general was a dutiful professional soldier who did not smoke and hardly drank, and he was not interested in acquiring money or estates. Fortunately he was a man of common sense, with a wry gift of ironic humour which saved him from the scars of disillusionment. He had long known that whoever tried to follow Bismarck would be criticized and ridiculed: 'It was clear to me that the person responsible for changing on to a different course would suffer for it, but this was no argument against undertaking it', he wrote nearly five years later.[3] At the time he remarked to some friends that he did not expect to remain chancellor for long.

Caprivi's appointment caused widespread surprise. Prince Henry refused to believe the press announcement: he thought the editors had got it all wrong, for he was convinced his brother would make Waldersee chancellor, while Caprivi would succeed him as chief of the General Staff. But if Waldersee had political ambitions, they were not immediate ones: 'I would be a fool to busy my mind with thoughts of the chancellorship', he wrote in his diary on 14 February, 'I shall stick to my old plan: first, at least one successor to Bismarck must ruin himself; then perhaps I might be persuaded.' Yet Waldersee, as his printed journal shows, was a poor judge of men and events. His confidence in his own position was shaken by an incident which occurred at the height of the resignation crisis: Waldersee criticized the Kaiser's proposed solution of a tactical problem which the General Staff had prepared as a military exercise, and he was surprised to find that William resented his remarks. Although there was an outward reconciliation, the embers of friendship between the two men merely smouldered fitfully. Caustic comments on the young ruler began to appear in Waldersee's diary: he was only interested in the navy; he humiliated senior commanders in front of junior officers; 'he literally pants for applause, liking nothing better than crowds who are yelling out

"Hurrah"'.[4] Many of these criticisms were echoed several times over by both ministers and generals in the next twenty-five years, but not by men who believed, as did Waldersee, that William would soon be looking to them as political saviours of the empire.

A slightly absurd episode in the autumn destroyed Waldersee's standing in William's eyes. Manoeuvres that September were held in Silesia and were attended by Francis Joseph and an impressive retinue of Habsburg dignitaries. Suddenly on the second day William assumed personal command of VI Corps, which he had not realized was intended by Waldersee to be the defeated force. Everything ordered by the Kaiser to improve the situation made its position more desperate, and he eventually finished up with his two divisions on opposite banks of the river Neisse, unable to support each other. William was angry at being made to look ridiculous in front of distinguished foreign observers, and he blamed Waldersee for allowing him to lose.[5] It was, he complained, even worse behaviour than he had shown over the military exercise in March. Immediately William began to look for a suitable command for Waldersee and, at the beginning of February 1891, he was succeeded as chief of the General Staff by Count Alfred von Schlieffen, a soldier with no political ambitions whatsoever. The Kaiser appointed Waldersee commanding general in Altona in the hope, as he remarked, that he would keep an eye on troublemakers in Hamburg – and in Fried-richsruh.

Schlieffen was not a man to challenge civil authority, and Caprivi's tenure of office was made secure by Waldersee's fall. The Kaiser himself had good grounds to be satisfied with Caprivi. A series of moderate reforms – in labour relations, to the taxation system, and to local government in the countryside – suggested willingness to make changes, but not dangerous ones. There was success, too, in foreign affairs: Caprivi was strengthening the Triple Alliance by seeking trade treaties to link the German, Italian and Austro-Hungarian economies; and although Bismarck's secret Russo-German 'Reinsurance Treaty' was allowed to lapse, Caprivi accompanied the Kaiser to Peterhof in August and made a favourable impression on the Tsar and his foreign minister. Yet basically the whole governmental system was unsound. Caprivi was alarmed at the extent to which policy depended upon the monarch's whim, and so were others in Berlin. 'He looks at events with the simplicity and confidence of a child', one prominent figure commented in April 1891. Two months later Baron Holstein wrote, 'I am curious to see how long the present regime will survive. I do not put much reliance on the Kaiser's constancy . . . . Let us hope he will reach maturity before there is any serious testing time. In any case if we don't want a republic we must take our princes as Providence sends them.'[6]

Providence, however, was by now straining the loyalty of many monarchists. To them William's tendency to give snap decisions, make spontaneous speeches, and indulge in dramatic gestures seemed the height of irresponsibility. In June 1891, for example, he drew up plans for increasing the size of the army and redeploying its strength: neither the chancellor nor the war minister were consulted. Caprivi indignantly submitted his resignation, but he was persuaded to remain in office. In mid-November William infuriated his ministers and offended Bavarian susceptibilities when, during a state visit to Munich he signed the ceremonial Golden Book of the Rathaus, adding to his autograph the grandiloquent tag, '*Suprema lex, regis voluntas*' ('The will of the king is the highest law'). His mother was as shocked as any of his subjects: 'A Czar, an infallible Pope, the Bourbons and our poor Charles I might have written such a sentence, but a constitutional Monarch in the 19th century . . . !!!', she wrote to Queen Victoria. Worse was to follow within a few days. The Kaiser travelled back from Bavaria to Potsdam. There he told recruits, paraded to swear loyalty to him, that should he order them to shoot down brothers, sisters, mothers or fathers they would have to fulfil his command 'without a murmur'. This 'terrible new speech', as his mother called it, offended opinion in England, France and even in Russia as well as provoking open criticism in Berlin. Caprivi's half-hearted explanation that His Imperial Majesty was warning young recruits against the menace of civil anarchy failed to satisfy anybody.[7] These ill-conceived phrases, at Munich and at Potsdam, lowered the Kaiser's prestige and authority at home and abroad. Outside observers began to wonder yet again if temperamentally as well as physically he lacked balance.

He continued to puzzle those nearest to him as well. Emotionally he remained uninterested in any woman apart from Dona, whose placidity frequently tried his patience. He much preferred the exclusive company of his own sex. No women joined the annual Scandinavian cruises aboard the *Hohenzollern*, where he indulged in puckish pranks which his suite generously attributed to a sense of humour – an imperial foot gently applied to the stretched posterior of an aide-de-camp dutifully carrying out his morning physical jerks might, with luck, bring down a row of admirals and generals like skittles across the deck. But his guests could never tell when he should be taken seriously. Kiderlen-Waechter, the diplomat assigned by the Foreign Ministry to these Scandinavian cruises for the first ten years of the reign, was better qualified than anybody else to assess William's mood at sea and yet even he could not always separate 'matters both great and small', as he admitted in a letter to Holstein. There was, for example, the incident of the Kaiser's beard. The *Hohenzollern*'s cruise up the fjords in July 1891 brought out the seafarer in William's repertoire more markedly than any previous voyage. Even the Sunday addresses a chaplain prepared for him to preach had a nautical appeal, although their five titles – 'Salute at Sea', 'On the High Seas', 'Signalling at Sea', 'The Great Turning Point', 'The Happy Homeward Voyage' – seem remote from the miraculous catch of fish on Lake Gennesaret, which was their ostensible theme. ('I leave out all dogmatic trash', he explained to the Dean of Windsor after the sermons were published.)[8] As the Kaiser delivered these addresses crew and guests could see he was growing a fine mariner's beard, which matured magnificently between 'Salute' and 'Turning Point'. It became the joke of the voyage, an adornment beside which the upturned moustaches would fade into insignificance. 'This will fix the portrait painters', he chuckled at dinner. 'People will collect the coins showing me without a beard.' But was it, Kiderlen-Waechter wondered, only a joke? One day the Kaiser suddenly brought his sound right hand down vigorously on a table and exclaimed, 'With a beard like this you could thump on the table so hard that your ministers would fall down with fright and lie flat on their faces!' Kiderlen was so disturbed by 'H.M.'s autocratic tendencies' that he thought the beard worthy of a special letter from Bergen to Berlin, although he told Holstein that 'it would perhaps be better to say nothing to the Chancellor of my observations, to avoid causing him unnecessary annoyance'.[9]

The beard was shaved off once the homeward voyage was happily completed, but the autocratic tendencies remained. They asserted themselves dramatically in February 1892. Caprivi, anxious for political support from the Roman Catholic Centre Party and conscious of a genuine sense of grievance among the stricter Lutheran conservatives, encouraged Count Zedlitz, the Prussian Minister for Ecclesiastical Affairs, to introduce a schools bill which would have given both the Lutheran and Catholic Churches some control over education. The bill was fiercely opposed by liberals, socialists and radicals but, as Waldersee wrote in his journal on 21 February, 'no one really knows what the Kaiser wants'. Three days later, William made his annual speech to the provincial assembly of Brandenburg. He had not bothered to let Caprivi or Zedlitz know what he intended to say, and this is not surprising. He began by suggesting that 'fashionable' Germans who liked to criticize the government should emigrate, thus ridding the Reich of 'grumblers we do not need'. Predictably he then reverted to a pet theme – the calm days ahead for the ship of state when she emerged from the present storm. On this occasion he treated the Brandenburgers to a confused historical travelogue in which Sir Francis Drake, bemused on a peak in Darien, saw for the first time 'the broad waters of the Pacific . . . lit with golden rays from the rising sun'. A leap in time and place brought his audience nearer home, with the Prussian victories of Rossbach in 1757 and of Dennewitz in 1813: 'I am helped to press forward on the path Heaven has marked out for me', he declared, 'by my feeling of responsibility to the Ruler of all and by the firm conviction that He, our old ally of Rossbach and Dennewitz, will not now desert me. He has taken such incredible trouble with our old homeland and with our dynasty that we may assume He has not done this for nothing. Nay, people of Brandenburg, on the contrary, we are called to greatness; and to days of glory will I lead you. . . . My course is right, and I shall continue to steer it.'[10]

His aides-de-camp welcomed this ragbag of double negatives as a revelation of Divine Will. Others who read the speech were more critical, even Phili Eulenburg. 'Everyone is asking with one derisive accord, what may be these days of glory to which he is *now* going to lead us?', he noted in his diary. 'I wish I could put a padlock on his mouth', wrote the Kaiser's mother to Queen Victoria, 'I tremble for him – with all his rashness and obstinacy, etc., he is a big baby'. The German press was less indulgent: one Prussian daily sarcastically suggested that, if 'the grumblers' followed His Imperial Majesty's advice, the exodus would be so great that Germany would become a third-class power in a matter of months; and both in Berlin and Cologne the speech was interpreted as an assertion of antiquated royal absolutism. In London *The Times*, despairing of William's statesmanship, sardonically commended him as a theologian of originality. *Punch* depicted him as Jove, with a quiver filled with barbed speeches, and quoted from Dryden's *Alexander's Feast*:

With ravished ears,
The Monarch hears,
Assumes the God,
Affects the nod,
And seems to shake the spheres.

For some months *Punch* was banned from the imperial palaces and from the *Hohenzollern* because of this cartoon. The Kaiser's rollicking sense of humour stopped short of his own person.[11]

The speech did not clarify his attitude to the schools bill or to any other immediate issue. Caprivi was left in doubt for another three weeks then, on 17 March, the Kaiser attended a Crown Council and spoke out against educational reforms which favoured Roman Catholic schools. Zedlitz and Caprivi resigned office. The Kaiser was surprised and personally pained by their action. He had, as he informed both Phili Eulenburg and Queen Victoria, been seized by a strange fever on hearing of the reactions to his Brandenburg speech, and his doctors ordered him to rest. To precipitate a ministerial crisis at such a time was, in his eyes, unpatriotic, and he blamed Caprivi for not seeing that it was his duty to gratify a royal master whose health was broken 'by strain and over exertion'.[12] He left next day for one of his hunting-lodges, suffering, as the British ambassador said, from 'a nervous breakdown'. In the end, Caprivi was persuaded to remain as chancellor, but he did so less from sympathy with William in his depths of self-pity, than from fear he would otherwise turn again to Waldersee. Caprivi agreed to drop the schools bill. At the same time he eased the burden on himself by handing over the post of Prussia's chief minister ('minister-president') to Count Botho zu Eulenburg, cousin of 'dear Phili'.

By the beginning of April the Kaiser was back in Berlin, although still in an excitable state of mind. On Saturday, 2 April, he unexpectedly visited the British embassy. He told the ambassador, Sir Edward Malet, that as an admiral in the Royal Navy he thought he should pass on to the British Admiralty intelligence reports he had received on torpedo-boat bases which the French were constructing between Dunkirk and Brest. 'As he was putting on his coat in the hall', Malet wrote privately to Lord Salisbury, 'he said that he hoped to go to England for 2 or 3 days "if Grandmama lets me".' The remark embarrassed Malet. He knew that, while the Kaiser enjoyed 'feeling quite at home ... in dear old Osborne', the Queen found her grandson's presence exhausting, not least because his manners and his strictures intensely irritated his uncle, the Prince of Wales. No doubt Malet should have dissuaded him from another visit; but could he have done so? Already Caprivi had been snubbed for hinting that, since the Kaiser's competitive zeal at Cowes lowered Hohenzollern popularity among the British ruling class, he might be advised to race elsewhere. Moreover, whenever the Kaiser was subjected to criticism at home he became conscious of his dynastic link with Britain, momentarily as Anglophile as his mother: 'I am a good deal of an Englishman myself', he had told Queen Victoria proudly the previous July. It was hard to expect Malet to puncture his illusions at a time when he had come to the embassy clearly under nervous strain and bringing, as he thought, information of service to his English friends. Fortunately Malet had a ready excuse for silent acquiescence. 'It was impossible for me', he explained to Salisbury, 'to tell him before the servants that the Queen strongly objected.' Before the end of the month the Kaiser had invited himself to Cowes for regatta week, although this year he agreed to stay on his yacht rather than in the cramped accommodation of Osborne. With a sigh the Queen resigned herself to another round of 'friendly rivalry' between uncle and nephew, at least for that summer; but a week before the Kaiser's arrival a cypher telegram from Windsor to Berlin asked Malet plaintively if he 'could hint that these regular annual visits are not quite desirable'.[13]

Yet the regatta of 1892 passed amicably. William, so the Prince of Wales informed his son, was 'not the least grand, and very quiet, most amiable in every respect'. This is not surprising: he had reason to be on his best behaviour. Cowes Week coincided with a change of government in Britain. In July a general election had given the Liberals a slim parliamentary majority, threatening a reversal of British policy towards the other European powers. The prospect worried the Kaiser, more so indeed than it did his officials in the Foreign Ministry. For the past six years Lord Salisbury had worked closely with Germany and her allies, Italy and Austria-Hungary. Although he consistently avoided the commitments of a formal alliance, the Kaiser was convinced he could count on Salisbury's goodwill. He was less sure of Gladstone and Rosebery, since on past record the Liberals were inclined to appease the French and the Russians. William hoped in that August for some continuity in policy, with no 'new course' marked out on British charts. Fortunately Salisbury agreed with him and saw to it that Rosebery was well briefed, as soon as it was known that he had accepted the Foreign Office. If in 1892 there was less disruption in foreign affairs than when the Liberals last came to power, some at least of the credit rests with the Kaiser's restraint and good sense during his days at Cowes. Significantly the Queen no longer laboured her objections to his annual visit. William himself, in acknowledging the gift of a clock the following January, told her he was counting the hours 'till the moment when I can again sight dear Osborne rising out of the blue waters of the Solent'.[14]

Next summer William invited Phili Eulenburg to join him in the new *Hohenzollern*. For two and a half years Eulenburg had been head of the Prussian diplomatic mission to Bavaria, and the Kaiser was considering moving his friend to one of the greater embassies. London was a first choice, since the ambassador, Paul Hatzfeldt, was in poor health. Cowes could provide William with an opportunity to see how Eulenburg was received in English society. The summer months of 1893 had been difficult in Berlin, with Caprivi struggling to pass through the Reichstag a bill increasing the size of the army by eighteen per cent and having, as a compromise, to cut the length of conscripted service from three years to two. The parliamentary debates severely taxed William's temper and he was anticipating that Cowes would serve as a pleasant interlude, free from political wrangling, Not, perhaps, strictly speaking a holiday: he was determined to sail furiously, convinced that his three-year-old cutter *Meteor* would hold off any challenge from the Prince of Wales's new yacht, *Britannia*. He arrived off Cowes on Saturday afternoon (29 July), ebullient as ever, and keyed up for the Queen's Cup competition which would be decided on Tuesday.[15]

Unfortunately there was a war scare that weekend. For several months the British press had been alarmed by French activity in the Mekong delta and by Russian activity in the Pamirs: the current number of *The Nineteenth Century* carried an article by Curzon on 'India between Two Fires'; and it was generally accepted that the best answer to a Franco-Russian threat was closer collaboration with Germany and her two allies. On Sunday evening (30 July) the Kaiser dined with the Prince of Wales in *Britannia*. Shortly before midnight, Sir Henry Ponsonby, the Queen's private secretary, arrived with a telegram received at Osborne from the Foreign Secretary in which it seemed as if the French were threatening war after a naval incident off Bangkok:

59

Rosebery sought an urgent meeting with the German ambassador to see how far Britain might rely on German collaboration. So long as he was aboard *Britannia* the Kaiser remained heartily aggressive – Germany's growing strength had been a theme of his table-talk all the evening. But once back in *Hohenzollern* he dropped the mask. He poured out his worries to Eulenburg in his cabin: France and Russia had the initiative; neither the British fleet nor his own army was yet ready for war; above all, if Germany could not now, in this crisis, appear as the decisive world power, then all the prestige he had built up in the past five years would be shattered. 'I really have never seen him so overcome', Eulenburg wrote. Kiderlen and another German diplomat were summoned to the Kaiser's cabin in the small hours of the morning in order to help Eulenburg convince him that his fears were groundless. It was a complete nervous collapse. 'He looked very wretched – pale, and biting his lips nervously', Eulenburg wrote. 'I felt dreadfully sorry for him. He, coming here with his big talk about our ships, felt driven into a corner as it were. . . . To be put in one's place is always a bitter pill for one's dear vanity.'[16]

Within a few hours the war scare receded, for the messages from Siam were much exaggerated. But, so far as William was concerned, the episode was not closed. How had he come to be 'driven into a corner'? Had Rosebery over-reacted, or had the Prince of Wales and Ponsonby deliberately dramatized an incident of diplomacy in order to test his reactions? When later his ambassador forwarded to him Rosebery's explanation that he had thought it polite to keep the Kaiser informed of the situation so long as he was in England, William scribbled in the margin, 'What an old yarn! That doesn't need to be done through a private secretary deathly pale at twelve midnight.'[17] For the remainder of Cowes Week the Kaiser was unbearably arrogant, as though hiding from himself his weakness of will-power in the small hours of Monday morning. Later that day he insisted on showing the Prince how *Britannia* ought to be sailed; on Tuesday he won the Queen's Cup in *Meteor*, and sent a telegram from Cowes to Osborne (a mile away) so as to inform his grandmother of his success; on Wednesday he refused to call off a race against *Britannia*, even though it meant that he himself and the Prince of Wales were late for a state dinner given by the Queen in his honour. The Prince, for his part, contented himself by making slightly malicious remarks to Eulenburg over his nephew's pleasure in striking seamanlike attitudes. Socially it was not a good Cowes that year, and Eulenburg made it clear to William he had no wish to go to London as ambassador.

It was not only his English hosts who suffered from William's inner need to assert himself. Two furiously worded telegrams were despatched to the chancellor at the end of Cowes Week. Ostensibly they rebuked Caprivi for the way in which he was handling the transfer of responsibility from an outgoing imperial finance minister to his successor. But it is significant that all this fuss over minor procedural details followed William's discovery that Caprivi, so far from being alarmed by the weekend war scare, had welcomed it as a possible means 'of expanding the Triple into a Quadruple Alliance'. The Kaiser's extravagantly phrased reprimand infuriated him and he prepared another letter of resignation. But, as the *Hohenzollern* sailed back from the Solent to Kiel, Eulenburg set himself to heal the breach between sovereign and chancellor. He told the Kaiser that if he forced Caprivi out 'in the moment of his return from a pleasure trip' all Germany would place the blame on him, criticizing him for having spent a week sailing at such a time of political crisis. This rebuke, as Eulenburg reported to Caprivi a few days later, 'produced ... an explosion on which I need not enlarge to Your Excellency'. No one else could have spoken so bluntly and retained William's favour. But the Kaiser saw the force of his friend's arguments. He did not want another chancellor crisis; and on his return to the capital he treated Caprivi graciously and considerately. The letter of resignation was undelivered.[18]

Yet to a soldier of Caprivi's moral stature it was irksome to depend for political office on so brittle a character as Phili Eulenburg. He grumbled about intrigues at court and about the shadowy influence of figures like Baron Holstein, whose activities poached on other men's responsibilities. And when, in January 1894, the satirical periodical *Kladderadatsch* began to ridicule a camarilla behind the throne, Caprivi was not inclined to take action against editor or contributors even though it seemed as if confidential information was being leaked by some highly placed officials. The fable of 'the three men in the fiery furnace' described the activities 'once upon a time' of three royal servants, Insinuans, Intriguans, and Calumnians, who bore a strong resemblance to Eulenburg, Holstein and Kiderlen-Waechter. Of these three the most dangerous was Insinuans, who saw his sovereign more often than the others and who played the lute before him, 'singing to it bewitching melodies'.

Outwardly Eulenburg ignored these satires. He was about to take up a plum posting in the foreign service, the embassy at Vienna, and he did not want to brawl in the gutter with hack journalists. While Kiderlen fought a duel and Holstein – who had never met the Kaiser, and who was to do so only once in his life – raged venomously against enemies, real or imaginary, Eulenburg tried quietly to discover the identity of the satirists. Caprivi's reluctance to order an inquiry convinced Eulenburg the chancellor was a broken reed. Less than seven weeks after the 'fiery furnace' fable appeared in *Kladderadatsch*, Eulenburg was pressing the Kaiser to dismiss Caprivi. He admitted that this advice showed a change of mind, but he claimed that Caprivi's failure to take a firm line with the Reichstag was leading to an outcry in the press.[19] The Kaiser, he thought, might most effectively rule through a Junker landowner in whom he could have personal confidence – his cousin, Botho Eulenburg, for example.

There was, as usual, some truth behind Phili's reasoning: politically Caprivi was isolated, and all the noise was being made by Junker protectionists in the 'Agrarian League' or by Bismarckians anxious for revenge. But, while the Kaiser deplored the ridicule of *Kladderadatsch* and innuendoes in other newspapers, he could not miss their significance: it was unwise, for the moment, to advance any further the Eulenburg family. Besides, William did not wish to precipitate a constitutional crisis. His mind was full of trivialities of imperial status: for several months that winter he sought a personal reconciliation with the Prince of Wales, offering him high honorary rank in the German army in the hope he would himself be made colonel-in-chief of a Highland regiment. Queen Victoria deplored this 'fishing for uniforms on both sides', and would at first have nothing to do with it: no foreigner had ever been made colonel-in-chief of any British regiment; but in the end William had his way. While she was at Coburg that April the Queen made him honorary colonel of the First Royal Dragoons. It was not a Scottish regiment, but it pleased him: 'I am moved, deeply moved at the idea that I now too can wear beside the Naval uniform the traditional British "Redcoat"', he told his grandmother on 24 April.[20] He promised another visit to Osborne during regatta week – sacred, sacred Cowes.

This playboy attitude to affairs of state hid a natural disinclination for serious work which exasperated public figures and political commentators in Berlin. William certainly believed he was industrious: hours set aside each week for audiences with generals, admirals, ambassadors, heads of government departments, his chiefs of cabinet; long lists of promotions of officers in the army and navy, each promotion signed personally by the All Highest; important diplomatic despatches, read and annotated; plans for public buildings submitted to him as a formality but receiving 'improvements' sketched in the imperial hand; meetings of scientists or archaeologists; army units, warships, dockyards, forts, factories, model housing-estates – all inspected briskly and with a well-briefed mind. And yet, despite this sense of activity, it was hard to escape the impression there was something frivolous in his style of rule, that he was the crowned dilettante of his generation. His inability to concentrate for any sustained period of time – that old criticism made by Hinzpeter and his teachers at Cassel and Bonn – became more marked as his range of distractions broadened. 'This is not the time to play with a nation as though it were a big toy', Holstein grumbled to Eulenburg; and during Cowes Week in 1894 the oldest and most renowned newspaper in the capital, the *Vossische Zeitung*, published a survey of His Majesty's activities in the past twelve months, which showed he had spent at least 199 of the 365 days in travel, many of them at sea and out of direct communication with the government or his service chiefs.[21] At times, especially aboard the *Hohenzollern*, he seemed in a fantasy world. It was, for example, on a North Sea cruise in July 1892 that he told Eulenburg of the 'sort of Napoleonic supremacy' which he was establishing 'in the peaceful sense' in Europe, an anticipatory claim to leadership with, as yet, little relationship to reality. And it was while cruising in the fjords on 12 July 1894 that he drew, on a telegraph form, a detailed sketch and plan of the fast but economical light cruiser of the future – which, the experts confessed, would have capsized in the first swell on the German Bight. Like so much undertaken by the Kaiser, the sketch was, pictorially, an excellent piece of work.[22]

Had William abandoned his pose as officer of the watch and left day-to-day politics to the chancellor and his ministers while amusing himself with ships, uniforms and parades, then Germany might have worked out a practical and smooth system of government. But the Kaiser still thought as an autocrat. He saw nothing inconsistent in suddenly intervening on a grand scale after weeks of remote control, ruling spasmodically by telegram. Hence, in the autumn of 1894, he sought to settle the domestic crisis which had developed slowly through the summer months.

Basically, the problem was simple. The division of responsibilities between Caprivi, as chancellor, and Botho Eulenburg, as minister-president of Prussia, had not stood the strain of a largely peripatetic sovereign. The immediate issue concerned the spread of revolutionary socialism: Botho Eulenburg wanted repressive legislation; Caprivi did not think he could pilot an anti-socialist law through the Reichstag, and was too loyal to his principles to wish to make the attempt. At first the Kaiser supported Botho: on 1 September he gave Botho the impression he would become chancellor, as well as minister-president, and be given authority by the representatives of the German princes to hold elections for a new Reichstag on a restricted suffrage in place of the universal suffrage stipulated in the constitution. Yet, even now, William hesitated: this was the type of anti-socialist revolution from above which he had condemned Bismarck for having recommended in 1890; and he had no wish to imperil the tenuous federal links in the Reich by an autocratic *coup d'état* staged by a Junker clique who lacked support outside the older provinces of Prussia. The Kaiser was hopelessly confused. He snubbed Caprivi publicly and privately until eventually, on 23 October, the unfortunate chancellor wrote yet another letter of resignation. Within a few hours William, distressed at this newest constitutional crisis, came personally from Potsdam to the chancellery to plead with Caprivi that he should stay in office. The Kaiser then left for his annual shooting expedition on one of the Eulenburg estates. There, Botho was inconsiderate enough to offer his own resignation as William was on his way to the butts – he could not, he explained, work with Caprivi any longer.[23]

Fortunately for the Kaiser, Phili Eulenburg was present – his absences from Vienna were already causing resentment – and he was as willing as ever to give advice: 'The Kaiser came up to me with that pale, pinched look so familiar to me from all the innumerable bad hours we have been through together.' Anxiously he asked, 'Whom can you suggest? ... Don't you know anyone?' As it happened, Eulenburg had a candidate in mind. A few weeks previously the Grand Duke of Baden (who had helped unseat Bismarck) wrote to Eulenburg suggesting that the posts of chancellor and minister-president should be re-united under a statesman of experience, the veteran Bavarian aristocrat and diplomat, Prince Chlodwig zu Hohenlohe-Schillingsfürst; and Eulenburg now recommended Hohenlohe to the Kaiser 'as a stop-gap while another man was sought for'. There were objections: he was a Roman Catholic, and he did not know north Germany well – 'I'm on the spot for that', William quickly interjected. He returned to Berlin, still thinking he might somehow keep Caprivi and Botho Eulenburg in harness; but there was a press leak of confidential remarks made by the Kaiser to the chancellor, and William indignantly gave up all attempts at a reconciliation. On 26 October the newspapers were told that the chancellor and the minister-president had tendered their resignations. Three days later the official gazette announced that Prince Hohenlohe would succeed to both posts. At seventy-five he was a few months older than Bismarck had been at the time of his dismissal. From up at Friedrichsruh there came a scornful grunt of disbelief.[24]

6. Operetta Government

At first Prince Chlodwig zu Hohenlohe was reluctant to take over the burdens of the chancellorship. 'Have served 30 years, am 75 years old, and don't want to start something I cannot manage', he jotted down in a memorandum for his own use.[1] He complained he had no gift for speech-making, did not understand the political ways or legal customs of Prussia, and was not a soldier. The Kaiser made light of these objections. He emphasized the unique role of the Hohenlohes as a supra-national aristocratic family. They were, indeed, related by marriage to several reigning dynasties, including those of Germany and Great Britain. One of Prince Chlodwig's brothers was a respected member of the Prussian Upper House, another was a Cardinal at the Vatican, a third was Court Chamberlain to Francis Joseph in Vienna. The Prince's Russian-born wife retained close connections with the great families of St Petersburg and Moscow. It was easy for Hohenlohe, despite his initial reservations, to convince himself that his princely prestige would enable him to curb William's impetuosity as neither of his predecessors had done: they, after all, had not been addressed by the sovereign with the familiar '*Du*', nor sent letters of state which began '*Lieber Onkel*' ('Dear Uncle'). If he was called to move into the chancellor's gloomy palace on the Wilhelmstrasse, so be it. He was, he felt, entitled to more respect and consideration from the Kaiser than poor Caprivi had ever known.

William, however, saw the change of chancellor differently. He wanted a man of experience and understanding, someone who could handle ministers and party chiefs while admiring the genius which the imperial touch would bring to foreign affairs. Baron von Holstein, observing political life from his room in the Wilhelmstrasse, was disturbed by William's style of government: gunboat-diplomacy abroad, and a superficial dismissal of everyday problems at home. Less than a fortnight after Hohenlohe's appointment, Holstein described in a letter to Philipp Eulenburg how the Kaiser would receive 'Uncle' heartily in audience at Potsdam, say 'Why you've brought along a regular letter to Santa Claus!', and after a couple of minutes send him back 'to Berlin with his fat briefcase full of unfinished business'. 'This, my dear friend, is operetta government', Holstein commented, 'not one that a European people at the end of the nineteenth century will put up with.' Eulenburg, remote in his Viennese embassy, dismissed Holstein's fears: 'I am convinced that the Guiding Hand of Providence lies behind this elemental and natural drive of the Kaiser's to direct the affairs of the kingdom in person', he replied with airy grandeur on 2 December. But by Christmas Eulenburg was beginning to change his mind. Alexander III of Russia had died on 31 October 1894: his successor, Nicholas II, was twenty-six. While the Kaiser had looked upon Alexander III as basically hostile to Germany, he was certain 'Nicky' would be grateful for private advice, emperor to emperor. Soon, rumours of confidential exchanges began to circulate in the other European capitals. Eulenburg found the authorities in Vienna uneasy because it was said that, without consulting his Austrian or Italian allies, the Kaiser had offered diplomatic support to the Tsar if he wished to establish Russian control over the Dardanelles. 'Our relations with the new Tsar do not please me a bit', Eulenburg told Holstein on 11 January 1895. 'I am watching H.M.'s family politics with real anxiety.'[2] The danger lay not so much in anything the Kaiser could do on his own, as in what he might say and, even more, in what others believed he had said.

To William the accession of Nicholas came as a heaven-sent opportunity for restoring the old friendship between the rulers in Berlin and St Petersburg. William, who exaggerated the impact of dynastic sentiment on power politics, believed he could induce the Tsar to turn his armies away from Europe and thereby strengthen the prospects of peace on the continent. Already Nicholas was indebted to William who, six months previously, had exerted himself considerably to persuade his cousin, Princess Alix of Hesse, that she might follow the instincts of her heart and marry the heir to the Russian throne. As soon as William learnt of Alexander III's death he made a speech at Stettin in which he offered friendship to the new 'Autocrat of All the Russias'. A week later he sent the first of some seventy-five letters in which, over the next eighteen years, he set himself the task of winning and retaining

Nicholas's confidence. These 'Willy-Nicky' letters, dashed off in the Kaiser's characteristically flamboyant style of English, had two main objectives in foreign affairs: to open the Tsar's eyes to the sinfulness of alliance with republican France – 'Nicky, take my word for it, the curse of God has stricken that people for ever' – and to remind him of Russia's Holy Mission in farthest Asia, where his armies were 'to defend Europe from the inroads of the Great Yellow Race'.[3] Yet the letters also show how much William envied the unfettered powers of a Tsar: in February 1895, for example, he praised the 'capital speech' in which Nicholas dismissed petitions for a Russian parliament and constitution as mere 'senseless dreams'. In William's eyes the maintenance of autocracy was a task imposed on His emperors by the Lord of Lords.

At times it seemed as if William wished to rule Germany through a handful of court dignitaries. Criticism in the Reichstag, cool appraisals of his speeches in the press, or a show of ministerial independence made him toy with the idea of dictatorship. With a Bavarian as imperial chancellor and chief minister of Prussia and with Marschall, another south German, still serving as foreign secretary, it is hardly surprising if there was discontent in the old guard of Junker politicians, a few of whom continued to regret the association of Prussia with the other German states in a common Reich. 'Yesterday I was in Berlin where I was able to speak to some conservative deputies', wrote Waldersee in his journal on 7 February 1895. 'All were united in thinking that Hohenlohe is not capable of getting us out of the present hopeless position and that something drastic is needed. They are thinking of a kind of *putsch* and of me as an ideal leader for it.' Occasionally the Kaiser did, indeed, give the impression he was about to call in Waldersee and the army, but by now his political instincts were sufficiently shrewd to make him hesitate. Such a step would paralyse industry with strikes and raise barricades in the cities. He knew repression and restraint at home would be accepted by his people only if they could see that sacrifices were necessary for the well-being of the Fatherland. William believed he had found a new cause which, without sending armies marching across Europe, would kindle national and patriotic sentiment. On 8 January 1895 he delivered a resounding speech to members of the Reichstag in which he claimed that a substantial increase in the fleet was Germany's prime essential as a great power in that new year. Exactly a month later he spoke at the Prussian War Academy on a similar theme.[4]

William's deep-rooted interest in naval affairs had been fired by the enthusiasm of Captain Alfred von Tirpitz, a torpedo specialist whom he first met on exercises in the Baltic. It was intensified during the past year by a study of *The Influence of Sea Power upon History*, the famous account of the struggle for maritime supremacy in the seventeenth and eighteenth centuries which the American naval captain, Alfred Mahan, had published four years previously. 'I am just now not reading but devouring Captain Mahan's book and am trying to learn it by heart', the Kaiser telegraphed to his American friend, Bigelow, on 26 May 1894.[5] Mahan's main contention, that the growth and prosperity of nations depends ultimately upon command of the seas, corresponded closely with William's own beliefs. Recent events seemed to confirm Mahan's determinism: the successes of the Japanese that winter in their war against China over the future of Korea was a lesson in the merits of sea power; and so, in a different sense, was the French ability to sustain military operations in Madagascar, an island in the Indian Ocean which was two thousand miles from any other French colony and greater in extent than their homeland. Both of these undertakings held William's interest: so, too, did reports from German traders in Mozambique and the Transvaal, where President Kruger was impatiently awaiting completion of his railway from Pretoria to Lourenço Marques and Delagoa Bay, a line which would virtually free the economy of the Transvaal from pressure imposed by Cecil Rhodes, the prime minister of Cape Colony. If Germany had naval bases in the China Seas and southern Africa, then it seemed to William he might conduct a 'world policy' consistent with his empire's economic strength and prestige. At present it was galling that German naval vessels in distant waters should be dependent on British coaling stations to keep them at sea. On 2 November 1894, in his first conversation on foreign affairs with Hohenlohe, the Kaiser suggested the Japanese might be told that, as compensation for their victories against China, Germany would expect to be given the island of Formosa (Taiwan), and he pointed out that a coaling station in Mozambique was highly desirable in order to protect German interests in southern Africa. A fortnight later William sent his chancellor a note commenting on the imminent defeat of China: 'We dare not be caught out over this business nor can we allow ourselves to be surprised by events', he wrote. 'We too need a solid base in China, where our trading profits amount to four hundred million a year.'[6] He left it to Hohenlohe and Marschall, the foreign secretary, to discover ways of acquiring the outposts of empire which he was convinced a world policy demanded.

The task was beyond them. Laboriously they set about building up a league of European Powers who might act together in the Far East, and perhaps later in southern Africa. They were hampered in part by British hesitancy and isolationism, but even more by their sovereign's temperament. For the Kaiser's interventions in foreign affairs – often snap reactions to the whim of a moment – could destroy in a few hours the diplomacy of several weeks. His interests moved disconcertingly from region to region: the China Seas; Delagoa Bay and the Transvaal; the Bosphorus and the Dardanelles. Sometimes his attention was concentrated solely on the Reichstag: the only occasion upon which he went out of his way to congratulate his foreign secretary was when, on 2 March 1895, Marschall's discreet canvassing of the Centre Party persuaded the deputies to support the immediate construction of four new cruisers. At no time could William's ministers feel they enjoyed his confidence. In mid-February Eulenburg, responding to pleas from Holstein, had to write to William and beg him to show support for Hohenlohe and Marschall if he did not wish to plunge Germany into a severe constitutional crisis. William vigorously denied that he wanted another round of government changes ('If Hohenlohe goes, I'll go too'), but the general situation was hardly better than in the closing months of Caprivi's chancellorship. The Kaiser saw no reason to let Hohenlohe know what personal assurances he made to the Russians, nor tell Marschall what matters he had asked Eulenburg to raise with Francis Joseph. 'The eternal fight with H.M. is wearing us out', the exasperated Marschall wrote in his diary; and a few weeks later he complained, 'He interferes persistently in foreign policy. A monarch ought to have the last word, but H.M. always wants to have the first, and this is a cardinal error.'[7]

William's intervention was at its worst in Anglo-German relations. He believed he knew and understood the British better than anyone else in Berlin. At times his judgement was shrewd. He rightly saw that Rosebery's Liberal cabinet was so divided between 'imperialists' and radical 'isolationists' that it was not worth taking seriously any overtures Rosebery might make: better, he thought, to await the return of Lord Salisbury and the conservatives. But the Kaiser never perceived party subtleties in British politics. He attributed a continuity of outlook to Conservative foreign policy which it could not possess; he missed the significance of Joseph Chamberlain's growing enthusiasm for the colonies; and he made the odd mistake, again and again, of looking on Salisbury as a Bismarck with an Oxford accent, dismissing his innate shyness as guile and his flexibility of approach as opportunism. William suspected that Salisbury took refuge at Hatfield to avoid responsibility for unpopular decisions (as Bismarck had been known to do at Friedrichsruh), and he ascribed to Salisbury an influence over London newspapers which no prime minister of England has ever enjoyed. Yet when Salisbury succeeded Rosebery in June 1895 the Kaiser was pleased with the change of government. A general election, which followed in July, gave the Conservatives and Unionists a huge majority, and William took the unusual step of sending Salisbury a telegram of congratulation, direct from Potsdam: 'Hope you are none the worse for your stupendous climbing of the ladder considering the height of the tempest and the number of rungs.'[8] Even allowing for his taste in nautical imagery, it is a strangely phrased message: had he in mind the un-dropping of the pilot?

A week later Cowes Regatta got off to a damp start. The *Hohenzollern* steamed up the Solent in pouring rain on the afternoon of 5 August. Prince Henry had arrived the day before with four large cruisers, for the Kaiser was determined to make an impressive appearance that summer. He was elated at the completion of the Kiel Canal, which he had opened on 20 June, and he was conscious of the presence at Cowes of USS *Chicago*, a light cruiser commanded by the redoubtable Captain Mahan, whom William had met briefly at the regatta in the previous year. But this time it was not a happy Cowes Week. The German warships tended to 'block the course of the racing vessels' as well as firing off salutes 'every few moments'. The Prince of Wales thought it tactless of his nephew to celebrate the silver jubilee of victories in the Franco-Prussian War aboard his warships at the Royal Yacht Squadron's regatta, and the Germans complained that 'fat old Wales' snubbed their sovereign in public. Worst of all, there was a misunderstanding between the Kaiser and the prime minister. Salisbury was able to talk to William after dinner at Osborne on the evening of his arrival, although their conversation was interrupted by the Prince of Wales and the obligations of what was essentially a social occasion. On the following day Salisbury received an invitation to call on the Kaiser at a time when he was already committed to an audience with the Queen at Osborne. A heavy rainstorm induced him to stay at Osborne until half-past seven, and he was then forced to cross to Portsmouth, since (as he explained in a letter to the German ambassador) there were 'certain appointments' in London which he 'could not fail to meet'. Next morning Queen Victoria wrote to Salisbury. Her letter was mainly concerned with difficulties caused by her grandson's eagerness to have Lord Wolseley, or another distinguished soldier, as the new ambassador in Berlin, but she also remarked, 'The German Emperor is a little sore at your not coming to see him, having waited hours for you thinking you would come after seeing me.' Salisbury sent a more detailed letter of apology to Hatzfeldt, the German ambassador, and hoped the incident was closed.[9]

So it should have been; but William, who interpreted every incident in personal terms, remained vexed. It is not clear why he had asked Salisbury to call on him. Possibly he hoped to invite himself to Hatfield. He had already arranged, at the end of the week, to travel by train to Westmorland for a few days shooting before re-embarking on the *Hohenzollern* at Leith, and it seems he contemplated making a detour to visit Hatfield, where he could have held confidential discussions with the prime minister, just as in the past he had broken train journeys at Friedrichsruh for talks with Bismarck. Kiderlen, describing the Cowes misunderstanding in a letter to Holstein, commented that 'at any rate the visit to Hatfield . . . has definitely been abandoned'.[10] The Kaiser's special train did not go as far east as Hertfordshire. He was disappointed in Lord Salisbury. When, on 25 August, a hostile article appeared in the *Standard* he assumed it was inspired by the prime minister himself.

Yet if, over the next two months, the misunderstanding deepened, the responsibility lay with the German ambassador and the Kaiser's style of diplomacy rather than with Salisbury. The most urgent question in Europe that summer was the future of the Turkish Empire. Sultan Abdul Hamid had shown, in recent months, that he could retain control of his huge dominions only by permitting his Kurdish irregular troops a free hand to terrorize potentially dissident national minorities, especially the Armenian Christians. So bestial was Ottoman rule that Lord Salisbury began to consider the desirability of ending the Sultanate and partitioning Turkey-in-Europe. At the end of July he discussed the problem in general terms with the German, Russian and French ambassadors. Hatzfeldt, however, misrepresented him: he gave the impression in Berlin that Salisbury was already prepared to agree with Germany on a precise plan for dividing up Turkey. When the Kaiser met Salisbury at Osborne on 5 August he was surprised to find him so uncommunicative.[11] It does not seem to have occurred to him that Salisbury did not follow up the remarks attributed to him by Hatzfeldt because he never made them.

At the end of August William took the initiative himself. Characteristically he chose as an intermediary, not the British ambassador, but the military attaché, Colonel Swaine, to whom he felt he could talk 'as one soldier to another'. Swaine was invited to dine at Potsdam on 29 August. To his consternation, he found he was the Kaiser's sole guest. After dinner William began to talk about Constantinople, which he had visited six years before: the Sultan would respect whichever power first sent its warships to anchor off his palace, the Yildiz Kiosk. The Kaiser argued that Salisbury should order the British fleet through the Dardanelles: 'Nothing will result until a British man-of-war appears in the Golden Horn with an ultimatum', and then 'the Sultan would be on his knees'. Germany would support such action provided 'you do not spring this upon us like a thunder-clap out of a blue sky'. He then outlined a partition scheme from which Russia, Austria-Hungary, Italy and Great Britain would profit while Germany remained a disinterested observer. Syria might be offered to Russia, a proposal which would encourage France and Russia to 'fight it out' and thereby put an end to their friendship. 'The next great war will be between the Russians and the Japanese', he predicted, and he added 'My interests are to drive the Russians into Asia'. It was a typical Kaiser's-eye view of the world, an irresponsible survey delivered without reference to Hohenlohe, Marschall, Holstein or any other member of the foreign service.[12] There is no evidence they ever learnt of their sovereign's proposals, although later in September he took Hatzfeldt partly into his confidence.

Salisbury found Swaine's report awaiting him in London on 2 September and immediately had it printed and circulated to members of the cabinet. They were suspicious: the Kaiser seemed eager to make mischief between Britain and Russia and between France and Russia. Since he had not used the customary diplomatic channels it did not seem necessary to reply to what was, technically, table-talk. Eventually, in the first week of October, Swaine was authorized to tell Hatzfeldt there would be no change in British policy and that, so far as Anglo-German relations were concerned 'Africa is and will remain a stumbling block to both Powers'. Once again, almost casually, Salisbury rebuffed the Germans and William's latent resentment came to the surface. He began to complain of Salisbury's treachery and double-dealing. There would be no more extravagantly phrased personal telegrams despatched from Potsdam to Hatfield. On 24 October he treated the unfortunate Colonel Swaine to a stern lecture on the folly of 'England's policy of selfishness and bullying'. 'The Colonel', William told Marschall 'appeared to be deeply disturbed and much moved'.[13]

There followed an even stranger tempest in a teapot. Sir Edward Malet, ambassador for the past eleven years, presented his letters of recall two days later. The Kaiser received him courteously and gave him a signed engraving of his 'Yellow Peril' cartoon.* But Malet left Berlin under a cloud: no court dignitary bade him farewell at the station. On his final visit to the Foreign Ministry, Malet warned Marschall that continued encouragement of the Boers in the Transvaal would harm Anglo-German relations, and the Kaiser insisted on regarding these remarks as impertinent. William spent the last days of October on Eulenburg's estate of Liebenberg, where his host noted he was 'very indignant over Malet's behaviour'. By the time he returned to the capital, this indignation was boiling up to frenetic anger and on 3 November he roundly abused the British chargé d'affaires, Martin Gosselin, at an official reception: Malet, so William insisted, had dared to use the word 'ultimatum', and Gosselin should see to it that people in London remembered 'We are not Venezuelans.' Malet denied having spoken so forcibly and Salisbury tried to reassure the Kaiser. Gosselin attributed William's strange behaviour to the influence of Eulenburg who, so he informed Salisbury, 'seems to possess mesmeric powers over the Emperor' and he wondered if William was 'subject to hallucinations'.[14] Over the next two months his moods were as incomprehensible as the actions of his great-great-grandfather, George III, during the onset of 'the royal malady' in 1788. At Christmas, for example, the Kaiser gave orders for his wife's younger sister, Princess Louise Sophie and her husband Frederick Leopold of Prussia, to be

---

* 'It shows the powers of Europe represented by their respective Genii called together by the Arch-Angel Michael – sent from Heaven to *unite* in resisting the inroad of Buddhism, heathenism and barbarism for the Defence of the Cross', William explained in a letter to Nicholas II on 26 September 1895 (N.F. Grant (ed.), *Kaiser's Letters to the Tsar*, p. 19). The original drawing was sketched by William, who handed it over for completion and embellishment to the distinguished painter, Hermann Knackfuss, of Kassel.

placed under house arrest for a fortnight since she had committed a light-hearted breach of court etiquette;[15] and, in the family circle, he remained an extremely heavy-handed father to the fourteen-year-old Crown Prince and his brothers. Throughout the remainder of the winter, and well into the summer, the Kaiser complained intermittently that he was suffering from 'ear-trouble'.

His nerves were also strained by disputes over domestic politics. Shortly before his angry outburst to Gosselin on the evening of 3 November, William discovered that government ministers had that day decided to drop repressive legislation in which he was intensely interested. This rebuff – a 'mutiny', as he excitedly called it – was followed by the start of a long conflict between the Kaiser and his war minister, General Walther Bronsart von Schellendorf, who proposed to modernize Prussian court-martial procedure; and at the same time William was angry with Hohenlohe, and most of his ministers, for their lack of enthusiasm for naval expansion.[16] William's behaviour was totally unpredictable. Five days before Christmas he button-holed the British military attaché for the third time in four months and complained to him yet again of Salisbury's policy: 'You are courting a crash', William told Swaine, 'but I suppose the German Emperor with his twenty army corps will see that no great harm comes to you' for 'the Protestant nations should keep together'.[17] Hohenlohe was alarmed by William's language and conduct but decided 'it was not worth having a row with the Kaiser', as he noted in his diary on 29 December. Baron Holstein wrote to Eulenburg in Vienna and complained that William was 'a quite superficial ruler', a man 'denied the gift of political tact'. Eulenburg, the one person with the ability to manage William when he was under great strain, thought that 'something must be done' but – perhaps because of the Christmas festivities – shirked decisive action. On Christmas Day itself William wrote a long letter to Eulenburg hinting at secret plots and intrigues around him and declaring that he was prepared to oust his enemies in the government and then 'rule in the Prussian spirit' through a compliant chancellor. For this role William suggested their friend Bernard von Bülow, the ambassador in Rome. 'Bülow will be my Bismarck', he told Eulenburg – who weakly sent a telegram back to Potsdam agreeing with everything William proposed.[18] Like Hohenlohe (with whom he discussed William's strange behaviour on 28 December), Eulenburg believed that so long as the Kaiser was governed by emotion rather than reason it was best to humour him and hope the mood would pass without any grave crisis in affairs. This time it did not.

In the early afternoon of 31 December 1895 news reached Berlin that, two days previously, Dr Storr Jameson with six hundred armed police of the South Africa Company had 'invaded' the Transvaal as the preliminary to an anti-Boer rising in Johannesburg. German capital accounted for a fifth of foreign investment in the Boer republic and German-born settlers held high positions in President Kruger's administrative service and the banks. The German Government could not ignore developments in the Transvaal where, as *The Times* admitted, many people in Berlin thought that the Reich possessed virtually 'a moral protectorate'. The Kaiser reacted belligerently to news of Jameson's raid. 'I hope that all will come right', he wrote to the Tsar, 'but come what may, I never shall allow the British to stamp out the Transvaal.'[19] Yet, despite his bluster, the Kaiser's nerves were as taut as at Cowes, when he was surprised by the war scare of 1893. At the Opera Gala on 1 January a senior German diplomat found him incoherent with wild speculation. Earlier that day he had inserted an attack on the War Minister's plan for court martial reforms into his customarily conventional New Year greetings to the generals. Bronsart, who at once offered to resign as war minister, was received in audience next morning and abused so violently that, as he told Hohenlohe later in the day, 'Had it been anyone else, I would have reached for my sword.' 'The War Minister thought H.M.'s condition not normal and he was very worried about the future', noted Hohenlohe in his diary.[20] Fortunately by the evening it was known that Jameson and his force had been captured by the Boers and, as the international crisis receded, so William began to recover his self-control. There was no need for precipitate action: a grandiose gesture would satisfy German national pride, and that was something much closer to William's taste.

At ten on the Friday morning (3 January 1896) he arrived in the Wilhelmstrasse, accompanied by three admirals.[21] By now, as the foreign secretary noted, he had 'developed some weird and wonderful plans': ships and marines were to be moved about the ocean; a formal protectorate proclaimed over the Transvaal; an international congress summoned to Berlin; a high-powered mission sent to Pretoria to discover what military aid Kruger required. Hohenlohe and Marschall liked none of these suggestions. At last Marschall proposed the Kaiser might offer Kruger congratulations on having rounded up the Jameson raiders. A colonial specialist drafted a suitable message. Holstein, at hand in an antechamber, objected to this latest instance of peremptory diplomacy, but Marschall assured him that William's original ideas were even worse. At twenty minutes past eleven the fifty-three word telegram was on its way to Kruger:

I wish to express my sincere congratulations that you and your people without asking the help of friendly powers, have succeeded in restoring peace through your own actions against armed bands which broke into your country as disturbers of the peace and in preserving the independence of your country against attack from without.

The Berlin newspapers carried the text of the Kruger Telegram before nightfall. It was in the English press on Saturday and, as the public houses emptied that evening, Londoners indulged in their first widespread anti-German demonstrations: German seamen were beaten up in dockland; German clubs were attacked; a number of shops whose owners bore Germanic names had their windows broken. Jameson was a music-hall hero, and abuse of him ran counter to what the prime minister called, 'the taste of the galleries in the lower class of theatre'. The Kaiser did not realize how deeply the telegram wounded British sensibilities. When, eighteen months later, his brother Henry rode in the Queen's Diamond Jubilee procession to St Paul's, a cockney voice was heard to call out, 'If yer wants to send a telegram to Krooger, there's a post office round the corner.' William had offended the people, not their leaders.

Salisbury and Joseph Chamberlain spoke soberly and sensibly, trying to minimize misunderstandings in which newspapers delighted. Queen Victoria ignored the irate protests of her eldest son and, on 5 January, sent William a masterly letter in which, writing as his grandmother and for his own good, she explained patiently how much she regretted he should have sent Kruger a message 'considered very unfriendly towards this country, which I am sure it is not intended to be'. Although the errant grandchild was spared a spanking, he was placed firmly in the corner.[22]

The Queen's letter reached Potsdam while William was in conference with 'Uncle Hohenlohe' and the original draft of his reply is in the chancellor's handwriting. It was, commented Victoria in her journal, a 'lame and illogical' explanation: William maintained he had rejoiced, not at the discomfiture of English officers and gentlemen, but at the defeat of filibusters acting in defiance of their government, for 'rebels against H.M. the most gracious Queen are for me the most execrable beings in the world'. Since William's pride recoiled from a letter of total apology, he added an irrelevant final paragraph which emphasized his dignity as head of the Prussian dynasty: he was 'glad to say' that the house arrest recently imposed on his sister-in-law and her husband 'has had a very salutary effect and . . . ceased today'.[23]

English press attacks on Germany continued for several weeks. Inevitably they stirred up latent Anglophobia in Berlin and the great trading cities. William hoped he might exploit this mood so as to gain approval in the Reichstag for a rapid growth of the navy. 'To impress seafaring Powers, a fleet is needed', he wrote in a hurried note to Hohenlohe two days after sending his telegram to Kruger. Hohenlohe agreed with him, but the navy secretary, Hollmann, was a realist. He did not think that Reichstag deputies who still regarded the navy as their sovereign's expensive toy would be inclined to support a rapid shipbuilding programme because the newspapers abused the British. William was disgusted: on the evening of 24 January he bluntly informed Hollmann that he would shelve demands for a large fleet until he could find ministers and a Reichstag who shared his patriotic zeal. Later that week he sent for Tirpitz, by now a Rear-Admiral, to tell him he would soon take over as navy secretary from Hollmann; William added that, 'if need be' the chancellor would be replaced by someone from Tirpitz's own generation (presumably Bülow who, like Tirpitz, was born in 1849). But, as Hohenlohe and Eulenburg realized, William remained emotionally so unstable that it was difficult for anyone who listened to him to distinguish serious plans from pipe dreams. The British ambassador, Sir Frank Lascelles, wrote privately to Lord Salisbury on 20 February and warned him of the Kaiser's persistently 'wild state of excitement'.[24]

By now Swaine was back in England and a new military attaché, Colonel Grierson, installed in the British Embassy. Early in March, without consulting Marschall, William set out to repair Anglo-German relations. Characteristically he began by greeting Grierson, when he was out riding on Tuesday, 3 March: 'Remember what I say', he warned, wagging his finger knowingly, 'Russia is at the bottom of your troubles, Russia is your implacable enemy.' That evening the Kaiser came to the British Embassy and stayed talking to the ambassador from ten until half past one in the morning: private information from Russia made him believe the Tsar would soon take foreign affairs in his own hands and follow a policy against Austria in the Balkans and against 'England's' Indian empire; Lord Salisbury should renew the agreements he had reached in 1887 with Italy and Austria-Hungary and thus come nearer to the Triple Alliance. Lascelles told Salisbury he felt the Kaiser's views were 'somewhat imaginative'.[25] When, eight weeks later, William again singled out Grierson and warned him of Russian designs – this time on Egypt – it was assumed in London he was merely out to make mischief.[26] No one believed him any more, or took his diplomatic initiatives seriously.

Meanwhile there was no sign of the new 'Prussian spirit' in government of which William had written to Eulenburg at Christmas. Rear-Admiral Tirpitz, though promised an early summons to office, found in March that Hollmann had gained the Reichstag's approval for a new battleship and three cruisers and, with this success, was for the moment back in the Kaiser's favour. It was suggested that Tirpitz might look for a suitable coaling-station in the China Seas, and in April he left Hamburg to take command of the German Cruiser Squadron in the Far East. The conflict with Bronsart over the reform of military justice was harder to settle. By the spring it seemed as if William could not escape from the courts-martial dispute. It even followed him to the Eulenburg country estate, where he liked to hunt with Phili by day and talk music and aesthetics in the evening. As he was about to set out for a shoot on 18 May he received a telegram from Hohenlohe: the chancellor said he intended that afternoon to promise the Reichstag a courts-martial bill drafted 'in accordance with modern legal opinion'. William was depressed: 'He looked at me half afraid, half miserable, questioning me with his beautiful blue eyes', wrote Eulenburg later. 'Dear Phili' hastened to the rescue, sending Hohenlohe a mild reprimand for having delivered such a statement without approval from their All-Highest sovereign. Hohenlohe was incensed: he would not serve as dummy for a ventriloquial emperor. Bavarians, no less than Prussians, could when they wished bring 'spirit' into government. 'I am no chancellery official but Imperial Chancellor, and it is for me to know what to say', he replied tartly to Eulenburg.[27]

This fine response was unfortunately kept from the Kaiser's notice. William was enjoying such good sport in the fields that Eulenburg was reluctant to spoil his happiness by repeating the chancellor's precise words: a summary was enough for a holiday evening. Yet Hohenlohe's dignified conduct had an odd effect. It convinced Eulenburg that he, at least, should be retained in office as a safeguard against the wild men of the political Right. During the 1896 summer cruise in Norwegian waters Eulenburg persuaded William to keep Hohenlohe as chancellor while gradually introducing his own nominees into the government.[28] Bronsart was so shabbily treated that he offered his resignation, and in August 1896 the courts-martial bill was allowed to fade into the background. Meanwhile William agreed with Eulenburg that, at an appropriate moment, Bülow would take over the Foreign Ministry from Marschall and Tirpitz replace Hollmann at the Navy Office: but not yet.

Throughout 1896–7 Eulenburg's influence was greater on William than at any other time in their friendship. 'Phili' shrank from the responsibilities of high office, but was convinced he understood the Kaiser's psychology as did no other person. William's errors, he believed, sprang from bad counsel, generally tendered by ministers unworthy to serve him, and increasingly he sought leave from his post in Vienna to bring comfort to William's 'troubled soul'. At the end of October 1896 Eulenburg wrote to Bülow in Rome and described how he had found the Kaiser 'suffering terribly, poor thing' because Marschall was prosecuting the Berlin commissioner of police for slandering the government: 'I could only grasp and squeeze his dear hand and say that Prussia was strong enough to have escaped real damage', Eulenburg added.[29] It is impossible to assess the depths of homo-eroticism in their friendship at this time, although Eulenburg's emotional possessiveness pervades the fragments of his correspondence so far printed.

So, too, does a muddled mysticism. When, as Eulenburg once wrote, he stood in 'proximity to the mightiest throne on earth' there seemed to him every reason for his 'beloved Kaiser' to rule as the splendour of his titles demanded.[30] Such an attitude merely encouraged all the absurdities of 'operetta government' – empty boasts of royal power, vague menaces to party politicians, capricious intervention in foreign affairs. And under Eulenburg's influence William became more and more conscious of those spectral ancestors who looked down on him from their celestial gallery. On 22 March 1897 he celebrated the centenary of his grandfather's birth, a ruler who, he declared, 'would have been canonized had he lived in the Middle Ages'. To commemorate the centenary the Kaiser spoke at a banquet in the Berlin palace: he told his guests that his grandfather was present with them in spirit (which may have been a trick of orator's licence) but he then announced with startling emphasis 'and he certainly paid a visit last night to the regimental colours'.[31] Soon it was being said that, in expectation of this ghostly inspection, William II had appointed himself special aide-de-camp to William I for the occasion. Such excursions into mysticism may have meant something to Eulenburg, but they confounded the more worldly members of Berlin society.

Other aspects of William's behaviour aroused greater resentment. In the last week of April the newspapers reported that Prince Henry had read to the officers of his flagship a telegram from his brother in which the Kaiser referred to Reichstag opposition deputies as 'rascals' and 'scoundrels who knew no Fatherland'. Three weeks later a prominent radical Liberal deputy, Eugen Richter, led a verbal onslaught in the Reichstag on irresponsibility in the highest places. Never before had the sovereign been attacked so scathingly in the chamber; and not a deputy rose to speak in his defence. 'The Kaiser's position is growing weaker every day', wrote Holstein to Bülow on 22 May; and even William himself told Hohenlohe that the tone of the newspapers reminded him of the early days of the French revolutionary Convention.[32]

In early June 1897 the Kaiser decided on action. The plan agreed with Eulenburg the previous summer was implemented, although 'Phili' himself and some of William's personal secretariat advised him to wait until August or September. But William's timing was right. Bülow was brought from Rome to the foreign ministry and Tirpitz, who was already on his way home from China, hurried to the Navy Office: Hohenlohe remained a tired, but distinguished, figurehead chancellor.[33] Since the Reichstag was coming to the end of a long and stormy session, the ministerial changes passed off far more peacefully than Eulenburg had anticipated. High summer was, politically, a close season: journalists on holiday, and no parliaments until November. By mid-July, when the *Hohenzollern* sailed north again, Eulenburg was convinced that if Bülow and Tirpitz once captured the imagination of the German public there was now an opportunity to rally the masses behind William II as an embodiment of the national will to greatness.

7. World Powers

At the end of the first week in August 1897 the *Hohenzollern* carried William and Dona up the Gulf of Finland for a six-day visit to St Petersburg. The 'kind, splendid, even lavish hospitality' – to use William's own words – was in a grandiose style. The principal Petersburg newspaper, *Novoe Vremya*, believed the success of the visit was evidence of closer understanding between the two empires, especially in the Far East. William himself remembered 'pleasant hours' when the two rulers exchanged views on the principles they should follow 'to procure to our countries the blessing of Peace'. But at least once in their talks he raised a specific problem: would Nicky object if German warships anchored off the northern Chinese port of Kiaochow? A Russian squadron had wintered there two years previously, but the Tsar made it clear that he would accept a German presence at Kiaochow, provided his naval authorities in the Pacific were consulted in advance. He did not, at the time, mention this conversation to any of his ministers.[1]

On 14 November 1897 German marines from the Far Eastern cruiser squadron landed in Kiaochow Bay and seized control of the town and harbour. Five months later the whole district of Kiaochow was formally transferred from China to Germany on a ninety-nine years' lease and subsequently declared a colonial protectorate within the German Empire. The decision to acquire Kiaochow was the Kaiser's own, first mooted by him as early as November 1896, in the belief that Germany needed a colony with a port which would free the navy from dependence on the dockyards of Hong Kong and serve as a terminus for railways to Peking and northern China. The naval authorities had hoped for a base farther south and the foreign ministry disliked trespassing in a region where Russia and Japan were already competing for influence. But the Kaiser brushed aside all objections. After his visit to St Petersburg he was certain he could count on Nicky. He argued that

Germany would benefit from a spectacular success in foreign policy, something which would capture and hold the imagination of the people. All that now concerned the Kaiser was the question of timing. On 1 November, the Feast of All Saints, two German Roman Catholic missionaries were attacked and murdered by Chinese brigands in southern Shantung. The news reached Berlin four days later. It gave William the opportunity for which he had been waiting. He telegraphed to the Tsar: 'Trust you approve according to our conversation Peterhof my sending German squadron to Kiaochow, as it is the only port available to operate from as base against marauders.' He added by way of explanation, that he felt obliged to safeguard the religious missions of his Roman Catholic subjects. The Tsar's reply was non-committal – 'Cannot approve nor disapprove your sending German squadron to Kiaochow' – but it was good enough for William. His admiral, who had himself recommended Kiaochow as a base, was ordered to sail into the bay. Bülow was in Rome. There he received a jubilant telegram from his Kaiser:

Hundreds of German traders will be delighted to learn that the German Empire has at last gained a sure foothold in Asia: hundreds of thousands of Chinese will tremble when they feel the iron fist of Germany lying heavily on their neck; and the entire German people will rejoice that their government has taken firm action. Once and for all time I shall show that the German Kaiser is no person with whom to take liberties nor to have as an enemy.[2]

Whether many of the 350 million Chinese trembled at the acquisition by Germany of 200 square miles in Shantung may be doubted, but William was right in his belief that his own subjects would applaud his action. It expressed the dominant sentiment in German society at the close of the century, the need to find an outlet for the energy of a unified people seeking to raise itself from continental mastery to world power. Kiaochow was important, not as a place, but as a status symbol and as proof that 'our dear master' (as Bülow called William) was aware that the new economic strength of the Reich needed a 'world policy'. Germany was a young nation growing fast. In 1898 one out of every three Germans was under the age of eighteen, and the birth rate was still rising. The manufacturing activity of the German labour force was increasing five times as rapidly as its British counterpart. Academics and industrialists preached the need for a form of imperialism (*Weltpolitik*) which would, in some mysterious way, retrospectively justify the unification of Germany by giving her people a sense of world mission; and, at the same time, it would satisfy the need for overseas markets. William and Bülow did not invent *Weltpolitik*: they harnessed it.

Not everyone in the administration was pleased at the Kaiser's initiative. Some Bismarckians in the foreign service feared he had again destroyed the fragile friendship with Russia. Others expected war. Tirpitz told Hohenlohe there would be a conflict with China; the naval High Command prepared for operations against the Japanese; the Minister of War gloomily predicted the worst in Europe and checked mobilization plans. But William remained elated. He hunted on the Eulenburg estate as usual in November, for he saw no reason to stay in the capital. There was none of the nervous strain he had shown during earlier crises. He was not surprised that the seizure of Kiaochow should begin a scramble to lease ports from the Chinese: the Russians acquired Port Arthur, the British Wei-hai-wei, the French Kwangchow. Not a shot was fired. The traditional mistrust between the British and the Russians in the Far East worked to Germany's benefit: each rival was more suspicious of the other than of the newcomer.[3]

Muraviev, the Russian foreign minister, was less accommodating than his emperor, but the Kaiser knew him as a lightweight and was unimpressed by his blustering objections to German policy. William was determined that the Tsar should welcome Germany as a partner, not a competitor. Both empires, he assured Nicholas, were committed to spreading Christianity through the East, guarding civilization from the Yellow Peril. On 4 January 1898 he sent Nicky a drawing which showed the figures of Russia and Germany 'as sentinels at the Yellow Sea for the proclaiming of the Gospel of Light and Truth in the East'. 'I drew the sketch in the Xmas week under the blaze of the lights in the Xmas trees', he explained. So convinced was William that his sketch would create a good impression that he showed it to Hohenlohe on New Year's Eve. The chancellor was too old to welcome dynastic diplomacy by visual aid but, as he drily told Holstein, 'I did not risk attempting to dissuade him'.[4] There is no evidence that the sketch impressed the Tsar, but by March the Russians had certainly resigned themselves to sharing guard-duty on the Yellow Sea with their German neighbour.

Hohenlohe, too, was honoured with a topical card that Christmas: a picture of bluejackets manning the guns of a warship. Above the bluejackets was inscribed the Latin tag, *Ultima ratio regis* ('The final argument of the king'). Below them William had written, 'Good luck for New Year '98.'[5] Now that Germany had gained her foothold in Asia, the navy had returned to the forefront of the Kaiser's mind. It was to remain there throughout the year, and beyond.

When Tirpitz took over as navy secretary from Hollmann early in June 1897, he immediately began to plan a High Seas Fleet. His energy was astonishing. On 15 June he presented William with a two-thousand-word memorandum on the future character of the navy. It was a revolutionary document, and easily won the Kaiser's enthusiastic support. Tirpitz argued that warship design should be based on the type of threat likely to face an individual country. 'For Germany, the most dangerous enemy at the present time is England', he proclaimed as a basic thesis. The only way to challenge British seapower effectively was to concentrate on building battleships rather than cruisers and follow a strategy which placed 'the highest military potential' in the waters 'between Heligoland and the Thames'. Such a fleet would have no difficulty in meeting the lesser challenge offered by the Russian and French navies, but it could not be built up immediately. Tirpitz proposed to submit a parliamentary bill – the 'Navy Law' – which would determine and secure revenue for warship construction until the year 1905. By then he calculated that Germany would possess, in home waters, a fleet of nineteen battleships and twenty-four cruisers. Vessels serving in African and Asian waters would be reduced in number. Early in August a draft Navy Law, providing for seven battleships, two large cruisers and seven small cruisers was presented to the Kaiser. When he opened the Reichstag session on 30 November 'the development of our battle fleet' figured prominently in his speech from the throne.[6]

Earlier appeals for a large navy had been received with widespread indifference. But Tirpitz was a master propagandist. He established a special news section in Berlin to answer hostile criticism in the national and provincial press. A comprehensive study, *The Sea Interests of the German Reich*, provided Reichstag deputies with the facts needed for any debate. Outside parliament, local naval associations sponsored talks and meetings, many addressed by university professors. Between September 1897 and March 1898 the German Colonial Society organized 173 lectures on the need for a navy and distributed 140,000 pamphlets and more than 2,000 copies of Mahan's *Influence of Sea Power*. All this agitation – the most professional exercise in public salesmanship perpetrated in pre-Nazi Germany – secured passage of the Navy Law

through the Reichstag by a comfortable majority on 26 March 1898.
The Kaiser was overwhelmed with pride and joy. He had, he confessed
privately, never anticipated there could be such a change of heart in the
Empire. But he knew whom he should thank. The credit for 'winning
over fifty million stubborn, short-sighted and bad-tempered Germans
. . . in eight months' belonged to that 'truly mighty man', Admiral
Tirpitz, he told Hohenlohe.[7] If Bülow was to be his Bismarck, then
Tirpitz had already staked a claim to be his Roon.

The agitation for the Navy Law aroused such enthusiasm that conservative supporters of the monarchy were reluctant to see Tirpitz's
mass movement dissolve once the Reichstag had given the shipbuilding
programme its approval. Early in April 1898 a group of businessmen,
industrialists and aristocrats founded the Navy League, to foster
national consciousness throughout Germany. The League was independent of political parties and claimed to be above them. It therefore
became the principal instrument of monarchist loyalty in the Reich.
For William this was a significant development. Propaganda for the
navy was propaganda for an all-German institution and naturally
encouraged German patriotism whereas discussions about the future of
the army (in which Bavaria, Saxony and Württemberg clung tenaci-
ously to relics of independent traditions) invariably aroused par-
ticularist sentiment. Anyone, in town or village, could join the Navy
League for a mere fifty pfennigs a year, but it drew its funds not so much
from individual members as from great combines such as Krupp and
Stumm, their satellite financial concerns, and the General Federation of
German Industrialists. Their resources enabled the propaganda begun
by the German Colonial Society to be stepped up considerably. Within
two years the Navy League had a quarter of a million members, within
seven years a million. Public servants who sought advancement did
well to associate themselves with a cause favoured by their sovereign
and his intimate advisers. But, self-interest aside, there was genuine
enthusiasm for the navy as a symbol of 'world policy' and for the
Kaiser, whom even his critics conceded was 'the true creator of our
fleet'. By 1906 one adult male in every twelve belonged to the Navy
League or one of its associate bodies. This figure was three times as high
as the membership of the principal tacitly anti-monarchist organ-
ization in the Reich, the Social Democratic Party, although in an
election the socialists could count on over three million supporters.
After 1905–6 the Navy League became more rabidly nationalistic than

its imperial patron and was therefore at times an embarrassment. But at first the League was a welcome sounding-board for William's prophecies and opinions. When, on 23 September 1898, he declared in a speech at Stettin that 'Our future lies on the water' he was reiterating points he had stressed many times before. The Navy League ensured that the Stettin speech, unlike its predecessors, was known and remembered throughout Germany.[8]

William's words were reported in most British newspapers, and yet the speech at Stettin prompted editorial comment only in the *Morning Post*. In general the British press had come to accept the need for Germany to increase her fleet. When the Navy Law was first announced in the autumn of 1897 some commentators feared Tirpitz's programme would stimulate French and Russian shipbuilding and thereby upset the balance of naval power. Only the conservative weekly, *Saturday Review*, was from the outset suspicious and prepared to link the Kruger telegram, Kiaochow and the Navy Law in one long Catonian warning of Germany's growing might: *Germaniam esse delendam* were the closing words of an article on 11 September, which delighted Anglophobes in Berlin. 'William the Witless wants a navy', the *Saturday Review* commented in lighter vein for the Christmas number of 1897. 'By 1904', it added, 'perhaps England may have to determine what she will do with the ships of His Sacred Majesty.' At the same time, for eight weeks in the autumn of 1897, the *Naval and Military Record* carried a serial story by Colonel Cornwallis Maude in which Britain, already holding off the armies of France and Russia, was unexpectedly confronted with a German invasion ordered by the Kaiser without a declaration of war. Yet this tale, prototype for a familiar genre ten or fifteen years later, was not especially hostile to Germany or to William himself. Basically it was a war-game fantasy and went almost unnoticed. Most dailies reported Tirpitz's naval programme calmly and sensibly: the *Daily Telegraph* on 1 December 1897, the *Manchester Guardian* a day later, and *The Times* on 28 March 1898 all conceded that Germany was wise to re-assess her naval policy when faced with hostility from France and Russia and new problems caused by distant commitments. There was as yet in London no sense of menace in the German shipbuilding programme. Salisbury was too concerned with French colonial pretensions in Africa to follow the *Saturday Review* in its tirades against Germany.[9]

Occasionally German writers, too, considered an invasion of

England, though less imaginatively than Cornwallis Maude. The Kaiser himself was fascinated by a naval staff plan prepared for him in 1897 which suggested seizure of the Scheldt estuary as a stepping stone to the east coast of England.[10] Yet over all these conjectures there remained a certain academic unreality. Now and again Tirpitz and his sovereign chilled each other's spine with fearsome tales of a British surprise attack, the Royal Navy seeking to destroy Tirpitz's creation before it became powerful. No doubt this nightmare owed something to the publication in 1897 of Mahan's considered analysis of Nelson's action against the Danish fleet at Copenhagen. Non-navalists, however, refused to take such fears seriously. Hatzfeldt, who had served as ambassador in London since 1885, discounted the likelihood of war between two nations whose commerce benefitted mutually from the preservation of peace. He emphasized that Germany was recognized as an efficient and industrious rival for world markets, but not as a potential enemy. The grandiose schemes of *Weltpolitik* did not stir Hatzfeldt's imagination. More than once, he complained of the 'cattle market diplomacy' of the Wilhelmstrasse. To him 'world power' implied the partnership of Britain's navy and Germany's army. Nothing would have pleased him so much as the conclusion of an Anglo-German alliance.[11]

Salisbury knew Hatzfeldt well and liked him; however experience made him sceptical of approaches from the German Embassy which did not always match the mood in Berlin. But in the spring of 1898 Salisbury fell ill. For five weeks his nephew Balfour looked after foreign affairs, prompted by the impulsive and energetic Colonial Secretary, Joseph Chamberlain. In the last week of March Hatzfeldt met Balfour and Chamberlain at two private dinner-parties and sought their views on Anglo-German relations. Balfour was non-commital: Chamberlain, to his surprise, favoured an alliance – Britain and Germany could jointly safeguard China from further foreign incursions. Hatzfeldt was delighted, but his report of Chamberlain's proposals aroused suspicion in Berlin. 'Chamberlain must not forget that in East Prussia I have one Prussian army-corps against three Russian armies and nine cavalry divisions close to the frontier', William wrote in the margin. 'No Chinese wall separates them from me and no English battleships can keep them at bay.'[12] He wanted nothing more to do with 'Brummagem Joe' (as the Kaiser liked to call Chamberlain): it was a trap to entangle Germany with Russia.

In the second week of April, however, William was visited at Wilhelmshohe by Baron von Eckardstein, honorary counsellor of the embassy in London and an influential figure in London society. Eckardstein received the impression that the Kaiser was eager for an Anglo-German alliance, and reported back enthusiastically to Hatzfeldt. The ambassador was puzzled: he suspected Eckardstein had embellished the Kaiser's remarks, for his account did not tally with the letters and telegrams from Berlin. But Hatzfeldt seized on one reported reaction of the Kaiser: his desire to hear something from Salisbury himself, rather than from other members of the cabinet. On 15 April Hatzfeldt sent Salisbury a nineteen-page letter in which he welcomed the improvement in Anglo-German relations and suggested that Queen Victoria, who was resting in the south of France, might profitably meet her grandson at Coblenz during her homeward journey, thereby letting the world see that the British and German nations were no longer rivals in empire. This proposal was speedily and firmly quashed by Salisbury. He suggested that, as grandmother and grandson had not met for three years, the Kaiser might come to Windsor in the early winter.[13]

With Chamberlain, Salisbury was as practical as ever: 'I quite agree with you that under the circumstances a close relation with Germany would be very desirable', he wrote, 'but can we get it?' He was worried over the Kaiser's susceptibilities. If Eckardstein was correctly representing William's views, then some offer should be made, a 'mutual defensive arrangement' perhaps. On 11 May Salisbury at last had a long personal interview with the ambassador. Unfortunately neither man seems to have understood the other, and the British and German accounts of this meeting are totally at variance. Salisbury told Lascelles he had welcomed the prospect of 'a general alliance with Germany ... so long as it dealt with general European interests', but added that he had raised various practical difficulties. Hatzfeldt reported to Bülow that Salisbury was principally concerned with European problems, and quoted him as having said, 'You ask too much for your friendship.' In Berlin it was assumed the talks were at an end. On 30 May Willy let 'dearest Nicky' know the British had been angling for an alliance. In reply, the Tsar telegraphed news of Salisbury's 'tempting proposals' to Russia earlier in the year, but added that these offers were turned down 'without thinking twice about it'. Mischief and malice were speedily eroding the veneer of dynastic friendship.[14]

At this point an older champion of good relations between London and Berlin sought to take over from Hatzfeldt and Eckardstein. The Kaiser's mother made repeated efforts that summer of 1898 to bring about an understanding between the two countries. Her son treated her intervention with pained surprise. In a long letter on 1 June he reviewed – not entirely dispassionately – the contacts between successive British and German governments since his accession: 'In the Siamese Imbroglio . . . I staunchly stood by England and volunteered my help', he wrote in his best English. 'Instead of thanks or of help in our colonising enterprises I got nothing whatever, and for the last 3 years have been abused, ill-treated and a butt to any bad joke any musikhall singer (*sic*) or fishmonger or pressman thought fit to let fly at me.' If the idea of an alliance is genuinely meant, he asked, 'Why in the name of all that is diplomatic use and sense, does not the Prime Minister make a real proposal?'[15] Vicky (the Empress Frederick) continued to act as an unofficial intermediary throughout the summer: 'I do know for a fact that William *is most* anxious for a *rapprochement* with England, and *hopes* with all his heart that England *will come* forward in some sort of way and meet him half-way', she wrote to Queen Victoria in mid-July. On 21 August she invited William to Friedrichshof for a meeting with the British ambassador, who had recently held private talks with Chamberlain and Balfour in London. On that occasion Lascelles told William that 'in some influential quarters' in Britain there was 'a wish for an alliance which should be strictly defensive and should take effect if either party were attacked by two Powers at the same time'. This unexpected offer impressed William: never before in his reign had the two countries seemed so close to alliance. But no one in Berlin shared the Kaiser's optimism. What gains were there for Germany in such an understanding? Bülow, on taking up office, had been told by Eulenburg, 'You will always achieve all you desire so long as you do not omit to express your admiration whenever H.M. has earned it.' This was the advice he now followed. The Kaiser was congratulated on his brilliant exposition of German policy to Lascelles; but within three days Bülow had succeeded in convincing William it was impossible to reach any general agreement with Britain without making it appear in St Petersburg as if Germany was taking sides against Russia.[16] The link with St Petersburg remained in being: the alliance project swiftly became a historical curiosity.*

* Something, however, was gained from all this diplomatic activity. On 30 August 1898 the British and Germans concluded an agreement to collaborate in southern Africa if, as seemed

In October 1898 William's love of travel induced him to undertake a journey to Constantinople, Jerusalem and Damascus.[17] This 'expedition to the Orient', as it was derisively called by some of his critics, aroused stronger feelings than any previous royal visit. It was bad enough that William and Dona should accept hospitality from Sultan Abdul Hamid, who had been ostracized for the past three years for his failure to safeguard the lives and property of the Armenian Christians in his empire. It seemed even more deplorable that William and Dona should then sail down to Haifa and travel to the Christian holy places under the protection of the Sultan's Syrian bodyguards (and the management of Thomas Cook). The press, especially in France, poured scorn on the Kaiser's pilgrimage. In the twelfth century the Crusader monarchs were reluctant to wear kingly apparel in a city where their Saviour had once ridden on an ass and 'worn a crown of thorns', but William's delight in the show business of majesty knew no such restraint. On 29 October 1898 he made his entry into Jerusalem, mounted on a black charger, wearing white ceremonial uniform, his helmet surmounted by a burnished gold eagle. Hermann Knackfuss, the most favoured of court painters, was at hand to ensure that this historic occasion was preserved on canvas with a minimum of artistic licence: the dust, flies and beads of perspiration were omitted; the Kaiser's sense of grandeur faithfully retained.

'Revolting', wrote the Tsar's mother to her son. 'All done out of sheer vanity, so as to be talked about! . . . That pose of Ober-pastor, preaching peace on earth in a thunderous voice as though he were commanding troops, and she wearing the Grand Cross in Jerusalem, all this is perfectly ridiculous and has no trace of religious feeling – disgusting!'[18] But was it all a pose? William had a deep, though highly personal, religious faith. Dona, too, was pious: she contributed to the founding of four dozen churches. A few days after leaving Jerusalem Willy told Nicky, 'The thought . . . that His feet trod the same ground is most stirring to one's heart, and makes it beat faster and more fervently': there is no reason for doubting his sincerity. But he was also excessively conscious of Germany's imperial past. No Christian sovereign had entered Jerusalem since the Hohenstaufen Emperor

---

likely, the Portuguese wished to dispose of their colonial possessions in order to stave off bankruptcy. At the same time the Germans agreed not to seek a naval base in Delagoa Bay. This undertaking was a clear sign of waning interest in the Boers, a tacit repudiation of the Kruger telegram.

Frederick II captured the city in 1229. If a Hohenzollern Emperor could not take Jerusalem by storm, then at least he could make certain he was hailed as a conqueror come in peace.

Telegrams to the Tsar, the Sultan and Queen Victoria ensured they missed no detail of his rapturous progress. Yet, as he admitted in his letter to Nicky, he was disillusioned by 'the way Religion is understood in Jerusalem', the conflicts between the Christian sects and the air of political intrigue. 'My personal feeling in leaving the holy city was that I felt profoundly ashamed before the Moslems and that if I had come there without any Religion at all I certainly would have turned Mahometan', he wrote.[19] He tried to be dispassionate, visiting Catholic and Orthodox shrines, praising 'the prettiness' of the English church in a message to his grandmother. Against the wishes of several members of his suite, he even received a five-man Zionist deputation which had come all the way from Vienna and was headed by the formidable Theodor Herzl: German imperial protection to settle Jewish communities in Palestine? It was a tempting suggestion and held William's interest, momentarily.[20] But, more and more, he was fascinated by the Moslems. The people of Damascus greeted him ecstatically and he responded to their adulation as though he were a deprived child. The Sultan of Turkey and the three hundred million Moslems who, throughout the world, respected the Sultan as their spiritual leader could now 'rest assured that the German Kaiser will ever be their friend', he declared in a speech at the tomb of Saladin. Once more he had spoken unfortunately: the two temporal rulers with the greatest number of Moslem subjects were his grandmother, Queen-Empress Victoria, and the Tsar of All the Russias. Neither was pleased. 'Cook's Crusader', as *Punch* called him, seemed to be exchanging the Cross for the Crescent.[21]

The principal consequence of these visits to Constantinople and Damascus was increased German economic penetration of the Middle East. A German company had begun building railways in Asia Minor five years previously, and a line already ran for two hundred and fifty miles through Anatolia from Eskisehir to Konya. George von Siemens, senior director of Germany's biggest bank, the *Deutsche Bank*, was in Constantinople at the time of the Kaiser's visit and succeeded in securing concessions for harbour works on the Asiatic shore of the Bosphorus. These concessions were followed, in the spring of 1899, by formal authority to build a line linking the Bosphorus to the Persian

Gulf. This 'Baghdad Railway' project was potentially of greater economic value to Germany than the Kaiser's first essay in world policy, the seizure of Kiaochow. A 'trade and resources map of Asia Minor' published in Halle at the time of William's visit to the Ottoman Empire sold remarkably quickly in Germany, where industry was booming. Bülow insisted that the Baghdad railway and its subsidiary ventures were examples of German commercial enterprise, no more and no less. But William, like Bonaparte, saw in the Orient a sector of the world where traditionally glory was to be gained in splendour. Cecil Rhodes, visiting Berlin in March 1899, found William no longer actively concerned with southern Africa. To Rhodes he seemed 'a man of grand ideas' whose vision was, at the time, fixed on Mesopotamia. Significantly the German Admiralty began to look for coaling-stations on the Yemeni coast and in the southern Persian Gulf: a German Aden would serve as a staging-post for the Far East – or for India.[22]

At first the new German interest in the Middle East did not alarm the British. *The Times* even smiled benevolently on Germany's sense of mission in the East. The anger of the French press was sufficient in itself to ensure that the leading conservative newspapers in London treated William sympathetically, for Anglo-French relations were bad at that moment because of the colonial confrontation at Fashoda. But the Damascus speech left people in England uneasy. Although William sent his grandmother several charmingly phrased messages, Victoria was irritated by his behaviour. A tart note to Lord Salisbury from Balmoral complained that 'the German Emperor is better informed about our Navy than I am'; and a telegram from William in Malta on his way home left her unmollified – he had inspected the Mediterranean Squadron and found HMS *Caesar* 'the most fighting ship I ever set my foot on'.[23] If William had sailed home up Channel the Queen would have invited him to Windsor, but she was in no hurry to send an invitation and, as he decided not to risk winter gales in the Bay of Biscay, the situation did not arise. Salisbury was sorry William did not come to Windsor: 'The attitude of France makes it desirable that the world should believe in an understanding between Germany and England', he told the Queen. Shortly before Christmas William commented to the British ambassador on the 'excellent' condition of Anglo-German relations, adding that he was convinced there would be war between Britain and France in the coming year. But, as Holstein explained to Hatzfeldt, he did not wish to be entangled in other people's quarrels: 'His Majesty sees clearly the advantages . . . of abandoning our position as spectator as late as possible.'[24]

No one, however, could describe him as a disinterested onlooker. On 20 January 1899 he called, once again, at the British Embassy, in order to let Lascelles know that France and Russia had invited Germany to join them in a coalition against Great Britain but that 'he had no intention of doing so'. He also warned Lascelles of a secret treaty between Russia and Afghanistan which would result in a military threat to India later in the year.[25] These crude attempts to frustrate settlements between Britain and Russia over rival railway schemes in China or in Persia left Salisbury unmoved. But they angered Queen Victoria. 'William's fortieth birthday', she wrote in her journal on 27 January, 'I wish he was more prudent and less impulsive at such an age'. Four weeks later she wrote to Nicholas II telling him how the Kaiser 'constantly says that Russia is doing all in her power to work against us'. The Tsar was assured that the British Government did not believe in these reports. She hoped that if William 'should tell things against us to you', such mischievous behaviour would not lead to misunderstandings.[26] Within a fortnight of the Queen's letter, the Russians had accepted British proposals for the agreement on railway construction in China which Salisbury had sought for eight months. This agreement, and the settlement at the same time of disputes in Africa with France, annoyed William. He was childishly vain over world policy, resenting any development which did not confirm his prejudices and predictions. Bülow played up to his master's vanity. In February 1899, for example, Bülow completed arrangements for the purchase from Spain of the minute Caroline Islands in the western Pacific (population: 65,000), reporting to the Kaiser that 'this success will stimulate people and navy to follow your Majesty along the road which leads to world power, greatness and eternal glory'.[27] To mark Bülow's achievement William created him a Count, the honour Bismarck had received after Prussia's triumph over Austria in 1866.

In one sense, Bülow was right: the German people as a whole delighted to follow their sovereign in his fancies and follies of grandeur. They were glad he was master of the Carolines and, within a few months, of the Pelews and most of the Mariana Islands, too. Moreover they shared his indignation that, during disorders in the Samoan archipelago, the British had opposed a German-sponsored chieftain and had permitted German property to be damaged. From March to

October 1899 grievances over Samoa plagued Anglo-German relations. They prompted William to send his grandmother an astonishing
letter in which he complained at length of Salisbury's treatment of
Germany ('Lord Salisbury cares for us no more than for Portugal, Chile
or the Patagonians'). The Queen was indignant: 'The tone in which
you write about Lord Salisbury I can only attribute to a temporary
irritation on your part', she replied. 'I doubt if any Sovereign ever wrote
in such terms to another Sovereign, and that Sovereign his own
Grandmother, about their Prime Minister'.[28] Salisbury, as he wrote
privately to Lascelles on 10 May, was 'puzzled' why the Kaiser should
look on him as an enemy:

> I cannot make out what I have done to deserve that distinguished reputation
> ... It is a great nuisance that one of the main factors in the European
> calculation should be so ultra-human. He is as jealous as a woman because he
> does not think the Queen pays him enough attention . . . I can only submit, as
> is my duty, to be belaboured for other people's offences. I must console myself
> with thinking that five years ago he hated Lord Rosebery as much as he does
> me now.

Some months previously Eulenburg had warned Bülow to remember
that 'William II takes everything personally'; and the Kaiser's attitude
towards Salisbury confirms this judgement. Once he convinced himself
that the prime minister thought little of his gestures towards England
nothing would induce him to change his mind. 'My feelings towards
him have never been very acute in any direction', Salisbury assured
Lascelles, but increasingly he began to look for subtle motives in every
word and whim of William, expecting a Bismarckian mastery of policy
which never existed.[29]

Nevertheless Salisbury still believed Anglo-German relations would
benefit from a visit by the Kaiser to his grandmother. It seemed
probable he would descend on Cowes once more. The Samoan dispute,
however, dragged on through the summer of 1899, and William
excused himself from the regatta when Dona broke a fibula ten days
before the racing began. In mid-September Hatzfeldt warned Salisbury
that William felt so strongly over Samoa that there was a danger he
would be recalled as ambassador and that German policy would turn
decisively against Great Britain. Salisbury was reluctant in principle to
give way, but he yielded to pressure in the cabinet from Balfour and
Chamberlain. The Samoan dispute was settled by an agreement which

enabled Germany to acquire the island of Upolu, where William believed a naval coaling-station could be set up. Immediately, the Kaiser agreed to come to Windsor. He was delighted with the Samoan settlement. Upolu, like the acquisition of the Carolines, was a success for 'world policy' and the partnership of Kaiser and foreign secretary. An ecstatic telegram was despatched to Bülow: 'You are a real magician granted to me quite undeservedly by Heaven in its goodness.'[30]

William and Dona, with a large suite (including Bülow), arrived at Windsor on 20 November 1899. They stayed there five nights, and then went for a couple of days to Sandringham, as guests of the Prince of Wales. It was a difficult time for any ruler to visit Great Britain. The long-expected conflict with the Boers had begun five weeks before, and public sympathy in Germany was overwhelmingly on Kruger's side. So long as William was in Berlin, he reflected German opinion. He took advantage of the patriotic mood among his subjects to announce a Second Navy Law, which would be introduced in the Reichstag early in the coming year. Yet his attitude to the war was realistic: 'I am in no position to go beyond strict neutrality for I must first get myself a fleet', he remarked. 'In twenty years' time, when the fleet is in being, I shall be able to talk differently.' Once at Windsor, however, he became as English as his surroundings. 'From this tower the world is ruled', he told his military aides in a burst of admiration as they waited for the Queen at the foot of the Round Tower. It was, he confided to Bülow, 'the finest reception and the most inspiring impression of my life'. He did not meet the prime minister – for Lady Salisbury died at Hatfield on the first day of the German visit – but he talked at length with Balfour and Chamberlain. The Queen was relieved to find that both William and Bülow deplored 'the shameful attacks on England' in the German press. To Balfour the Kaiser patiently explained how the German General Staff thought the British army could win in South Africa. With Chamberlain he was more cautious: an alliance between Britain, America and Germany – a favourite project of Chamberlain – he dismissed as contrary to the traditions of all three countries; he did not want to find himself forced into a conflict with Russia; but he listened sympathetically to suggestions of limited Anglo-German agreements for co-operation in potentially dangerous areas, such as Asia Minor and Morocco. Through the Queen's private secretary, the Kaiser sent a message to Lord Salisbury: no alliance, 'for we know that is impossible, but an understanding, "Yes".'[31]

Yet in the weeks which followed the Windsor visits there seemed little chance of understanding. Two days after William's departure, Joseph Chamberlain made a speech at Leicester in which he developed his ideas for an Anglo-Germano-American alliance, despite the coolness so recently shown by the Kaiser to the proposal. German newspapers were hostile. They hinted that some sort of bargain had been reached at Windsor. Bülow, forced on the defensive, delivered an important speech in the Reichstag on 11 December in which he asserted that Germany could live in peace and amity with 'England' only on a basis of equality. To William's delight, he shifted the emphasis away from verbal quarrels to the naval problem: 'We must build a fleet strong enough to prevent an attack . . . from any power', he said.[32] The context showed clearly that, in rallying support for the new Navy Law, he was deliberately implying a challenge from the Royal Navy.

In the first week of January it was learnt in Berlin that British warships had intercepted three German vessels suspected of carrying supplies for the Boers. This 'piracy' excited public opinion still further against England and was exploited by the Navy League in its demands for more and more battleships. The newspapers which condemned 'England's buccaneering adventure' also made public Tirpitz's famous theory: if Germany had a modern and concentrated High Seas Fleet, not even 'the strongest naval power' would risk attacking it for fear of being subsequently left too weak to face a coalition of other navies. There was never much doubt that the Navy Law would have a smooth passage through the Reichstag, even though, unlike its predecessor, it set no limit to the cost of construction. Despite brilliant speeches by the socialists Karl Liebknecht and August Bebel, the Navy Law was carried on 12 June 1900 by 201 votes to 103. By 1916 Tirpitz could expect to have at sea a fleet of 38 modern battleships and 58 cruisers. Over the next five years a battleship would be launched, on the average, every four months.[33]

Once again the Kaiser celebrated passage of a Navy Law with champagne. 'As my grandfather did for the army, so will I for my navy', he had told officers of the Berlin garrison on New Year's Day.[34] Yet, in spite of Navy League propaganda and outbursts of England-baiting in the newspapers, William maintained better relations with the British than in the previous winter. Detailed notes on the military conduct of the Boer War were sent to the Prince of Wales at Christmas. Five weeks later, as though emphasizing his Englishness, William introduced sporting allusions, to which his uncle took ready exception: the Prince could see no parallel between 'our conflict with the Boers' and the Lords Test Match of the previous summer (in which Australia beat England by ten wickets). But William, undaunted, continued to show goodwill. He congratulated the Queen on the relief of Kimberley. More significantly, he sent to the Prince of Wales full details of attempts by the Russians to form a continental league which would 'enforce peace' in South Africa. The Prince and Queen Victoria warmly thanked William; but the prime minister had doubts about the whole affair, suspecting that the Kaiser was over-dramatizing a conventional diplomatic initiative.[35]

Lord Salisbury's scepticism sprang, in part, from William's odd behaviour. Before writing to the Prince, William had let Lascelles know of the Russian move but had, at the same time, minimized its significance: 'The British Government', he told the ambassador, 'would be a set of unmitigated noodles if they cared a farthing' for anything Russia might do. A week later he discussed the incident again with Lascelles: it showed, he said, the deplorable character of the Tsar ('He is as weak as Louis XVI'). 'I let you know', he explained, 'because I am the grandson of your Queen, for whom I have always retained the deepest devotion.' Bülow, so Lascelles reported, was worried by his master's indiscretion. It is now clear that Salisbury was not entirely wrong in his assessment: the Russians contemplated joint 'amicable pressure' rather than the coercive measures implied by William's dramatic warning.[36] Yet, whatever his methods and motives, William's later claim to have befriended the British during the Boer War has some basis in fact. He defied the Anglophobe envy of 'official' Berlin and, by insisting on strict neutrality, ruled out hostile intervention by any effective league of continental powers.

That summer of 1900, however, attention was suddenly and startlingly shifted from Africa to the Far East. In China resentment against foreign domination exploded in the so-called 'Boxer Rising'. Europeans were besieged for three months in the diplomatic quarter of Peking. On 20 June the German minister, Baron von Ketteler, was murdered while attempting to negotiate with Chinese officials. The British, French and Americans set about raising impromptu relief forces. But Ketteler's murder seemed to the Kaiser as great an insult to Germany's world-power status as had been Gordon's death at Khartoum to the British. William wished to avenge Ketteler by a massive punitive expedition, with token contingents from other nations serving under a German commander-in-chief, someone who could win the glory that had come to Kitchener at Omdurman. For this task William selected Waldersee – although he was disappointed that Salisbury refused to be prodded into proposing the general himself.[37] On 27 July William inspected the German contingent at Bremerhaven, presented Waldersee with his Field-Marshal's baton, and made a speech which included the most unfortunately phrased of all imperial perorations:

Just as the Huns under their King, Attila, a thousand years ago made for themselves a name which men still respect, so should you give the name of German such reason to be remembered in China for a thousand years that no Chinaman, be his eyes slit or not, shall dare to look a German in the face. Carry yourselves like men, and the blessing of God go with you.

Apart from this passage – which later led propagandists to abuse Germans as 'Huns' – it was a splendid occasion, though one commentator acidly observed that Waldersee was receiving 'laurels on account'.[38] It was a pity, for many people's prestige, that by the time Waldersee reached China the Legations were relieved, and the emergency virtually over.

Lord Salisbury assumed that William wished Germany 'to do something really big in China'. Apart from the Bremerhaven speech there had been the usual warning of Franco-Russian intrigues ('I have heard some of this before', Salisbury commented drily) and complaints by letter to the Prince of Wales that it was impossible for him to understand the Chinese policy of 'the great men in Downing Street'.[39] Yet, in reality, William's objectives were more modest. He explained them to Lascelles on 22 August: an Anglo-German agreement for an 'open door' in trade along the Yangtse where, he said, 'German commercial interests are second and not too far inferior to those of England'. Most of the cabinet welcomed the proposal: Salisbury was uneasy. Enquiries were made to check trade figures for the Yangtse valley, and it was found that the value to Great Britain was three times as high as to Germany. Once again, as over Samoa, Salisbury was obdurate. But he bowed to his colleagues' will, and at last, on 16 October 1900, an agreement was reached by which the two powers agreed to keep open all trade with China and to preserve the integrity of the Chinese Empire.[40]

Gradually opinion in the British cabinet was coming to favour alliance with Germany. Chamberlain was well disposed and, early in the new year, Eckardstein reported Chamberlain and the Duke of Devonshire as speaking of a possible alliance while the Prince of Wales was staying at Chatsworth. But the Prince had other matters on his mind. From Osborne he had learnt that Queen Victoria's health was failing, and he had recently heard (though he was pledged to secrecy) that his favourite sister, the Kaiser's mother, was stricken with cancer. On Friday, 18 January, the Prince was summoned urgently to Osborne. His brother, the Duke of Connaught, was that day in Berlin attending the bicentenary celebrations of the Prussian kingdom. He, too, was called to the Queen's bedside, and William thus heard of his grandmother's deterioration in health almost as soon as her two sons. He at once decided it was his duty to be present at Osborne. He cancelled his remaining engagements for the bicentenary weekend and on Saturday morning sent an uncoded telegram to the Prince of Wales announcing he would reach London the following evening.[41]

The British public was deeply moved by his action. He reached Osborne on Monday morning, and remained at his grandmother's bedside for much of the night. The family found him dignified, subdued, and helpful in small details: for once he forgot to be William the Grand. For the last two and a half hours of the Queen's life, he assisted her doctor to support her on her pillow, his right arm pinned beneath her, strained as it had been so often under Hinzpeter's tuition in his boyhood. When, early in the evening of Tuesday 22 January, Queen Victoria died, William was as much an intimate member of her family as her English children and grandchildren. Indeed, next day, as the new King, Edward VII, left for the traditional accession council in London, the Kaiser remained in charge of the arrangements at Osborne. It was at his suggestion that a Union Jack was draped on the walls of the room in which his grandmother's coffin lay in state. Despite protests from Dona in Berlin, from Bülow and from Eulenburg, the Kaiser remained in England for the funeral on 2 February and the interment in the Mausoleum two days later. He was present, so he said more than once, as a bereaved member of the royal family and not as sovereign of the German Empire. Edward VII, sentimentally touched by his nephew's devotion, wondered if he had misjudged the man. Impulsively he raised him to the rank of Field-Marshal in the British Army. Modestly William took little notice of his forty-second birthday, observing strict mourning. Inevitably there were political conversations, in which he again held out promise of an Anglo-German alliance. There was, too, an amicable meeting with Lord Salisbury, whom he had not seen since the misunderstanding at Cowes in 1895. 'I believe there is a Providence which has decreed that two nations which have produced such men as Shakespeare, Schiller, Luther and Goethe must have a great future before them', William declared in a speech at luncheon on the eve of his departure.[42] To many it seemed as if Queen Victoria in death had brought about that reconciliation between London and Berlin which she and Albert sought so earnestly forty years before.

On 5 February William was cheered through the West End as he began his homeward journey. Many buildings flew German flags as well as Union Jacks. At Charing Cross station he was so overcome with emotion that he gripped his uncle's hand in a farewell gesture of good faith towards the new king. As the train pulled slowly out over Hungerford Bridge, William could be seen standing stiffly and impassively at the salute. Next morning *The Times*, which was not noted for sympathy towards Germany, printed a long and favourable account of William's movements. At the foot of the column *The Times* added a verse tribute, contributed by a Mr J. Rhoades.[43] Although his two stanzas are deficient in craftsmanship, they leave no doubt of the feeling towards the Kaiser that week in London:

> Sorrow's dear dues are paid, 'tis time to part;
>   Your country calls you o'er yon billowy bar,
> That severs land from land, not heart from heart,
>   To travel fast and far.
>
> Farewell, Sir, mists between us may have been,
>   But this salt mist that doth the eyelids wet,
> Your English tears for love of England's Queen,
>   England will not forget.

8. Admirals All

William returned from his grandmother's funeral glowing with Anglophile enthusiasm. For much of the following fortnight he remained in civilian clothes, which was regarded in Berlin as an English habit, and he wore a red enamel tiepin bearing a VRI monogram set in diamonds. His table talk was of Osborne and Windsor, and of how well 'they' did this or that in England. Before leaving London he had advocated an alliance between 'the two Teutonic nations', one in which the British 'would keep the seas, while we would be responsible for the land'. 'With such an alliance', he declared, 'not a mouse would stir in Europe without our permission.'[1] Imperial impromptus of this kind seemed to Bülow wildly irresponsible while Anglo-German relations remained so delicately poised; and at Westminster they were treated with considerable caution. Lord Lansdowne, who became Foreign Secretary in October 1900, confessed privately he thought a formal alliance was 'a very stiff fence to ride at', but he was prepared to attempt the jump. On 12 March 1901 he circulated to his cabinet colleagues proposals for Anglo-German collaboration in the Far East, and in the last week of May he instructed the Permanent Under-Secretary at the Foreign Office to draft a formal defensive agreement, which would have operated in Europe as well as in China. Yet little progress was made with either of these proposals. The Germans would never accept a basically anti-Russian combination in the Far East, while the British could not accept the burden of defending the frontiers of all three Triple Alliance Powers (Austria-Hungary and Itaty as well as Germany). Hatzfeldt and Eckardstein continued to urge Bülow to conclude some agreement, if not over the Far East at least over the future of Morocco, but Bülow was in no hurry. He assumed – and William agreed with him – that there was no natural ally for England apart from Germany. 'We can wait. Time is on our side', Holstein had telegraphed to the London embassy while the Kaiser was in England; for the British to be drawn into the Franco-Russian camp was, as Holstein remarked, 'beyond the limits of the possible and the probable'.[2]

Queen Victoria's death was followed seven months later by the death of her eldest daughter, the Kaiser's mother. If William was moved by this bereavement, he hid his emotions from his uncle who crossed to Germany for the protracted funeral ceremonies. William entertained Edward vii to luncheon at Wilhelmshohe on 23 August, chaffing him heartily over the behaviour of 'those unmitigated noodles' in the British Government and complaining that nothing had come of his 'earnest desire' for 'a definite and binding Treaty of Alliance'. This tiresome banter seemed inconsiderate and out of place. Edward returned to Homburg, where he was taking the waters, exhausted with keeping his temper: 'One always felt there was electricity in the air when the Emperor and King Edward talked', his private secretary recalled thirty years later.[3] Victoria had mediated with stern impartiality between uncle and nephew, finding excuses for William's behaviour which would never have occurred to her son. Now, however, there was no one to soothe Edward's ruffled feelings. Queen Alexandra disliked and despised William – 'Ach, the fool', she was heard to say at Sandringham in November 1899 on learning how William was including in his suite Herr Haby, a barber responsible for pluming the imperial moustaches upwards each morning.[4] Both Edward and Alexandra continued to regard the ruler of Germany as a rude, conceited youngster who showed no signs of mellowing to maturity.

For most of his subjects too, he was still 'the young Kaiser', though by now he was in his forty-third year. This youthfulness sprang in part from the restless energy which had amazed Bismarck at the start of his reign and which he retained in undiminished vigour. Moreover nearly all his entourage were older and fatter men, beside whom he seemed trim and sprightly. His hair was not allowed to appear grey until he was in his fifties; and his abstemious eating habits, together with his liking for physical exercise, kept his weight down to seventy kilograms (about eleven stone). He was by now the father of six sons: the crown prince ('little Willy') was nineteen in the summer of 1901 and the youngest son (Joachim) was ten. With all his sons he was a strict disciplinarian, although not a martinet. He was more indulgent towards his daughter, Princess Victoria Louise, who at the time of her grandmother's death was still a month short of her ninth birthday. Dona remained dutifully loyal to her husband and, with the turn of the century, he came to acknowledge his dependence upon her to a greater extent than in earlier years. For Germany as a whole the imperial family was a symbol of respectable domesticity, primly setting standards which Berlin society could never attain.

The Kaiser regarded the deaths of the two Victorias, his grandmother and his mother, as bringing down the curtain on the Second Act of his life. Other prominent characters also left the scene. Hohenlohe, a mere extra on the stage for the past three years, finally resigned on 16 October 1900, complaining that 'everything in foreign affairs . . . is settled by H.M. and Bülow' and that he personally had been told nothing about Waldersee's China expedition.[5] Bernard Bülow took over as chancellor while Otto von Richthofen, a convinced colonialist, succeeded Bülow as state-secretary for foreign affairs. A few months later Hatzfeldt's health gave way and he handed over the London embassy to Count Paul von Wolf-Metternich, a distant relative of the great Austrian chancellor. General von Hahnke, a friend to William in his days as a regimental officer and chief of the military secretariat since his accession, was succeeded by General Dietrich von Hülsen-Häseler, a versatile soldier who had long been a howling success in evening entertainments aboard the *Hohenzollern*, sometimes as a conjurer, occasionally in drag. One of William's confidants had fallen from grace: Kiderlen-Waechter, for ten years the Foreign Ministry's representative on the summer cruises, commented too loudly and too caustically on some of his master's foibles – and found himself posted to Bucharest as minister. Philipp Eulenburg remained the Kaiser's favourite friend, surviving both the disgrace of his only brother (a divorce case revealed strange sexual habits) and the discovery by William that Eulenburg paid hush-money for several years to the husband of a former mistress. Frequently William criticized Eulenburg's casual style of conducting embassy business in Vienna, but he continued to seek his company as often as possible, and on the 'first day of the new century' created him a Prince. No one else at court could talk so richly on such varied and stimulating topics. The only friend who seemed at times to rival 'dear Phili' in popularity was Prince Max Egon von Fürstenburg, at whose castle of Donaueschingen in Baden William was a guest each November, and occasionally in May as well; but Fürstenburg was a hearty extrovert who appealed to a different side of William's nature from the musical and artistic Eulenburg.

By now, however, William was widening his circle of close acquaintances. In June 1899 Albert Ballin, chairman of the Hamburg-America Steamship Line, organized an elegant dinner on the eve of the Kiel Regatta.[6] This dinner became an annual event, high in the German social calendar, and it ensured the lasting friendship for Ballin of his imperial master. The two men shared a love for ships and the sea, a restless wanderlust, a liking for the conventionally ornate in visual art, and a genuine desire to see German business on top in world markets. Their friendship, which was sufficiently intimate for William to accept criticism from 'the genial Jew', had considerable social significance. Through Ballin the Kaiser came to know Jewish banking and commercial notables within German society, a class against whom his wife Dona, his friend Eulenburg and the Prussian aristocracy in general were strongly prejudiced. Although, like so many of his contemporaries, William often spoke disparagingly of Jewish press barons and Jewish socialists, he was never rabidly anti-Semitic and enjoyed cordial relations with other Jewish businessmen besides Ballin. He particularly respected the technical and organizational skills of Walter Rathenau, son of the founder of the great *Allgemeine Elektricitäts Gesellschaft* (AEG) combine. The transcript of a conversation between the Kaiser and the thirty-two year old Rathenau in February 1900 has survived. It shows both the limits of William's scientific knowledge and his inquisitive mind. The Kaiser had attended a lecture by Rathenau on 'Electrical Alchemy' and was clearly out of his depth but, to impress those around him, he assumed a heartily partisan manner, denouncing petrol as an expensive foreign product much inferior to electrical power as a means of propelling vehicles. It does not appear that Rathenau and his colleagues were especially gratified by their sovereign's patronage. Rathenau, too, found something child-like in his personality.[7]

William was prepared to pick Jewish brains and enjoy the hospitality of his wealthier Jewish subjects, but inevitably he was impressed by the new racial mysticism fashionable in Germany at the turn of the century. In 1901 he read the famous work by Houston Stewart Chamberlain, *The Foundations of the Nineteenth Century*, which had been published in Vienna two years previously. Chamberlain, born four years earlier than the Kaiser, was the son of a British admiral but spent his adult life in the German-speaking lands, married a daughter of Richard Wagner and developed the theory that all worthwhile civilization and culture was Teutonic in origin. He claimed that since the German people alone possessed the highest qualities of language and national soul, they were destined to serve as the inspiration for all humanity. Chamberlain's woolly-minded Nordic nonsense appealed to Eulenburg, who invited Chamberlain to visit him at Liebenberg while the Kaiser was a guest there in the last week of October 1901. Bülow, too, was summoned to meet this newest prophet of Germanism, although significantly he did not bother to recall this occasion in his comprehensively anecdotal memoirs. At the time, so Eulenburg wrote later, William 'stood completely under the spell' of Chamberlain; and when, soon afterwards, he received a letter from Chamberlain praising the Prussian royal house and commending its present head as 'the foremost German of them all', his enthusiasm knew no bounds. He replied to Chamberlain's letter on New Year's Eve: 'First I read your wonderful letter by myself and then I read it out to everybody gathered around my Christmas table. All social ranks and all generations listened silently and were deeply moved.'[8] In the past other writers had commented favourably on the nature of imperial sovereignty, but no one before Chamberlain described the Prussian kings' moral and spiritual mission in language corresponding so closely to William's own mysterious concept of Divine Guidance. Yet, although they maintained a fitful correspondence for the remainder of Chamberlain's life, the Kaiser soon came to treat his doctrines with reserve. For however much Chamberlain might laud the ruling dynasty, his Pan-Germanic teaching was fundamentally divisive rather than unitary; and William was shrewd enough to perceive this weakness. Austria-Hungary and Germany were, in different degrees, both multi-national empires; assertions of racial supremacy cut across existing loyalties within them and were therefore a danger to the established order of states. William welcomed the tone of Chamberlain's doctrines but feared their consequences, for he was more far-sighted than Eulenburg.

Four days after thanking Chamberlain for his 'wonderful letter' William was writing to Nicholas II in a totally different style.[9] This time he was concerned, not with a philosophic abstraction, but with a subject on which he had long held strong opinions – the importance of sea power and the role of Germany's new fleet. Nicholas was informed of the progress in constructing the latest armoured cruisers and battleships, and he was also given unsolicited advice on the means of maintaining Russian naval influence in the Persian Gulf. Behind William's lavish assurances of friendship lay a new assumption in policy: if the prospects for Anglo-German collaboration were bad, then it was essential to reach some form of understanding with Russia, in the hope that the Tsar and his ministers might be able to influence their ally, France, and thereby lessen the risk of war in Europe at a time when Germany was challenging Britain's world-power status.

Throughout the period 1902–5 William took every opportunity to show goodwill towards the Russian imperial family, although sometimes expressing himself unfortunately. In August 1902, for example, he visited Reval and joined Tsar Nicholas in watching Russian war-ships at manoeuvres. While they were on the quayside, William, exasperatingly hearty that day, made a pun on the Tsar's patronage of international disarmament and introduced him to Bülow as 'the Admiral of the Pacific'. Although Nicholas responded coolly to this latest title, William was so pleased with his pun that, as the *Hohenzollern* sailed away, he signalled the Russian imperial yacht, 'The Admiral of the Atlantic bids farewell to the Admiral of the Pacific', a valediction acknowledged by a curt 'Goodbye'. Within a few weeks English journalists had learnt of the exchange of signals but not of their punning origin, and the Reval meeting was represented in some sections of the British press as an attempt by the two emperors to divide the oceans of the world between them, much as Napoleon and Alexander I had sought to partition Europe at Tilsit nearly a century before. Undeterred by Nicholas II's embarrassment, William continued to sign himself 'Admiral of the Atlantic', or 'A of A', in his letters to St Petersburg until the summer of 1904, when Japanese victories against Russia's squadrons in the Far East at last convinced him that the use of such grandiose naval ranks was tactless.[10]

'The German Navy – at Whom Is It Aimed?' asked a leading article in Harmsworth's *Daily Mail* on 29 September 1902. The reader was left in no doubt of the answer. And by now the Admiralty, too, was alive to the threat of naval rivalry, realizing the newest battleships were short-range vessels designed for action in the North Sea and not on distant oceans. Plans were made for the establishment of a naval base at Rosyth, facing the key German ports across the North Sea, although not announced in parliament until 5 March 1903. Throughout that winter Anglo-German relations were in a strange state of transition. William stayed at Sandringham for a week in November 1902 and then travelled to Lowther Castle for a few days' shooting with his friend,

Lord Lonsdale; but the dynastic connection, stressed during his last visit to England, had worn thin and William's reception by press and public alike was icy. 'Thank God he's gone', Edward VII was heard to remark as peace returned to Sandringham.[11]

In May 1903 King Edward paid a state visit to Paris, which was returned by President Loubet two months later. These exchanges helped to soften French hostility towards the British. They were followed by negotiations in London which sought to settle outstanding colonial disputes between the two countries. Reconciliation with France was accompanied in England by alarmist rumours concerning German intentions: the most popular holiday reading in the summer of 1903 was Erskine Childers' *Riddle of the Sands*, a thriller centred upon an attempt to decoy the Royal Navy away from the North Sea so as to facilitate a German invasion from the Frisian Islands. The diplomatic pattern of Europe was changing in ways neither Bülow nor the Kaiser had anticipated. Much of the bargaining between Britain and France concerned Morocco, the one remaining independent Sultanate in north-west Africa, and a country in which Germany had commercial and strategic interests. In March 1904, when it was clear an Anglo-French agreement was imminent, William was cruising in the Mediterranean aboard a Hamburg-America liner put at his disposal by Albert Ballin. Bülow, from his desk in Berlin, advised William to land in Morocco and assert Germany's concern with the Sultanate on the spot. But William was hoping to emulate his uncle and reach an understanding with President Loubet. He had no wish to offend the French, and countered Bülow's suggestion with a strange proposal that Germany should lease Port Mahon in Minorca from Spain and there establish a Kiaochow for the Mediterranean. Few moves could have been better calculated to seal Anglo-French collaboration, for Port Mahon guarded the approaches to Toulon and was astride the seaway from Gibraltar to Malta. It was not a sensible suggestion, nor was his comment that the British could always be offered coaling rights there. In the event, the Germans did nothing. The Anglo-French Entente was completed by a treaty signed on 8 April 1904. Four days later Bülow told the Reichstag he was glad the British and French had removed causes of friction between their two nations: he was convinced neither country would injure or overlook German interests in Morocco or elsewhere in the Mediterranean.[12] Privately, within the German Foreign Ministry, the Anglo-French understanding was seen as a major diplomatic defeat. The only consolation was that no one thought the *entente cordiale* would survive the first threat of conflict.

Meanwhile, on 8 February 1904, the Japanese attacked the Russian fleet at Port Arthur without a declaration of war, and so challenged the strategic balance in the Far East. Throughout the eighteen months of hostilities in Manchuria the Kaiser supported Russia while the British sympathized with the Japanese. Germany profited materially from the war, concluding a valuable trade agreement with Russia in July 1904. But for Germany the chief importance of these events lay in their possible effect on Europe. If hostilities broke out between France and Germany, Bülow asked the General Staff in the third week of April 1904, did the Russians possess the strength to intervene effectively against Germany along their frontier through Poland? Schlieffen, the chief of the General Staff, had no doubt of the answer: Manchuria was crippling, and would continue to cripple, the Tsar's armies in Europe. He was convinced that if war came to Europe, Germany would gain a rapid victory in the West; and there were many staff officers ready to join Schlieffen in welcoming a new march on Paris. On 1 May the Kaiser seemed to be sharing their views. That day he opened a new bridge across the Rhine at Mainz and spoke belligerently of past triumphs and of Germany's present strength in the field. Foreign commentators interpreted his outburst as a gesture of defiance, a snook cocked at the *entente cordiale*; but this oversimplified his reactions. The Mainz speech was for home consumption. It pleased high-ranking officers disgruntled by the vacillations of 'world policy' by focusing attention on the traditional arena of battle west of the Rhine. Yet William was unlikely to give Schlieffen free rein. He was still obsessed by 'my navy'—a court official records how that season His Imperial Majesty insisted on wearing admiral's dress uniform to the opera for a performance of *Flying Dutchman* – and Tirpitz certainly did not want a war in 1904 or 1905: the newest battleships were only just coming into service and battle plans for the High Seas Fleet were far from complete.[13]

William was, however, determined to impress the British with his growing fleet. In June 1904 Edward VII was invited to the Kiel Regatta, where every available warship was moored as though for a grand review. At the state banquet William expressed delight that his uncle should have been 'greeted by the thunder of the guns of the German fleet', although Edward, in replying, merely commented on the joy with which he was looking forward to sailing at Kiel. Tirpitz personally tried to minimize the fighting strength of the German navy – his fears of a new 'Copenhagen' had increased after the surprise Japanese attack on Port Arthur – but British officers noted the efficiency of the German warships with some concern. When a German squadron visited Plymouth in mid-July it was received coolly and its movements were followed with suspicion. The first British war plan for destroyer operations against the German fleet was drawn up in that same month by, the Director of Naval Intelligence, Rear-Admiral Prince Louis of Battenberg, who had accompanied Edward VII to the Kiel Regatta (and who was a brother-in-law both of Prince Henry of Prussia and of Tsar Nicholas II).[14] There remained, however, several British naval officers who regarded 'the youngest Navy in the world' (as William described his fleet) with almost affectionate indulgence. Foremost among these British seamen was Rear-Admiral Montagu, a friend of the Kaiser's from past weeks at Cowes, who maintained a regular correspondence with William from October 1903 until the beginning of 1914. Admiral Montagu was 'very proud to feel' that improved cutters and gigs he had introduced into the Royal Navy were being modified for service in German warships too. Probably he was not aware that his highly personal letters to William were carefully annotated by the 'All-Highest', handed over to members of his naval staff and, at times, forwarded to the chancellor. Yet occasionally even Montagu gave a blunt warning which William could hardly ignore: 'Don't build any more fleets, Sir, or some day Germany will want to fight us', the Rear-Admiral wrote on 17 October 1904.[15]

Five days after Montagu sent this letter – and while it was being circulated round the naval secretariat in Berlin – the British and the Russians were brought close to war by the Dogger Bank incident. The Russian Baltic fleet, on the first leg of its voyage to the Far East, encountered English fishing smacks on the Dogger Bank, mistook them for Japanese torpedo-boats, opened fire and killed seven fishermen. British warships subsequently trailed the Russians down Channel and across the Bay of Biscay until the Russians, under pressure from their French allies, agreed to land the officers responsible for opening fire at Vigo and submit the incident to international arbitration. On 27 October William personally used the Dogger Bank incident to urge Nicholas to take the lead in forming 'a powerful combination of the three strongest continental Powers' (Germany, Russia and France) to resist the Anglo-Japanese partnership. Two days later Nicholas telegraphed back, welcoming the proposal but leaving Germany to take the initiative: 'Would you be willing to draft and frame the outlines of such a treaty and inform me of it?', he wrote. 'France is bound to join her ally once it is accepted by us.'[16] This telegram marked the peak of William's personal diplomacy: the text of a draft treaty was cabled to St Petersburg, and William waited throughout the month of November to see if his ideal of a Germano-Russian alliance, supported by France, would reach fruition. But Nicholas changed his mind – or had it changed for him by his ministers – and informed William he could take no action until the matter was thrashed out with the French. Already the Kaiser had been shocked to learn that the Tsar wished to refer the Dogger Bank incident to international arbitration: 'It is intolerable to permit foreigners to judge the actions of one's officers in the course of their duty', he commented. Now he was disgusted at Nicholas's weakness over the projected treaty. 'My opinion about the agreement is still the same', he wrote in English shortly before Christmas. 'It is impossible to take France into our confidence *before* we two have come to a definite arrangement.' The French president and foreign minister were 'no doubt experienced statesmen', he added, 'but they not being Princes or Emperors I am unable to place them – in a question of confidence like this one – on the same footing as you my equal, my cousin and friend'. Germany and Russia would continue in their 'present condition of mutual independence', he concluded; but he was deeply disappointed. 'The first failure I have personally experienced. Let us hope this is not the beginning of a series of similar experiences', he told Bülow.[17]

This rebuff left Bülow free to press an alternative policy on William: to show the world how worthless were England's fair words by humiliating France over Morocco. Technically, on this question, the Germans possessed sound legal grounds for complaint. In 1880 the French, Spanish, Germans, Italians, British and Americans had concluded a convention at Madrid which virtually guaranteed Moroccan independence. French attempts to establish economic and indirect political control over the Sultanate ran counter to the Madrid agreement. Germany was represented at Tangier by a young and ambitious diplomat, Richard von Kühlmann, who revived the earlier suggestion that the Kaiser might pay a courtesy visit while cruising in the Mediterranean. This proposal was taken up by Bülow and Holstein, and German newspapers were told on 21 March that His Imperial Majesty would land for four hours in Tangier during his spring cruise. William, however, was reluctant to set foot in Morocco: he did not wish to provoke the French; and he suspected that a densely packed North African town was a natural haven for anarchist assassins. 'Telegrams must be sent forthwith to Tangier saying it is doubtful if I shall land there as I am travelling incognito and have no wish for audience or receptions', he informed Bülow shortly before setting out on his cruise.[18]

But on the last day of March 1905 the liner *Hamburg*, with an imperial suite aboard which included nine admirals, duly anchored off Tangier. It was a squally morning and as the German visitors watched the thirty-one year old Kühlmann, in a Bavarian Uhlan's full-dress uniform, ascending a heaving rope ladder to the deck the possibility of not landing in Morocco again crossed William's mind. Yet he was no coward: the bouncing waters of the bay and the high-spirited Berber steed awaiting him on shore were challenges to be mastered, as others had been in his boyhood. William acquitted himself well. He controlled the strange horse firmly and discreetly, despite the commotion in the narrow streets. Nor was his public speech rashly provocative. There was no comprehensive gesture of patronage, as at Damascus seven years before. He reminded those who could hear him above the general bustle of excitement that the Sultan was lord of a free and independent country and he announced that Germany would support his efforts to keep Morocco open for peaceful competition in trade among all nations.[19] After receiving generous gifts, William returned to the *Hamburg*, which crossed the straits to Gibraltar, a mere fifty miles away. There for the first time the Kaiser saw the consternation caused by what Edward VII called his 'political-theatrical fiasco'. He does not seem to have realized, before landing at Tangier, how sensitive were the British to any suspected intriguing by Germany for a naval station so close to such vital trade routes. The cool reception he received at Gibraltar made him petulant. To Prince Louis of Battenberg, who was now in command of the Second Cruiser Squadron, he insisted that Germany would never permit France to gobble up Morocco as she had Tunisia in the early 1880s. 'We know the road to Paris and we will get there again if need be', he told Prince Louis. 'They should remember no fleet can defend Paris.'[20] But then, as though emphasizing his confidence in the maintenance of peace, he resumed his holiday cruise in the Mediterranean; and while the government weighed the prospects of war, William was sightseeing in Sicily and on Corfu, visiting for the first time the Achilleion Villa which he was to purchase two years later.

If the Germans wished to disrupt the Anglo-French Entente they were behaving maladroitly. There was never any danger of the British apathetically observing the humiliation of France so long as German admirals were being touted round such strategically important waters. But at first Bülow and Holstein appeared to be gaining a diplomatic victory. The Germans wanted an international conference on Morocco's future and refused to negotiate with France alone. Bülow's firmness forced the French foreign minister, Delcassé, out of office on 6 June, and the new French Government was more pliable than its predecessor. The French agreed to a conference of the signatory powers of the Madrid Convention: Bülow, supported in this policy by William, undertook to discuss Morocco privately with the French before the conference began, and also accepted offers of mediation from President Theodore Roosevelt. Since the conference could not assemble before the end of the year, the Germans believed they had plenty of time to improve relations with Russia and the United States and to ensure that, if votes were taken at the conference, Great Britain and France would be isolated. A group of hawks in Berlin, including Schlieffen and Holstein, were uneasy at this latest shift of policy, and the chief of the General Staff spent the closing months of 1905 perfecting the famous 'Schlieffen Plan' for defeating France in a thirty-one day campaign in the West; but William was pleased with Bülow's statesmanship. As one of the honours distributed on 'little Willy's' wedding day, Bülow was created a prince*; and while Schlieffen's staff officers were revising their war plans, the Kaiser took up his discarded project for a Russo-German partnership with which a friendly France could be associated. He would cultivate the Russians personally while leaving Prince Bülow to handle negotiations with the French.[21]

On 10 July William went to sea again. This time he sailed aboard the *Hohenzollern* on the still, lake-like summer waters of the Baltic. While off southern Sweden he received a message from Nicholas II inviting him to meet the imperial yacht *Polar Star* at Björkö on the Finnish coast seventy

---

* The Crown Prince married Princess Cecilie of Mecklenburg-Schwerin on 6 June 1905, the same day on which Delcassé was forced to resign as French foreign minister. It is often said that Bülow was created a prince in recognition of his role in unseating Delcassé, but this is not strictly speaking correct. Bülow's honour was announced in the morning newspapers: Delcassé's downfall was not known in Berlin until the evening.

miles west of Kronstadt. William, who had no senior minister or official on board, telegraphed to Bülow for the abortive draft treaty prepared in the previous November. He copied it in his own hand shortly before arriving at Björkö on Sunday, 23 July, and carried it in his pocket when he crossed to the *Polar Star* next morning. The treaty provided that each country would help the other if attacked by a third power: it would be effective as soon as peace was signed between Russia and Japan; and, so as to limit Germany's obligations, William inserted on the original draft a clause confining the treaty to Europe. Nicholas, taking William into what had been his father's saloon, read through the text three times while the Kaiser – as he wrote later to Bülow – prayed hard that God would guide the Tsar wisely. 'It was as quiet as death; no sound but the waves, while the sun shone brightly into the dark cabin. I could just see the *Hohenzollern* gleaming white with the imperial standard fluttering in the breeze. I was just reading on the black cross the letters "God with Us" when I heard the Tsar's voice beside me saying (in English), "That is quite excellent. I agree". The two sovereigns signed the treaty and, now that the strain was over, William found his eyes filled 'with tears of pure joy'. His thoughts remained on higher things, and in particular on that peripatetic spectral audience who were regular viewers of such occasions: 'Frederick William III, Queen Louise, Grandpapa and Nicholas I have certainly been near us at this moment', he told Bülow. 'By God's grace', he added, 'this morning of 24 July 1905 at Björkö is a turning point in Europe's history: a great burden has been lifted from my beloved Fatherland, which will at last be freed from the terrible Gallo-Russian pincers . . . God has ordained and willed it.'[22]

There is no doubt William had gained a remarkable success. His strength of personality impelled Nicholas to sign a treaty running counter to the policy pursued by his ministers since his accession. When he questioned the position of France in this new alignment, the Kaiser confidently explained that, with Moroccan difficulties out of the way, 'we shall be good friends of the Gauls'. But Bülow was furious. He could not share his sovereign's mood of religious exultation; he only saw an independent initiative which, if it went unchecked, would leave the Kaiser's ministers as little more than clerks. Bülow claimed that by inserting the words 'in Europe', William had robbed the alliance of its greatest potential value since it would now be impossible to threaten the British garrisons in India. Very sensibly William pointed out that the legendary threat to British India was 'a complete illusion'. But

Bülow continued to remonstrate and when the *Hohenzollern* returned from the cruise, William found a long letter awaiting him in which the chancellor asked to be relieved of his office. At this point William's self-confidence collapsed. He begged Bülow to stay in office: 'You cannot and must not repudiate me', he wrote. Had he not at Bülow's bidding gone to Tangier and 'mounted a strange horse in spite of the impediment that my crippled arm caused to my riding'? Had he not ridden 'between Spanish anarchists because you wished it, and your policy was to profit by it'? A postscript added that 'the morning after your request for resignation had been received would find your Emperor alive no longer – think of my poor wife and children'. The tear stains of this fevered appeal were, however, offset by a less melodramatic second postscript: William suggested that, as 'since Björkö I am on such good terms' with the Tsar, it would be a simple matter for him to send off a coded telegram proposing the immediate removal of the 'in Europe' limitation.[23]

Bülow was less concerned with the additional clause than with discrediting the dynastic diplomacy for which the Björkö Treaty represented so great a triumph. The Kaiser's grovelling letter was enough to gratify his professional pride: 'I loved him with all my heart, and not only for the goodness he had shown me', wrote Bülow later in his memoirs, 'I loved the highly-gifted man with his nobly endowed character, so lovable and so amiable, so natural and so simple, so magnanimous.' At once Bülow sent a message back to this paragon among emperors, assuring William that his genuine successes were a source of pride and not of jealousy; should he wish to retain his chancellor, Bülow would serve him 'in gratitude and humility'. William telegraphed a reply immediately: 'Warmest thanks. I feel reborn.'[24] The tiff was over. Bülow remained chancellor; he even tried to offer concessions over Morocco in order to cajole France into joining the Björkö alliance, nebulous though that connection remained.

This was a disastrous shift of policy, as Holstein saw at the time. Having brought the Moroccan affair to crisis heat as champions of the Sultan's independence, Bülow and the Kaiser were now anxious to forget about it: 'All that matters is for us to find a way out of this Moroccan business so as to keep our prestige in the world intact, while taking account as far as possible of German economic and financial interests', Bülow wrote on 8 September.[25] Over the next six months the mixture of threats and blandishments puzzled the French, who remained convinced that the Germans wanted war. This uncertainty also influenced the British, and at a particularly dangerous moment; for in the first week of December the Liberals came into office after ten and a half years of opposition, and Grey, the new foreign secretary, was determined to emphasize the continuity in foreign policy by assuring the French they could rely on British support. Grey approved staff talks between the British and French military commanders which had begun unofficially in the last days of the Conservative Government. By the time the conference on Morocco opened at Algeciras (16 January 1906) Germany's Moroccan policy had considerably strengthened the Anglo-French Entente.[26]

To William's dismay these diplomatic defeats were not countered by any improvement in Russo-German relations. The Tsar's ministers, too, disliked the Björkö agreement, not so much from pique at his show of independence as from conviction it was incompatible with the existing Franco-Russian alliance. Russia, racked by revolts in her European provinces and by defeat in the Far East, needed French loans and French investment; and it was unthinkable to treat France as a junior associate in a continental league of emperors. At first the Russians kept William and Bülow guessing, and there was an amicable meeting between the Kaiser and Witte, the Tsar's chief minister, at the hunting-lodge of Rominten in the last days of September. But barely a week later Nicholas wrote to William: 'I think that the coming into force of the Björkö treaty ought to be put off until we know how France will look at it.' By the end of November William admitted to Bülow that, from the tone of their personal correspondence, it seemed to him as if Nicholas was wishing to annul the Björkö agreement entirely.[27] Bülow, like Holstein, now wished to reverse policy and take a tougher line with France; but William was adamant. As the year 1905 came to an end he reflected on world affairs 'beneath the re-lighted candles of a Christmas tree': 1906, so he told Bülow, would be especially 'unfavourable for a war': infantry and artillery regiments were being re-equipped; and the fleet was not yet ready. Moreover the revolutionary movement in Russia had alarmed William considerably. So long as there was a socialist menace in Germany, it would be dangerous to risk sending troops out of the country: 'Shoot down the socialists first, behead them, put them out of action, if necessary, massacre the lot – and then war abroad! But not before!'[28] It was a curious Christmas sentiment for a man who regarded himself as an instrument of the

1 *Above:* The Crown Princess of Prussia in 1862 with her two eldest children, William and Charlotte.

2 *Above right:* Windsor, 1863: 'precious little William' and his grandmother's pet.

3 *Right:* Georg Hinzpeter in 1869, three years after becoming tutor to the future Kaiser.

4 Princess Augusta Victoria ('Dona') on the eve of her marriage to the future Kaiser, 1881.

5 With Bismarck at Friedrichsruh soon after his accession, 1888.

6 *Above:* A shooting-party on the
Eulenburg estate at Liebenberg,
October 1892. The Kaiser, who
appears to be wearing a dirk, has on
his right his host's cousin, Botho zu
Eulenburg, the Prussian
minister-president. Philipp Eulenburg
himself is to the Kaiser's left, with his
hands in his jacket pockets. The
toothbrush moustache visible between
the Kaiser and Count Botho was
sported by Kuno Moltke, and the tall
figure behind him is General Hülsen,
while to their right in the rear rank is
Kiderlen-Waechter (with drooping
moustache).

7 'My bosom friend – the only one I
have': Count Philipp zu
Eulenburg-Hertefelt as ambassador in
Vienna in 1898.

8 1901: the Kaiser rides with Edward VII at Queen Victoria's funeral.

9 The Kaiser in civilian clothes, February 1901.

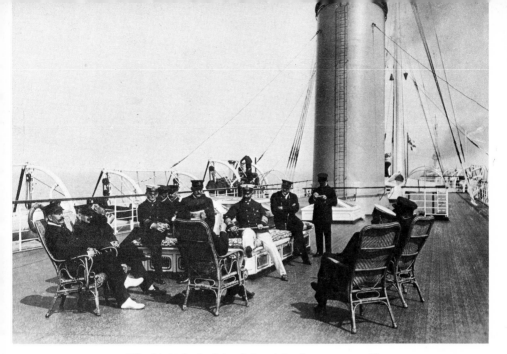

10 The 'Admiral of the Atlantic' relaxes on a cruise.

11 Admiral von Tirpitz: 'that truly mighty man'. 12 Warlord of the Second Reich.

13 On the terrace of the Achilleion, Corfu.

14 The Kaiser and Kaiserin, William and Dona, 1913.

15 The Kaiser and the younger Moltke watch military exercises at Coblenz in August 1914.

16 Germany's new idol: Hindenburg, 1915.

17 The Kaiser and his second wife, Princess Hermine, walk through Doorn.

18 Doorn: ducks, drakes and a dachshund.

Almighty; but fortunately Bülow by now understood that William's remarks were never more bombastic than when he was counselling peace.

The Algeciras Conference was a diplomatic disaster for Germany. Only the Austrians supported the German delegation, and their backing began to waver by the beginning of March. The other signatories of the Madrid Convention failed to understand what Germany wanted. They suspected the Germans were using the Moroccan issue as a ball to be kicked around in some oddly codified diplomatic game; not knowing the rules, they played safe and agreed to an Austrian compromise which maintained the Sultan's independence but entrusted the policing of the ports in Morocco to France and Spain, with a Swiss inspector responsible directly to the Sultan. William had begged Bülow to spare him the humiliation of a Moroccan Fashoda, and this at least Bülow achieved. President Theodore Roosevelt even sent his congratulations to William on the German success in ensuring that Morocco would continue to enjoy independence and an open door for foreign trade. But the European capitals saw the crisis differently. The Germans, it was said in Berlin and London and Paris, had wanted a conference on Morocco, and had found themselves isolated. In the Reichstag the opposition parties mounted an attack on Bülow on 5 April: the chancellor listened patiently while the socialist leader, Bebel, condemned his bankrupt imperialistic policy in Morocco and his sympathy for 'barbarian Russia'; but before Bülow could reply, he lapsed into unconsciousness. The chancellor's 'fainting fit' was such a newspaper sensation that it effectively distracted attention from the debate itself and from the final obsequies of the Algeciras Conference two days later.[29]

Inevitably the conference was seen by most contemporary observers as a personal defeat for the Kaiser. It was, after all, William's behaviour at Tangier which had placed Morocco on the diplomatic stage in the first place and many years were to pass before it was discovered that this dramatic entry was not of his own volition. William remained acutely conscious of the criticisms levelled against him, especially after the disappointment of Björkö. A quarter of a century later, exiled in Holland, he read with great attention and many marginal comments Harold Nicolson's biography of his father, the principal British delegate to the Algeciras Conference. At the close of the chapter on the Moroccan Crisis William picked up his indelible pencil and added a vituperative postcript:

Algeciras was the outcome of the totally wrong policy of Holstein-Bülow which forced me to go to Tangier. *The curse of constitutionalism!* Had I *not* been a *constitutional* monarch, tied to my 'advisers' by a constitution, but been free to govern like Frederick the Great then the visit to Tangier would never have taken place, and neither would Algeciras. France would have reached an arrangement suitable to herself. Bülow pursued prestige politics which, though abhorrent to me, everywhere aroused the suspicion that I had ordered him to do so, whereas he could hide behind me if they should fail – 'The Kaiser must not be made to look ridiculous, or be humiliated': a consequence of the impossible advantageous position enjoyed by the chancellor over the Kaiser.[30]

It is a point of view with which constitutional analysts might take issue; but as an instance of sustained resentment it rings clearly through the years. Over the Moroccan episode William forgot nothing and forgave nothing.

9. Scandals and Kaiser Crisis

The remaining months of 1906 passed peacefully enough for William. He watched, with some anxiety, the rapid construction and sea trials of the new British 'all big gun' battleship, HMS *Dreadnought*, which was to change the character – and the costing – of naval rivalry over the next few years. At home he railed against socialists and radicals who criticized the behaviour of German troops in putting down native risings in Africa; when the Centre Party joined the socialists in cutting military appropriations for South West Africa he became staunchly Protestant and denounced the Centre Party too. But, for most of the year, William was in a genial mood, playing heavy-handed jokes on humourless officers around him or giving authoritative value judgements on musical and artistic matters with which he had only a passing acquaintance. To his considerable delight on 4 July he became, at forty-seven, a grandfather for the first time. In Berlin the birth of a 'future heir to the throne of Prussia and to the German Empire' was celebrated with well organized rejoicing. There was even a congratulatory article in the London *Times* emphasizing, yet again, 'family ties which unite the Royal Houses of Prussia and of Great Britain'.

The Times, at that moment, owed a gesture of respect to the Hohenzollern dynasty. A few weeks earlier it had published a sensational full-page advertisement for William Le Queux's novel, *The Invasion of 1910*, and was rebuked by the prime minister in the House of Commons for such a 'mischievous publication'. The advertisement took the form of a large map of the British Isles, showing the advance of German invaders and including alarming captions, one of which mentioned the bombardment and sack of London. The book itself, which contained imaginary proclamations issued at 'Potsdam' and signed 'Wilhelm', was serialized in the *Daily Mail*. It became the best-seller of the year and was more popular – though less durable – than *The Riddle of the Sands*.

Sales soon surpassed the 75,000 copies of its German rival, *Seestern,
1906*, a thriller published in Leipzig at the end of the previous year and
describing a surprise English attack on the imperial navy.[1] William
personally treated this war-of-the-future fiction lightheartedly, taking
care some months later to let King Edward's private secretary see he
was himself in the habit of glancing at the columns of the *Daily Mail*; but
there was no hope of relaxing tension between the two countries so long
as yarns of this type remained popular. Dona, who never liked the
English, was confirmed in her prejudices. She could not understand
why, in August, William accommodated his arrangements to suit
Edward VII and travelled down to Friedrichshof to meet 'that fat old
gentleman'. But uncle and nephew were both worried by the rancour
which marked Anglo-German relations and, in particular, by the arms
race: William was determined to reassure Edward, especially as the
Reichstag had recently authorized a supplementary Navy Law, which
would supply the German fleet with six new battle-cruisers. Earlier that
year William had recalled, in a letter to his uncle, those hours of prayer
and vigil beside his grandmother's deathbed and, warming to his
theme, pictured the joy she would experience when 'from the home of
Eternal Light . . . she sees our hands clasped in loyal and cordial
friendship'. Each ruler was accordingly on good behaviour at Friedrichshof, avoiding topics which might unduly strain self-control.[2]
Edward promised to encourage a British minister to visit Berlin, for it
was one of William's lesser grievances that no member of the British
Government had come to the German capital since his accession. At the
end of August the Secretary of State for War, Haldane, duly travelled to
Berlin, where his mastery of the German language and his knowledge of
German literature made a deep impression. In September the Under-
Secretary of State for the Colonies, Winston Churchill, was the Kaiser's
guest at the autumn manoeuvres in Silesia. The two men talked for
some twenty minutes and Churchill, who had been warned by King
Edward not to be 'too communicative and frank' with his host, found
William 'very friendly . . . and a most fascinating personality'. The
power and organizational skill of the German military machine
staggered Churchill: 'I am very thankful there is a sea between that
army and England', he remarked on his return home.[3]

There followed, later that autumn, an absurd incident which was to
assume exaggerated importance. Every October the Kaiser was accustomed to spend a few days hunting with Phili Eulenburg at Liebenberg.

But this year William felt unwell. His physician was summoned and told him that he had a 'little cold'. 'No, it is a big cold', he snapped back. 'Everything about me must be big.' And he promptly cancelled his visit to Liebenberg. There was already a strained atmosphere on the Eulenburg estate. In April the Kaiser had ousted Baron Holstein from the political section of the Foreign Ministry, where he had been ensconced for thirty years. Holstein blamed his downfall on Eulenburg, with whom he had picked a quarrel four years before. By chance Eulenburg lunched at the palace on the day William counter-signed Holstein's resignation, and the Baron wrongly assumed these two events were connected. He tried to provoke a duel and began a whispering campaign to discredit 'dear Phili' and his Liebenberg circle of friends. The Kaiser's sudden cancellation of his annual visit caused uneasiness at Liebenberg: was it a genuine illness?; had he been listening to tales spread by Holstein's cronies? There was, as yet, no cause for alarm. Two days after rebuking his doctor William decided his cold was better. Belatedly he announced he would accept Eulenberg's hospitality after all.[4]

By now, however, the house party was beginning to break up. The Prince began to look for new companions who could amuse William after a day in the fields. In desperation he invited to Liebenberg the First Secretary at the French Embassy, Raymond Lecomte, an agreeable conversationalist whom Eulenburg had known for nearly twenty years. This, however, was an error of judgement: never before had a foreign diplomat come to one of these informal gatherings, where William liked totally to relax; and it was unwise to invite a Frenchman so soon after Algeciras. Moreover there was already gossip about Lecomte in Berlin. At the start of the year Holstein, of all people, had noted how Bülow was 'quite nervous about the possibility of . . . a scandal' because he thought Lecomte was a homosexual.[5] William arrived at Liebenberg on 7 November. His behaviour there was innocuous, but the news that Lecomte was among his fellow-guests added spice to rumours already circulating in the capital, where it was easy to represent Eulenburg as a sinister power behind the throne.

The unfortunate Eulenburg, like the royal favourites of earlier centuries, had made a host of enemies. Many were jealous of his influence: some – Holstein prominent among them – believed he treated power politics as a game; advancing public careers for the pleasure of destroying them again. He had not been a success as ambassador in

Vienna and, at the end of 1902, pleaded ill-health to retire from the foreign service; but there were several diplomats who envied him those years at the Habsburg Court. The military establishment was stung by his contempt for parade-ground pretentiousness; the business community resented his sharp tongue and disdainful dismissal of bourgeois values – he condemned Ballin's Hamburg-America liners, for example, as vulgarly ostentatious. Journalists who might have supported his attacks on the tawdry tastelessness of a militaristic society were thrown into hostility by his undisguised anti-semitism. Foremost among these journalists was Maximilian Harden, born the son of a Polish-Jewish merchant but accepting Christianity at the age of fifteen. Harden had attacked both Holstein and Eulenburg in the *Kladderadatsch* as long ago as 1893–4. Now he joined forces with Holstein and in his own journal, *Die Zukunft*, sought to discredit Eulenburg and what he called 'the inner circle of the Kaiser's Round Table'. Harden was helped, not only by Holstein, but by General von Hülsen-Häseler, chief of the Kaiser's military secretariat, by Prince Max von Fürstenburg and, it would appear, by the Kaiser's eldest sister, Charlotte, who had married Prince Bernard of Saxe-Meiningen. A group of Reichstag deputies, genuinely alarmed at the influence of the 'Round Table' also backed Harden. Chancellor Bülow's role in the Eulenburg affair is ambiguous. Although he owed his advancement almost entirely to Phili's backing, by the autumn of 1906 he was convinced his old patron wished to replace him by a candidate from the Liebenberg circle. Thus, while Bülow deplored Harden's activities, he made no attempt to defend Eulenburg or help to clear his name.[6]

On 14 November 1906 a Reichstag deputy asked the chancellor whether he would comment on rumours that a 'camarilla' (a secret group of intriguers) existed around the throne. Bülow replied obliquely, 'Camarilla is the name given to a poisonous foreign weed which has never been planted in Germany without doing great harm to the people.' Three days later Harden's weekly, *Die Zukunft*, attacked 'the nice people' around the throne, and especially the 'unhealthy latterday romantic visionary . . . Philipp Friedrich Karl Alexander Botho, Prince zu Eulenburg und Hertefeld', whom it accused of advising the Kaiser to act on his beliefs in autocracy and to decide every matter of executive policy himself. The next issue of *Die Zukunft* carried a disguised attack, playing on the esoteric language of the Liebenberg circle in which the commandant of the Berlin garrison was known as

'Sweetie' and the Kaiser, in his absence, as *Liebchen* ('sweetheart'). At this point Eulenburg, who was alarmed that William would discover his nickname, appealed to Bülow to see if anything could be done to silence Harden. The chancellor suggested that Eulenburg might go abroad and, in the second week of December, he left Germany for Switzerland. Harden's attacks ceased.[7] The Kaiser knew nothing of the whole business. He saw in the periodical press only such articles as were fed to him by his ministers or personal staff; and as yet nobody had the courage – or the heartlessness – to inform him of the campaign against his friends.

Prince Eulenburg's hasty departure for Montreux convinced Bülow he would no longer be able to intrigue for a change of chancellor. Three days after he crossed into Switzerland, Bülow took a political gamble and asked the Kaiser to dissolve the Reichstag, with a general election to follow in six weeks' time (25 January 1907). The election campaign was intensely nationalistic: Bülow and his conservative supporters sought to discredit the progressives and socialists by accusing them of lacking patriotic feeling in criticizing the army's action against the rebellious Hottentots of South West Africa. The 'Hottentot Election', as it is called, resulted in a striking victory for Bülow, and the party strength of the Social Democrats was almost halved. William, as Bülow wrote, was 'in high glee'. He interpreted the result as a vote of confidence in naval expansion and world policy. 'We've thrashed the enemy', he told a cheering crowd outside the royal palace in Berlin.[8] If the Moroccan crisis had momentarily weakened Bülow's hold, he was now firmly back in the saddle – 'my Bismarck' once more.

There was one discordant note. On the eve of the election Eulenburg returned home. The Knights of the Black Eagle, the senior order of chivalry in Prussia, had been summoned for their annual chapter and investiture. It was only a few months since Philipp Eulenburg had received the order from his sovereign and it would have been unthinkable of him to miss the ceremony if he wished to retain the Kaiser's confidence. But as soon as Harden discovered Eulenburg was back in Germany, he resumed his attack. *Die Zukunft* on 2 February for the first time suggested that Eulenburg's friendship with Raymonde Lecomte made him – to use contemporary jargon – a security risk. But the most devastating verbal onslaught came two months later, when Harden and Holstein discovered that Eulenburg would be in attendance on the Kaiser during a ceremonial visit to Wiesbaden. On 27 April *Die Zukunft* alleged that three imperial aides-de-camp were homosexuals and that all three were members of the Liebenberg Round Table and therefore close friends both of the commandant of the Berlin garrison (Count Kuno Moltke) and of Philipp Eulenburg. This was the decisive article. General Hülsen at last persuaded the Crown Prince it was his duty to bring the whole series of articles to the attention of his father.[9]

'Never shall I forget the pained and horrified face of my father, who stared at me in dismay when, in the garden of the Marble Palace, I told him of the delinquencies of his friends', the Crown Prince recalled in his memoirs fifteen years later; and he added, 'The moral purity of the Kaiser was such that he could hardly conceive the possibility of such aberrations.'[10] Perhaps not; but his reaction to the news was strange. Although there was no evidence against any of the men whom Harden had mentioned, the Kaiser demanded that Count Kuno Moltke and the aides-de-camp should resign their commissions, apparently on the assumption that, if innocent, they would already have taken action against Harden. A peremptory message to Eulenburg asked why he did not institute proceedings. But Eulenburg, who was suffering from a heart condition, was reluctant to do anything: he told William he was hesitating because of 'the political consequences of a possible trial' and in order to protect the throne. At the end of the month, however, William authorized Bülow to send Eulenburg one of the most harshly worded statements ever despatched by a sovereign to a close friend: it assumed that the accusations of 'unnatural vice' were justified, ordered him to return the insignia of the Order of the Black Eagle 'and avoid a scandal by forthwith leaving the country and going to reside abroad'.[11] Eulenburg vigorously asserted his innocence and asked the Crown Prosecutor to start proceedings against Harden as editor and proprietor of *Die Zukunft*. But the Prosecutor declared he could do nothing, since the public interest was not affected by the allegations. By now Bülow and many of Eulenburg's personal enemies were anxious to let the matter die down since it was discrediting German society in the eyes of foreign commentators. The French, in particular, were gloating. Lecomte had been recalled and the Paris newspapers enjoyed themselves by printing scandalous tales about numerous prominent figures in Berlin and Potsdam. Harden, on the other hand, genuinely believed he was exposing the great moral disease of the Reich, and hinted to Holstein privately that he possessed 'frightful material' which would have compromised the monarchy: 'I could make a scandal that would rock the world', he wrote in a letter to Holstein on 20 June.[12] But with Harden it was difficult to separate fact from fabrication.

The sordid affair dragged on for over a year. As William himself admitted in a private letter at Christmas, it dominated his thoughts and at times left him acutely worried. Understandably, he was deeply touched by the sufferings of old friends and even more by the agony which Harden's attacks caused their families. Kuno Moltke brought a libel action against Harden in which the magistrate allowed questions to be asked which were barely relevant and which tended to discredit the Liebenberg 'round table' as a whole. William hoped the court would clear his friends' names, and was angry when Harden was acquitted. He loathed Harden – 'No let-up until we have that fellow behind bars', he is said to have remarked on hearing that the law officers were preparing a new case against *Die Zukunft* – and he freely blamed the press attacks on 'Jewish insolence, slanders and lying'.[13]

The scandal grew in intensity with the passage of time. A second trial imposed a sentence of four months' imprisonment on Harden, but verdict and sentence were set aside on appeal. The most tragic figure of all was Philipp Eulenburg, the Junker aesthete, by now a sick man racked with chronic myocarditis. On 8 May 1908, after a year of innuendo and gossip, Eulenburg was arrested and taken to the Moabit Prison in Berlin to await trial for alleged perjury. At one of the earlier hearings he had denied under oath that he was guilty of homosexual practices, but his enemies had found a former valet, Jacob Ernst, who was willing to tell the court strange tales of his master's behaviour twenty-five years previously. When Eulenburg's trial began his health deteriorated rapidly and, after three weeks of hearings *in camera*, the trial was suspended. A second trial began on 7 July 1909, but once again the prince's health gave way and it was abandoned after a few hours. Ernst's evidence, whether true or fabricated, might have caused embarrassment to the Kaiser in open court, possibly justifying Harden's boast of 'rocking the world'. When William and Eulenburg took their 'excursion' holiday to the lakes of Upper Bavaria in 1886, Ernst had been in attendance on them. It is not clear how well William knew Ernst but, two years after the trip, Eulenburg certainly assumed he would remember the young man. In a letter to the then Crown Prince in May 1888 Eulenburg mentioned he had spent the previous day at the lakes and that 'Jacob still holds good to the old principles'.[14] Probably this cryptic comment alludes to fishing technique; but it was perhaps as well Jacob Ernst remained silent. Innocence was readily smeared that year.

No further action was taken against poor Eulenburg. He lived in almost total seclusion on his estates for another twelve years, the charge against him neither proved nor disproved. William and Eulenburg never met again. Officially no person of eminence in the government or at court might have social contact with the fallen favourite until his 'innocence' was established. Fortunately some men of spirit scorned this taboo and kept Eulenburg informed of what was happening in political life but, so far as William and Dona were concerned, yet another veil of hypocrisy was thrown protectively around the suspect virtue of the court. In 1927 William wrote to Eulenburg's son and assured him he was convinced of his father's 'absolute innocence': he had been the 'faithful martyr' of the 'first assault on the monarchy'.[15] But by then 'dear Phili' had been dead for six years. It was late to offer amends.

The most influential figure in German political life by the beginning of 1907 was not the chancellor nor one of the sovereign's close friends, but the fifty-eight year old navy secretary, Admiral Tirpitz. The fleet he was creating remained free from the scandals raised by the muckrakers in Germany's older institutions. While the army was infiltrated by new-fangled social ideas which threatened morale, Tirpitz's fleet was still a peculiarly personal possession of the Kaiser, largely independent of parliamentary control and reflecting his whims and prejudices. Yet, in 1907, the future of the navy was in doubt. Three years before, the British had appointed Sir John Fisher as First Sea Lord, a fire-eating admiral as ruthless and creative as Tirpitz himself. Under Fisher's direction the British fleet, already strengthened with the first dread-noughts, was re-formed to face the German challenge, after two centuries of rivalry with France. The naval arms race quickened in pace as Germany too began to build dreadnoughts, battleships with heavier armament and greater speed than their predecessors. This revolution in warship design, which began with the launching of HMS *Dreadnought* in February 1906, was actually to Germany's advantage, as Tirpitz early perceived. Provided they could find the necessary money for armaments, rival fleets could begin the construction of new capital ships on almost level terms. There seemed to Tirpitz no reason why Germany should not overtake Britain in this contest.[16]

One country had already decided the cost of dreadnought construction was prohibitive. Russia could not afford to enter the naval race. In June 1907 the second Russian-sponsored peace conference met at The Hague, with high on its agenda the possibility of cutting expenditure on armaments by collective pledges to limit warships and weapons. William disliked proposals for reducing his military budget, and Bülow told the Reichstag all talk of disarmament was impractical. Strangely enough, this view received strong support outside Germany: the Kaiser's friend, Vice-Admiral Montagu, writing from London on 7 May, hailed Bülow's speech as 'a masterpiece of sound reasoning';[17] but the subsequent attempts by the chief German delegate at The Hague to ridicule the conference rebounded against his country's reputation. The British Foreign Secretary, Sir Edward Grey, favoured confidential discussions between the various governments over their naval programmes before any shipbuilding plans were made known to the press or parliament. But both William and Tirpitz thought that this proposal was a trick, instigated by Fisher. While the delegates at The Hague were examining the prospects for disarmament, William and Bülow were discussing with Tirpitz means of raising additional taxation for the fleet so that the rate of constructing battleships could be speeded up.[18]

If the Hague Conference irritated William, another development in that summer of 1907 filled him with deep uneasiness. In earlier years there had seemed little likelihood of reconciliation between Russia and Great Britain. Now the two empires were settling their differences. The Anglo-Russian Entente, formally marked by an agreement signed on 31 August, was primarily concerned with Asian affairs; it was anti-German only in seeking to check Germany's influence in Persia. William sought personally to reassess the situation in two meetings: the Tsar, aboard his new yacht *Standart*, came to Swinemünde early in June, and Edward VII was once again at Wilhelmshöhe in mid-August. Little was achieved at either encounter: Swinemünde was no Björkö, but at least Edward VII in an expansive moment at Wilhelmshöhe felt able to assure his host of the great joy with which 'the whole English nation' would welcome a state visit. Tirpitz was eager to avoid tension with the British while a supplementary naval law was under discussion. If William undertook a goodwill mission to London, then there was little danger of Admiral Fisher ordering a surprise attack – a 'Copenhagen' – on the German fleet, a design he was suspected of harbouring.[19]

The state visit was arranged for the second week of November 1907. It nearly did not take place. On 31 October Edward VII was amazed to receive a telegram at Sandringham from William regretting that he would not be able to come to England as he had developed a cough on top of influenza. Later that same day, in Berlin, the Kaiser telephoned Bülow to tell him that, while resting on a sofa, he had fallen in a fainting fit and caught his head a stunning blow on the floor. This incident, as Dona confirmed soon afterwards to Bülow, took place entirely in William's imagination; and the British ambassador, on his way to discuss with Bülow the cancellation of the visit, was surprised to see the sick man riding at a gallop in the Tiergarten. That evening, at the theatre, William told his chancellor he now felt fit enough to travel to Windsor after all, as the afternoon's ride had cured him completely. The reason for this strange behaviour seems to have been the tone of the English newspapers. In preparing himself for the journey to England, William had come across the previous week's copies of *The Times*, which, under the headline 'Prussian Court Scandals', faithfully reported Kuno Moltke's action against Harden – 'unnatural vices', 'disgusting orgies ... at Potsdam', and similar salacious titbits.[20] Only firm self-control could have induced William to face London society at such a time.

Outwardly the visit went well. A spectacular banquet at Windsor was so lavish that some of the Germans thought it outshone even the opulence of St Petersburg. At a Guildhall luncheon in London William made an emotional speech, reminding the Lord Mayor that 'blood is thicker than water'. The University of Oxford honoured with a doctorate in civil law 'the most mighty prince, William II ... as skilled in the arts of peace as in the science of war' (*pacis artium haud minus quam rei militaris peritus*); and the King, declining to talk politics, organized shooting parties and accompanied his guests to gala performances at the London theatres. But it was clear to those who knew William that his nerves were taut, and the photographs show how much he had aged since the Eulenburg scandal burst on the public. Haldane and Sir Edward Grey thought he was badly briefed on the problems of the Baghdad railway and, at their second meeting, Grey was surprised at the vehemence with which he condemned the activities of the Jews within Germany, although insisting that he alone could restrain his people from violent outbursts of anti-semitism. Yet although William seemed to be living on his emotions, he still cut an impressive figure to the general public. Once more he was cheered in the streets of London and Windsor, and the theatrical strain in his temperament responded agreeably to the music of applause.[21]

On 18 November the state visit ended, and Dona and the ladies returned to Germany, but William stayed on in England for another three weeks. On the eve of setting out from Berlin he had asked Edward VII if there was a suitable residence in southern England on which he might take a short lease for a convalescent holiday. The King had several times visited Highcliffe Castle, near Bournemouth, the home of Colonel Edward Stuart-Wortley, and he asked the Foreign Office to see whether the colonel would be prepared, at ten days' notice, to lease his home to the German party for a fortnight.[22] Colonel Stuart-Wortley was not, as many books have said, already a friend of the Kaiser: he had never met him, although some years previously he had briefly entertained Prince Henry of Prussia in Malta. The colonel was related by marriage to the diplomat, Sir James Rennell Rodd (who had served in Berlin), while Mrs Stuart-Wortley was the daughter of a first cousin of Houston Stewart Chamberlain. The family, like so many in the English gentry, was dismayed at the tone of the newspapers and therefore welcomed any opportunity to improve Anglo-German relations. The colonel told the Foreign Office that he did not wish to let Highcliffe, but he was prepared to 'lend' it to the Kaiser and his party, provided he could remain on the estate and act as host for his guests. William accordingly moved into Highcliffe with a large retinue on the day the state visit ended. King Edward arranged for special postal services and a special train to be put at William's disposal. He also persuaded Mrs Rosa Lewis of the Cavendish Hotel in Jermyn Street, the most esteemed cook in London society, to cater for the Kaiser and his party throughout their stay on the south coast.[23] William's subsequent claim that, at Highcliffe, he was able to sample, 'as I had long wanted to do', the pleasures and comfort 'of English home and country life' was not, perhaps, strictly accurate, for the standard and style was markedly superior to the general level; but the illusion that, for once, he was a simple English country gentleman gave him great pleasure, and he stayed on for a third week rather than for the mere fortnight he had first envisaged. At least, as he remarked in a letter to H.S. Chamberlain, the people whom he met showed no desire to pry into German affairs; and that, at the moment, was a welcome relief for him.[24]

But there were enough tales of his table talk at Highcliffe to excite speculation in the London clubs and in Fleet Street. At the start of the third week of his stay in Hampshire, Colonel Stuart-Wortley received a letter from an old friend asking if he could arrange for the Kaiser to give an interview to the well-known journalist, W. T. Stead, who had already been received by Tsar Nicholas II. Stuart-Wortley raised the subject privately with William on 1 December: 'No, I cannot do it', he replied, 'Mr Stead endeavoured to gain an interview with me in Berlin, but Count Bülow advised me not to accord it. I have made a hard and fast rule not to accord any such interviews.' He doubted if he could trust Stead; anyhow, as he added, 'I do not require Mr Stead to put me right before the British public'. But he then began to talk freely to Stuart-Wortley, recalling his past efforts to improve relations with his grandmother's country. There was, for example, the time when Queen Victoria had appealed to him during the 'dark days' of the Boer War: 'I immediately set to work with my General Staff and, having considered the situation as it was, I recommended a certain line of military action. Queen Victoria thanked me most deeply. I do not wish to say that it was owing to my advice, but the strategy followed by Lord Roberts on arrival in South Africa was exactly what I had recommended.' Next day the Kaiser treated Stuart-Wortley to his version of how the pilot was dropped in 1890; Bismarck, he said, wished to call out the troops and shoot down the socialists in the streets, but 'I told Prince Bismarck that I would never incur before the Almighty the responsibility of shooting down my people'. On 7 December he accompanied the colonel on a morning visit to a neighbour at Waterford Lodge and, as they walked through the Hampshire lanes, the Kaiser talked of the possibility of war between the United States and Japan. (Curiously enough, thirty-four years later, 7 December became the 'day of infamy', when the Japanese planes attacked the American fleet at Pearl Harbor.) 'I foresaw the danger of the Yellow Peril twenty years ago', William told Stuart-Wortley during their walk, 'and that is why I built my fleet – just to be ready to lend a helping hand.' Only one British public figure came in for specific censure from William during these talks with the colonel – Admiral Sir John Fisher, the First Sea Lord, 'a most dangerous and overrated man . . . who rules the navy by undermen who take baits thrown by him in . . . the Fishpond'.[25]

William greatly enjoyed these three weeks at Highcliffe. He responded readily to the enthusiasms around him; thus he took care to send a huge bouquet of lily-of-the-valley and carnations to the eighty-seven year old Florence Nightingale, brought back into the public eye that November by the bestowal of the Order of Merit. His letters to Dona were full of delight, and at Christmas he told H.S.Chamberlain, 'I was in the position of a guest among the great British people who received me warmly and with open arms'. A postcard in English sent by William from Potsdam soon after his return home told Colonel Stuart-Wortley, 'I am quite in love with your lovely place! Shall only be too glad to come again.' Vice-Admiral Montagu assured him that 'your living a country gentleman's life for a bit has deeply touched our people'.[26] The Kaiser was convinced he had restored harmony between the two nations. Yet was it all superficial? While William was in England, Tirpitz's proposals for shortening the effective life of Germany's battleships were laid before the Reichstag. They speeded up the modernization of the fleet by twenty-five per cent each year: the race in building dreadnoughts was on. Confidential reports from the British naval attaché in Berlin confirmed the gloomy forecasts in the newspapers, one of his estimates even suggesting that by the autumn of 1911 the Germans would be able to have at sea two more dreadnoughts than the British. In parliament, and in the correspondence columns of the press, there was ample proof of alarm at these latest proposals. At times the mood in Britain verged on panic.[27]

On 18 February 1908 a registered letter in a pale green envelope with a Potsdam postmark was received through the ordinary mail in Whitehall. It was addressed to 'The First Lord of the Admirality (*sic*), Lord Tweedmouth, London' and was signed, 'William, I.R., Admiral of the Fleet'. The letter had been written by the Kaiser four days previously, on his own initiative and without the knowledge of his chancellor. It was a sincere attempt to minimize the 'German danger' by playing down the alarmist letters and sensational stories which he had read in the newspapers. The Royal Navy, Admiral-of-the-Fleet William declared, remained five times as strong as its alleged rival across the North Sea: 'The German Fleet is built against nobody at all. It is solely built for Germany's needs in relation with that country's rapidly growing trade', he explained.

The letter was treated confidentially by the British government. It was not shown to Fisher or any of the Sea Lords. Tweedmouth discussed the matter with Grey and the letter was shown to the King, to whom William had sent a courteous note informing him that he had written, as an admiral in the British fleet, to the First Lord. Edward VII was angry at this 'new departure', by which a foreign sovereign wrote directly to a senior member of the government. He made his objections clear to his nephew. When Bülow learnt from the British ambassador of the Kaiser's action, he too was exasperated by this latest instance of personal diplomacy. But Tweedmouth and Grey handled the matter tactfully. A polite but evasive reply, drafted and re-drafted many times over in consultation with the Foreign Office, was sent personally by Tweedmouth. He regretted the tone of the newspapers but, as a gesture of goodwill, enclosed a copy of the naval estimates which were presented to parliament while the reply was on its way back to Berlin. There the matter should have ended. Unfortunately a copy of the Kaiser's letter came into unauthorized hands while Tweedmouth was at a weekend in Hertfordshire; and an angry letter, headed 'Under Which King', appeared in *The Times* of 6 March from that newspaper's military correspondent. *The Times* became morally indignant at the thought of a British cabinet minister receiving a communication from the German Emperor when the naval estimates were under discussion. Lord Tweedmouth defended himself well, with a dignified statement in the House of Lords, but within a few weeks he was relieved of responsibility for naval matters. The newspapers were sure that the new First Lord, Reginald McKenna, would continue to take a sober view of the threat from Germany's shipyards.[28]

William was disappointed by the failure of his initiative and irritated by its consequences. When, on 8 March, the German ambassador sent a detailed and well-reasoned explanation for Britain's fears of a German fleet, William refused to acknowledge that Germany might, on occasions, have behaved ineptly: 'Nonsense. All English mistakes', he commented in the margin, and wrote at the foot of the despatch: 'The English must accustom themselves to the German fleet. And from time to time we should assure them the fleet is not built against them.'[29] This policy he followed throughout the summer of 1908, notably in conversations with Sir Charles Hardinge, the Foreign Office representative in attendance on Edward VII when he broke his journey to Marienbad at Schloss Friedrichshof in August. This meeting was preceded by an unofficial 'mission' to London by Ballin, undertaken with the approval of both William and Tirpitz. Ballin, who was alarmed at the naval rivalry, hoped the Friedrichshof conversations would ease the tension, but they were totally unproductive. The Kaiser seems to have resented Hardinge's manner and abruptly declined to consider any cut in the German naval programme. 'I would rather go to war than accept such dictation', he told Hardinge, and he insisted there was no good 'reason for nervousness in England'.[30] William was in earnest. He genuinely wanted better relations with Great Britain, but the popular press would not believe him, nor would a group of senior diplomats in the Foreign Office. Who, after all, expects to shake hands with a mailed fist?

That autumn the Kaiser repaid some of the hospitality he had received at Highcliffe. Colonel Stuart-Wortley was a guest at the imperial manoeuvres held near Metz between 8–10 September. Once again he held some interesting conversations with his host, and when he returned to England he contacted the son of the proprietor of the *Daily Telegraph*, proposing that he should 'write up' the Kaiser's remarks both at Highcliffe and at Metz. On 23 September he sent a neatly typed article which he described as 'a supposed communiqué . . . veiled as from a retired diplomatist' to the Kaiser in Berlin, and in his covering letter he emphasized the value of securing for William a fair hearing in the London press. William meanwhile had gone to Rominten for an autumn shoot: he acknowledged Stuart-Wortley's letter in a rather strange telegram on 30 September, which sympathized with the colonel on the death of his sister-in-law and added the slightly inconsequential information, 'I killed some very fine stags'. Eventually Stuart-Wortley received back his article on 19 October, with a covering letter signed by William at Potsdam four days before, although neither the letter nor three small amendments in the text were in the Kaiser's handwriting: 'It embodies all the principal items of our conversation during the recent manoeuvres and deals in a most reasonable and straightforward manner with the justified complaints that I have to make against certain organs of the English press', the letter declared. 'I firmly hope it may have the effect of bringing about a change in the tone of some of the English newspapers.'[31]

Stuart-Wortley sent the text to the *Daily Telegraph*, where it was printed on Wednesday, 28 October 1908. 'No newspaper has ever had a more important or a more interesting contribution', wrote the editor to Stuart-Wortley that morning. The 'interview', as it was incorrectly called, was based on the notes which Stuart-Wortley had taken at Highcliffe eleven months before, spiced with some Wilhelmine asides jotted down during the manoeuvres. References to purely German affairs and the Kaiser's strictures on Admiral Fisher were, not surprisingly, omitted. The English were blamed for their madness – 'mad as March hares' – in remaining suspicious of German intentions: one day, when faced by the menace of Japan, the British would be glad of the German fleet, and would appreciate his 'repeated offers of friendship'. The interview then told how William had refused to join Russia and France in a continental league during the Boer War and how he had sent a plan of campaign to Windsor which 'as a matter of curious coincidence' resembled the strategy later followed by Lord Roberts. 'I strive without ceasing to improve relations, and you retort that I am your arch-enemy. You make it very hard for me. Why is it?'[32]

William's remarks caused a sensation. Edward VII was furious at the historical licence which had crept into his recollections of dynastic exchanges during the Boer War; Nicholas II summoned the British ambassador to Peterhof and explained to him that Russia had only wished for peaceful mediation in 1900 and that William himself had suggested a Russian military demonstration on the frontiers of India; and in Tokyo the Japanese wished to know, a little plaintively, how they were at that moment threatening Germany and Great Britain. In general, the English were amused by William's gesture of goodwill: *The Times* thought that, if the fleet was for use in the Pacific, it was strange that a great naval force should be concentrated in the Baltic and the North Sea, 'many units of which notoriously lack coal capacity to make lengthy cruises of any kind'. But in Germany the newspapers were indignant. It was bad enough to be told that, as they had long suspected, their emperor was more sympathetic to the British than were most of his subjects: it was even worse to learn that he had actually employed the General Staff to draft a war plan for the British at a time when Germans of all classes warmly supported the Boers in South Africa. Why, moreover, was the German taxpayer subsidizing a fleet for service alongside the British in the Pacific, a region of small concern to someone living on the Elbe or the Rhine or the Spree? On 31 October Stuart-Wortley wrote to William confessing how 'disappointed and miserable' he felt at 'the fuss made by the villainous press in both this country and Germany', but he believed, so he said, that ultimately the tone of the newspapers would improve.[33]

He was wrong. The Berlin press had, on several occasions, enjoyed a 'Chancellor Crisis' but never before a 'Kaiser Crisis'; the whole concept of the sovereign's 'personal rule' was debated with a freedom which would not normally have been permitted. Only Harden's *Zukunft* was hurriedly confiscated for carrying its criticism of the monarch's impetuosity too far. In this crisis William was ill-served by his chancellor. Bülow had been shown the draft of Stuart-Wortley's article but had taken little interest in it, passing it on to subordinates in the Foreign Ministry. When the 'interview' appeared, Bülow duly offered his resignation 'for having failed under pressure of business to go through the English manuscript in person'; but William was desperate. He begged Bülow to stay in office and bolster the monarchy – 'Say what you like but . . . get us out of this', William told him.[34] He remained chancellor and advised William to go ahead with his programme of arrangements as though there were no crisis. A few days shooting stags with Archduke Francis Ferdinand, a visit to the airship trials – where he caused some amusement by hailing Count Zeppelin, a shade prematurely, as 'the greatest German of the twentieth century' – and then on to Prince Fürstenberg's estate at Donaueschingen where, for a change, he could shoot foxes. Meanwhile Bülow remained in Berlin to handle criticism of the Kaiser's conduct in the Reichstag. 'Always in my prayers, morning and evening, I remember you', William telegraphed to Bülow on the eve of the Reichstag debate.[35]

He was at Donaueschingen when the full report of the debate reached him. The tone of the opposition deputies did not surprise him, but he was deeply hurt by Bülow's performance; for the chancellor made him appear a well-meaning idiot who, in talking to Stuart-Wortley, had believed he was serving his country but was, in reality, 'laying on the colours too thick'. 'The knowledge that the publication . . . has caused much excitement and pain in our country', Bülow declared '. . . will induce His Majesty henceforth to maintain, even in his private conversation, that reserve which is equally essential for a coherent government policy and for the authority of the Crown.'[36] This, however, was not William's intention. He expected an acknowledgement of his attempts to win over and influence his English friends, not a contemptuous disavowal. Prince Fürstenberg found the Kaiser in tears at Bülow's treachery in trimming his sails to catch the prevailing mood of the country. Next evening, to lighten his guest's gloom, Fürstenberg laid on some after dinner entertainment. An orchestra played in the great hall of the castle and General Hülsen, head of the military cabinet, donned 'ballet skirts' and danced a *pas seul*, which one of the courtiers described as a beautiful performance and which was certainly no mere burlesque. The post-prandial pirouette, however gracefully executed, is a rare accomplishment in a general of fifty-six; and with good reason. Poor Hülsen-Häseler acknowledged the applause, retired panting for breath to the Long Gallery, and, still in balletic costume, slumped into unconsciousness. Two doctors failed to revive him.[37]

This macabre evening overturned the structure of William's nervous system. 'It took me four weeks to recover from the hard November days, partly a consequence of dear Hülsen's tragic and sudden death', William wrote to Archduke Francis Ferdinand in mid-December.[38] At times during these four weeks the Kaiser seriously considered abdication, and on 20 November the Crown Prince visited Bülow to let him know that he personally was ready to succeed his father if that was essential for the good of the Reich. From this misfortune, however, Bülow was determined to save the German people and he found a firm ally in Dona, who despaired of her eldest son's incorrigible frivolity. The Crown Prince was permitted to deputize for his father while William withdrew to the privacy of the Neues Palais. There he was mothered by Dona, who acquired a new domestic authority with the dispersal of the Liebenberg 'circle' and the absurd tragedy at Donaueschingen. William would not have recovered his composure after the shocks of the past eighteen months if it had not been for his wife. That month she remained with him for hours at a time, gradually mending his torn nerves and making the fountain of vitality flow once more within him. Dona, until now the ideal German housewife with no political interests, assumed importance as her husband's only loyal confidante, a hand to be held by a child lost unexpectedly in the dark. By the end of the year his letters were again ringing with self-assurance; but this time they rang without an echo in German policy. The Kaiser Crisis – or, as William called it, 'the unbelievable cowardice of the officials who left their master shamefully in the lurch' – created a gap between emperor and chancellor which nothing could bridge. 'Whether Prince Bülow will remain very long in office remains to be seen', commented the British ambassador with judicious detachment to Sir Edward Grey, soon after the *Daily Telegraph* incident. Prince Bülow himself, by the end of the year, was asking himself a similar question. The Kaiser's frosty attitude towards him left little doubt of the answer.[39]

10. The Danger Zone

By the beginning of 1909 William had learnt, painfully, there was no hope of achieving with Bülow the type of partnership his grandfather forged with Bismarck. 'Dear Bernard' was now 'that rogue'. For the moment, however, there were two sound reasons for retaining him in office: he had support from a majority in the Reichstag; and he seemed to understand the international crisis into which the folly of the Austrian and Russian foreign ministers had pushed Europe the previous autumn. For on 6 October 1908 – while the original draft of the *Daily Telegraph* 'interview' was in Germany awaiting William's approval – the Austrians annexed Bosnia-Herzegovina and thereby posed the Eastern Question again in an acute form, for the first time in thirty years.*

William was politically embarrassed by the Austrian action. 'I was only indignant that I was the last to hear of it', he commented later.[1] At the time, however, he feared that the Austrian initiative would weaken the prestige of Turkey, where many younger army officers were Germany's friends and clients. Bülow argued Germany had no choice: the Turks could be compensated, in cash; but it was essential to stand by

---

* By the treaty of Berlin (1878) Austria-Hungary was permitted to occupy the Turkish provinces of Bosnia-Herzegovina, which remained technically part of the Ottoman Empire. Subsequently the Austrians developed and exploited the provinces as though they were colonial possessions. The Austrian hold was threatened by a southern Slav movement among the inhabitants of the region, who favoured union with Serbia, and also by the 'Young Turk' reformers in Constantinople, who wished to restore Turkish authority. Russia, as the leading Slav nation, supported the Serbs and their sympathizers in Bosnia-Herzegovina, but the Austrian foreign minister believed he had struck a secret bargain with his Russian counterpart: Austria would annex the provinces while Russia would be compensated by concessions over the right to move warships through the Bosphorus and the Dardanelles. The Austrians, however, acted precipitately, before the Russians had completed diplomatic negotiations necessary to change the status of the Straits. Hence the intensity of Russian indignation over what was regarded by the Russian foreign minister as an Austrian trick.

Austria-Hungary, Germany's one reliable ally. Moreover here was a chance to lessen the threat to Germany of 'encirclement' by the entente powers: neither France nor Britain had direct interests in Bosnia-Herzegovina and were unlikely to support Russia; it would be a simple matter for the Germans to discredit and humiliate the Francophiles in St Petersburg responsible for shaping foreign policy. William welcomed the possibility of a diplomatic success and, though barely on speaking terms with his chancellor, permitted him a free hand throughout the Bosnian crisis. To his friend, Archduke Francis Ferdinand, William was openly bombastic: 'I hold myself prepared for everything that God may ordain', he wrote to him on New Year's Eve, 'I keep my powder dry and I am on my guard. You know that *you* may count on us.'[2]

Yet at heart William was anxious to avoid a war. The Austrian cause had little backing in Germany as a whole, and the crisis came at a bad moment for the navy leaders, who were still some laps behind their rivals across the North Sea. Significantly William's marginal comments on despatches from London show support for the idea of mediation, and during a state visit by Edward VII to Berlin in February 1909 he behaved with studied moderation and a semblance of tact. But there was a formidable war party in the German capital. It was led by Schlieffen's successor as chief of the General Staff, Helmuth von Moltke, nephew of the great strategist of 1866 and 1870. In January 1909 the Kaiser authorized Moltke to exchange letters with Conrad von Hötzendorff, chief of the Austro-Hungarian General Staff, so that the two allied armies could co-operate if there was a war on the continent. 'As soon as Russia mobilizes, Germany too will mobilize and, without doubt will mobilize her whole army', Moltke assured Conrad on 21 January.[3] Nor was Moltke alone in this warlike mood. General von Lynker, the unfortunate Hülsen's successor as chief of the Kaiser's military secretariat, also believed an Austro-German campaign would speedily dispose of Russia and France. He thought, as did Moltke, that it would be a long time before Germany had such a favourable opportunity for war; and he blamed William for holding back at such a moment. 'Over the past twenty-one years everything that has brought us down from the heights may be traced back to the Kaiser's influence', he complained.[4]

At this point the Kaiser was saved from the uncertainties of a war crisis by the initiative of a discredited companion. Kiderlen-Waechter's sharp tongue and delight in gossip had led William to banish him to the minor diplomatic post of Bucharest in 1898, but he was an intelligent man and after ten years in the Balkans his services were needed in Berlin. It is probable his disgrace had been engineered in the first instance by Bülow, and now that the chancellor was out of favour William was willing to receive Kiderlen once more, though he treated him with reserve. Kiderlen, believing Russia too weak to fight, acquired for the Kaiser a victory without war. On 21 March he drafted a telegram to St Petersburg, which Bülow signed: the Russians were to let the Germans know, 'with a precise answer "yes" or "no"', 'if they were willing to accept Austria's annexation of Bosnia-Herzegovina or whether 'events were to be allowed to take their course'.[5] The telegram was not, as has sometimes been said, an ultimatum, but its tone was sufficiently menacing to induce the Russians to give way. By the end of the month the crisis was over, peacefully.

William was delighted with this triumph on the cheap, although grudging Kiderlen his role in it. For once the diplomats had timed their decision well for, by mid-April, William was on his way to Corfu where he spent four contented weeks at his villa, the Achilleion, in an 'enchantingly gracious' mood. Then, in May, back to Pula and a meeting in Vienna with Francis Joseph. There, to his host's embarrassment, he delivered one of his more grandiose speeches: Europe was told that the continent had enjoyed peace that year because he personally had stood 'shoulder to shoulder ... in shining armour' with the 'august and venerable' ruler of Austria-Hungary. The imagery did not accord with the recollections of William's generals, for whom their War Lord's pose that spring had seemed singularly un-Wagnerian, but it gave a dramatic emphasis to an alliance which, after thirty years of partnership, tended to be taken for granted.[6]

He returned home to face a political crisis, though one which gave him a certain satisfaction. During Edward VII's visit to Berlin in February William had told him privately he no longer trusted Bülow and would soon replace him with a new chancellor. Bülow had long been conscious that the Bismarckian system of government was ill suited to an empire of sixty million subjects, which was by now the leading industrial power in Europe. Tentatively he began to propose reforms. But the old-guard Prussian conservatives would surrender none of their privileges. Bülow wished to impose death duties on the great estates: the Junkers saw no reason to balance the budget at their expense; and by mid-summer the chancellor's Reichstag majority had melted away. This was the opportunity for which William had waited ever since Bülow's 'treachery' during the *Daily Telegraph* debate. On 29 June 1909 Bülow travelled to Kiel and, in an audience aboard the *Hohenzollern* formally resigned the chancellorship, curiously enough in the same place and the same harbour as he had accepted appointment to the Foreign Ministry twelve years before. William wasted little time on him: it was regatta week, and Prince Albert of Monaco was waiting for a race to begin.[7]

The news of Bülow's resignation was rumoured in the press, but not confirmed for another fortnight. It was essential for William to consult the representatives of the other German states, and even he drew the line at re-ordering a government completely from the saloon of the *Hohenzollern*. Dona, seeking to assert her newly won influence, urged him to change his mind, and stick with Bülow after all. William, however, sensed the need for a different type of man, and indeed for a new style in government. Briefly he thought of appointing the Silesian aristocrat, Prince Lichnowsky, who had long experience of foreign embassies; but he chose instead a gentlemanly and tidy-minded bureaucrat, Theobald von Bethmann-Hollweg, a Caprivi without the military bark.[8] For the past four years Bethmann had been responsible for internal affairs, originally in Prussia alone and since 1907 in Germany as a whole. He was, as Bülow once complained, 'doctrinaire', more inclined than his predecessors to write lengthy, logical memoranda to serve as programmes of action at home and abroad. William knew he had little experience of foreign affairs, yet reckoned this no fault. Bethmann was by inclination a reforming conservative, willing to seek universal suffrage for the elections of the Prussian *Landtag* which had been based on a complicated three-tier voting system virtually unchanged since 1849. Abroad, he hoped to detach the British from the wiles of France and Russia by offering naval concessions in return for a political treaty. End the naval rivalry, he argued; secure a pact of neutrality with London; and, with this firm achievement in diplomacy, seek to reform and modernize the German constitution. From August 1909 until midsummer 1911 the search for an Anglo-German understanding was not far from the centre of Bethmann's mind.

William respected Bethmann's dutiful monarchism: he knew he now had a chancellor who would rally to his support if Reichstag deputies complained of his autocratic aberrations. He also approved of Bethmann's attempts to reach an understanding with the British, and he instructed Tirpitz to submit proposals which would provide a basis for naval discussions. But in September 1909 Tirpitz was by far the strongest personality in the German government, and his views were more devious than either William's or Bethmann's. He knew that, as yet, the High Seas Fleet could not hope to emerge victorious from a conflict. For the next 'four or five years' Germany would remain in a 'danger zone', and it was desirable to avoid complete estrangement from the British during this period. Tirpitz was willing to put forward proposals for limiting naval armaments, but he was not sincere. He did not wish them to be accepted. Nor for that matter did the German steel barons and shipbuilders, who were prospering comfortably from naval rivalry. There was, Tirpitz contended, no harm in discussions with the British so long as nothing was finally settled. At least it seemed unlikely the Royal Navy would 'Copenhagen' the High Seas Fleet while the politicians were talking of disarmament; and when Sir John Fisher retired as First Sea Lord in January 1910 the danger of a naval preventive war began to look even more remote.[9]

The Kaiser's feelings towards his mother's homeland were as ambivalent as ever. On 6 May 1910 Edward VII died, and William genuinely mourned the uncle whom he had more than once denounced to startled guests around his dining-table ('You can hardly believe what a Satan he is'). In Westminster Hall William stood silently beside the new king, George V, clasping his hand in friendship before the catafalque. Again he stayed at Windsor, where (as he wrote to Bethmann) 'memories ... kindle my sense of belonging to this place' which 'I am proud that I may call my second home'. Again he was cheered by an English crowd: Conan Doyle, reporting the king's funeral for *The Times*, thought the Kaiser looked 'so noble that England has lost something of her old kindliness if she does not take him back into her heart today'. William told Bethmann that the warmth of his reception was a 'good omen' for the new reign, offsetting the events of recent years 'which have been for me personally so unbearable'. And when, in February 1911, George V suggested William might wish to come to London in May for the unveiling of the memorial to their 'beloved Grandmother', the Kaiser accepted the invitation with alacrity and a beautifully phrased letter recalling those 'solemn hours in Osborne when she breathed her last in my arms'.[10]

The old diplomacy, however, owed more to Machiavelli than to Mrs Henry Wood, and the sentimental handshakes of royal cousins left scarcely a tear-stain on policy. William himself remarked privately, twenty years later, that his personal successes in London invariably outraged the 'anti-British mentality' which Holstein had encouraged among officials in the Foreign Ministry and they 'threw obstacles into my way, so as to upset my good relations with England'.[11] This was a shrewd comment but, as so often, an over-simplification. Bethmann-Hollweg believed that his government, which had as yet achieved nothing of note, needed a 'livelier tone' if it was to check a swing to the parties of the Left shown in recent by-elections. He hoped that if Kiderlen-Waechter were appointed foreign secretary he would gain a prestige victory for German diplomacy. William was uneasy. He warned Bethmann that Kiderlen would prove a vain and independent colleague, but he gave way and in June 1910 formally confirmed Kiderlen-Waechter's appointment as State Secretary for Foreign Affairs.[12]

In later years the Kaiser regretted such an error of judgement. On reading a history of these years in 1931 William commented in the margin that Kiderlen was 'an absolutely unprincipled, disobedient subordinate and a cynic'.[13] But in 1910 it seemed sensible to have an experienced diplomat in the Wilhelmstrasse, enabling Bethmann to concentrate on domestic problems. Kiderlen was certain he could rally patriotic voters behind a strong foreign policy in time for the Reichstag elections of January 1912. He wished to gain another success on the cheap, this time against the French and in Morocco, the very region where Germany had suffered such a diplomatic rebuff in 1906. The French played into his hands: for, in the spring of 1911, the government in Paris complained that the Sultan was no longer able to maintain order in the interior of Morocco, and sent an expeditionary force to do the task for him. Kiderlen argued that, since France was clearly about to establish a protectorate over Morocco, Germany was entitled to compensation.[14]

William was unenthusiastic. The word 'Morocco' recalled painful memories. It was tiresome of 'that louse' Kiderlen to conjure up ghosts from the recent past at such a time, for in early April William was off to Corfu again. During the winter, farmers had found limestone sculpture in the fields between the Achilleion and the city of Corfu. William was convinced there was a classical temple close to his villa. He intended to spend Easter supervising an extensive archaeological dig there. Not, however, an amateur one, for he summoned to the site the great Wilhelm Dörpfeld, who was profitably engaged at Olympia. The archaeologists obligingly discovered a Gorgon's head, centrepiece to the pediment of a temple of Artemis. Excited telegrams sped back to Berlin above the imperial cipher; and in reply came Kiderlen's wire about Morocco. 'If the French break the Algeciras Agreement, we can leave it to other powers, and especially Spain, to protest first', William telegraphed back to Bethmann; and he added, 'We can do nothing with warships . . . I therefore beg you to stand firmly at once against sending warships'.[15] Uneasily, he turned once more to the quest for the temple of Artemis.

By the end of the first week in May he was back in Germany, ready to cross to London for the unveiling of the statue to Queen Victoria in the middle of the month. At Karlsruhe, on 5 May, he studied a memorandum prepared two days earlier by Kiderlen which argued that, if the French were going to establish themselves in the town of Fez 'from anxiety for their nationals, we too have a right to protect our own'. Kiderlen accordingly recommended the despatch of warships to the ports of Mogador and Agadir where 'there are large German firms'. The ships would remain 'peacefully' in harbour, awaiting a French offer of compensation. Almost as an afterthought Kiderlen pointed out that because the ports were some 'distance from the Mediterranean, England would scarcely raise difficulties'. It was a powerful plea for action, promising to blot out the shame of 'earlier setbacks' and emphasizing the value of success in foreign policy to 'the future development of political conditions at home'. William agreed in principle, but he was concerned over the likely reactions of the British. Since he was going to London in the following week, final approval was withheld until he had tested English opinion.[16]

William and Dona spent three days in London, cheered in the streets and applauded by a standing audience at the theatre. Never, so William informed Bethmann-Hollweg, had he found the atmosphere at Buckingham Palace, 'so free, so open, or so friendly'. He held no political discussions with the English ministers, since both the British and German governments had emphasized that this was strictly a family visit. But shortly before leaving the Palace to travel home, he raised the Moroccan question with King George v. What exactly was said in this hurried exchange is not clear: one monarch had the subject at his fingertips, the other was caught unawares and with an eye on the clock. William received the impression that the King believed each country should strike its own bargain with France; George thought, in retrospect, William may have mentioned 'something about a ship', but he was certain he did not refer to the port of Agadir. When the Kaiser arrived back in Berlin he told Bethmann he had assured King George that Germany would 'never wage a war for the sake of Morocco' although she might seek compensation elsewhere in Africa if the French strengthened their position in Morocco. But the most important consequence of this, his last visit to London, was William's conviction that the English people and their rulers were well disposed towards Germany.[17] It seemed to him that Kiderlen was, after all, justified in assuming 'England' would not raise difficulties if there should be a naval demonstration at a southern Moroccan port.

On 26 June Kiderlen travelled up to Kiel – for it was, once again, regatta week – and there received the Kaiser's final approval of the Moroccan venture. Germany would use the presence of warships to extract colonial concessions from the French or, as an alternative policy, to establish a foothold in southern Morocco, where it was believed there were considerable mineral resources still untapped. From Kiel, Kiderlen triumphantly telegraphed back to the Wilhelmstrasse 'Ships granted'. He was disappointed on his return to find that the Kaiser's pet creation, the new navy, could not meet his requirements.[18] Kiderlen had intended to send two warships to Agadir and two to Mogador but, to his chagrin, Tirpitz had only one vessel in North African waters – and that one vessel hardly the pride of a fleet.

The gunboat *Panther* (1,700 tons displacement and a complement of 125 men) arrived off Agadir on the morning of 1 July. At noon the German ambassadors accredited to the countries which had signed the Algeciras agreement solemnly informed their governments of the German naval presence in southern Morocco. There followed four months of international crisis, in which Europe seemed at times closer to a general war than for forty years. Kiderlen intended the *'Panther*'s leap' to startle the French, but there was much less excitement in Paris than in either Berlin or London. A change of government in France during the last days of June had brought to power Joseph Caillaux, who was known to favour Franco-German collaboration, and there was in Paris none of the chauvinistic fervour of 1870. The German press, on the other hand, hailed the news from Agadir as proof that the Reich was once again pursuing a vigorous foreign policy. But to Kiderlen and the Kaiser the most surprising reaction came from London; for the British Government, which William had expected to be readily acquiescent, insisted on treating the incident as a grave threat to peace. Sir Edward Grey demanded an explanation from the German ambassador, whom Kiderlen left without clear instructions for three weeks. Exasperated by Germany's silence and by rumours of Franco-German negotiations, the British Government decided to adopt a stern tone; and Grey therefore welcomed the offer of the Chancellor of the Exchequer, Lloyd George, to deliver a strong warning in a speech which he was to make to city bankers at the Mansion House on 21 July. Lloyd George did not mention the *Panther*, Agadir, or even Germany by name; but it was assumed by the press, at home and abroad, that when he declared Britain would not be treated 'as if she were of no account ... where her interests were vitally affected', he was presenting the current crisis as an issue of peace or war.[19] There were, in consequence, violent attacks on the English warmongers in the newspapers of Berlin and Cologne.

The Kaiser, meanwhile, was at sea, spending July in the *Hohenzollern* on his customary cruise down the Norwegian fjords. Even before receiving reports of the Mansion House speech, he had been so critical of Kiderlen's performance that the foreign minister twice submitted letters of resignation to Bethmann-Hollweg (who took care not to pass them on to the *Hohenzollern*). William thought Kiderlen was demanding territorial concessions in central Africa from the French which no government could make and hope to stay in office. He insisted to Bethmann there must be no mobilization of Germany's forces while he was on his cruise, and the foreign office representative in attendance reported back to Berlin that William was unlikely to approve of any measures which would lead to war. Lloyd George's warning disturbed him little – 'a courteous gesture to Paris, where they are howling for help', he commented – but he was alarmed by reports that the Admiralty had cancelled the goodwill visit of Vice-Admiral Jellicoe's squadron to Wilhelmshaven. When William disembarked at the end of his cruise, on 29 July, he immediately received a report from Kiderlen and instructed him to moderate the demands he was making for colonial concessions from the French. There seemed no good reason why the whole business should not be settled within a week.[20]

To William's dismay, the crisis now took an unexpected turn. The conservative newspapers in Berlin became so intensely patriotic that it was difficult for Kiderlen to control the passion he had unleashed. There was talk of 'national dishonour', of 'unspeakable shame', of 'humiliation'; and the Kaiser personally was presented as a champion of appeasement. He had not received so bad a press since the *Daily Telegraph* incident; and he found his generals insistent on taking a tough line. Moltke told his wife, on 19 August, he was so 'sick and tired of this unhappy Moroccan affair' that he was beginning to despair of the future of the Reich, unless 'we can bring ourselves to present a determined claim which we are prepared to back up at the point of a sword'; and the Kaiser's principal naval adviser, Admiral von Müller, commented enigmatically, 'War is not the greatest of evils.'[21] On reflection, Müller thought it was essential to postpone the conflict with England until after the Kiel Canal had been broadened, so that dreadnoughts might move freely between the North Sea and the Baltic. Tirpitz, too, was anxious to get Germany clear of the 'danger zone' before there was any risk of his fleet being engaged in battle: 'With every year that passes we shall be in a more favourable position', he wrote to his deputy in the Navy Office on 12 August, and he listed the work still awaiting completion – forts on Heligoland, the widened canal, new dreadnoughts, new submarines. The earliest possible date for emerging from the 'danger zone' would be the spring of 1914.[22]

By the middle of August it was clear that only a handful of generals and conservative deputies were prepared to imperil Europe's peace over Morocco. Neither Bethmann nor Kiderlen wanted war, not least because they recognized Germany would have to fight it alone, since the authorities in Vienna refused to regard the Moroccan dispute as a question of vital importance to Europe as a whole. William himself finally decided in favour of a peaceful settlement at a conference in Schloss Wilhelmshöhe on 17 August, but he continued to be worried by the tone of the press and therefore retreated cautiously. Indeed, ten days later, he visited Hamburg and delivered a speech in his most reckless style: no nation, he declared amid warm applause, had the right 'to dispute the place in the sun to which we are entitled'.[23] Yet it remained – in Germany, at least – an artificial crisis. When, in the second week of September, a succession of newspaper articles suggested that patriotism was about to be sternly tested, the German middle class replied by a run on the banks and panic selling on the stock market. The mass of the German people turned readily back from catastrophe. To welcome a *Panther*'s leap was one thing: to leap over the brink of war for Morocco was quite a different matter.

Two more months elapsed before the Moroccan affair was settled by formal agreement. On 4 November Germany recognized the right of the French to 'protect' Morocco, receiving in exchange a sizeable segment of the French Congo, a largely swampy region adjoining the German Cameroons. The Kaiser, putting a bold face on a limited achievement, sent his congratulations to Bethmann-Hollweg on emerging successfully from a 'delicate crisis'. Privately he expressed a hope – not for the first time – that he had heard the last of Morocco. In this he was disappointed. The Reichstag debate on the Moroccan agreement, two days of set speeches on 9–10 November, saw sustained attacks from both conservative and liberal deputies on the inept foreign policy of the past five months, and by implication on the sovereign who had tolerated such alternations of bravado and retreat. The Crown Prince was present on 9 November; and the newspapers took pains to point out that he applauded, not Bethmann's defence of his policy, but the demagogic attacks of the conservatives.[24]

Bethmann and Kiderlen had hoped a crisis abroad would distract attention from domestic grievances, but the Agadir incident, and all the excitement of the newspapers, seemed remote to the working-class voters. The Reichstag election of January 1912 made the Social Democrats the largest single party in Germany, with more than a third of the total poll. In a chamber of 397 deputies there were 110 socialists. Bethmann-Hollweg could still muster enough support from the parties of the right and centre to get essential legislation through the chamber, but the election result was a considerable shock to the Kaiser. The Social Democrats were basically republican in ideology, and he began to fear for the stability of the throne. That January marked the bicentenary of the birth of Frederick the Great, and William appropriated 'old Fritz's' legendary reputation to bolster Hohenzollern morale. The anniversary of his birth fell on 24 January: William, however, decided that the celebrations would take place five days later, on his own fifty-third birthday. One hundred thousand copies of a special study of Frederick by Reinhold Koser, the director of the state archives, were presented on that day to students in the Prussian gymnasia and high schools.[25] It was a propaganda exercise which the more dogmatic socialist intellectuals treated with derision, but most German Social Democrats were less revolutionary than their leaders and William may well have been wise in following the electoral reverse with an improvised dynastic festival. Republican socialism remained a bogey, rather than a serious threat to the monarchy. When, in the spring of 1912, the socialist deputies mounted an attack on the Kaiser for permitting the army to be used against miners striking in the Ruhr there was uproar in the Reichstag, but no serious disturbances in the country as a whole. Germany was still an empire of barracks where obedience was a primary virtue and spiked helmets constricted the enquiring mind.

Even before the 1912 election William was turning away from the civilians who had muddled into and out of the Agadir adventure. His doubts about Kiderlen-Waechter were confirmed and, although he insisted that Bethmann was 'exceedingly sensible', he believed Germany needed someone with a heightened instinct for statecraft at the helm. 'I must be my own Bismarck', he announced to his naval chiefs on 9 December.[26] Tirpitz was more practical: Agadir, he maintained, had shown the need to cut down England's naval lead as rapidly as possible; and he therefore sought a substantial shipbuilding programme to be embodied, in a navy bill, as part of the budget proposals for 1912. But by now the General Staff, strengthened by younger officers of personality such as the chief of operations, Major Ludendorff, was demanding an army bill. In 1910 the Germans had spent the equivalent of forty million pounds on the army and twenty million on the navy. The Prussian war ministry pointed out that this proportion of expenditure was absurd since Germany remained essentially a continental power. 'In a future war', Moltke wrote in a memorandum for William on 2 December 1911, 'the decisive events will be on land and must be brought about by the army. It is on the strength of its army that Germany's power continues to rest.'[27] William accepted the implications of Moltke's memorandum: he had himself noticed deficiencies during the 1911 manoeuvres. In his New Year address to the military commanders he guaranteed that the army's essential needs would take precedence over those of the navy. As though to hold him to his word, an 'Army League' was founded later in January, with a retired general as its president and funds from heavy industry to assist its propaganda. The Army League never had the popular appeal of its naval forerunner, but it remained a powerful pressure group and one which prided itself on its instant readiness for war, uninhibited by any talk of a 'danger zone'. By the second week in February 1912 William was resolved to ask the Reichstag for an Army Law as well as a Navy Law that summer.[28]

Meanwhile he was following, with great interest, the political drama in England, where the struggle over Lloyd George's radical budget was resolved by a constitutional conflict between the Lords and the Commons. The year 1911 – with its unusually hot summer – was marked by extraordinary unrest in Great Britain: extensive strikes; suffragist militancy; mounting resistance in Ulster to the principle of Home Rule. The German embassy in London kept Kiderlen well informed of opposition within the Liberal Party to the government's defence policy, and some of these reports were forwarded to Bethmann and the Kaiser. William, too, remained in touch with Tory friends who thought little of their 'dangerously radical' government. Vice-Admiral Montagu, for example, commented on the changes which brought Winston Churchill to the Admiralty from the Home Office in the last days of October, 1911: 'Fancy, Sir, Mr W. Churchill now First Lord!', the Admiral wrote to William on 6 November. 'He was no use before, so they put him there to keep quiet. We are in an awful mess . . . No constitution. Territorials failing fast. The people only think of football or strikes.'[29] Vice-Admiral Montagu, a sincere champion of Anglo-German friendship, looked upon his correspondence with the Kaiser as a personal affair, and he cannot have foreseen that his letters were regularly circulated to the naval secretariat in Berlin, frequently in translation and with annotations. It is unlikely that William, who was Churchill's host at the manoeuvres of 1906 and 1909, took Montagu's comments too seriously; but by the end of the year 1911 he had certainly come to despise the British politicians and to think far less of British military potential than in earlier days. 'Nonsense, coward, weakling', William wrote at Christmas on a report from his ambassador in London which favoured an Anglo-German understanding; and some weeks later he assured his guests aboard the *Hohenzollern* that 'The English are all sheep. Mr Balfour is a sheep, Mr Chamberlain is one, Sir Edward Grey is the biggest.'[30]

William's sudden Anglophobia was no doubt a reaction against the suspicion he had been too well-disposed towards his 'English friends' during the Agadir crisis. As if to give the lie to this impression, he emphasized to Archduke Francis Ferdinand his conviction that 'only strong power and brutal force impress these people on the other side of the Channel', adding in the same letter that 'politeness is considered weakness'.[31] But he was inconsistent. While flourishing a big stick for the benefit of the archduke, he was prepared to welcome a renewal of contacts between his friend, Albert Ballin, and Sir Ernest Cassel, the German-born international banker who was a close confidant of the Churchill family. Cassel, coming to Berlin at the end of January 1912, suggested there might be a series of Anglo-German conversations: it was hoped that Germany would call a halt to any future shipbuilding programme in return for colonial concessions and a pledge that neither country would join any coalition designed to attack the other. William responded favourably to this vague, and largely exploratory, proposal. As a sign of goodwill he entrusted Cassel with a copy of the newest German naval programme, assuming that Churchill and Grey would be able to assess it calmly and judiciously before the naval bill was announced publicly in Berlin. At the same time the British were told the Kaiser would welcome a visit from a member of the government, preferably Grey himself or Churchill.[32]

The British cabinet was hesitant. There was only one minister familiar with the German scene (and, indeed, with the German language) and that was Lord Haldane who, though now in the Lords, remained Secretary of State for War, as he had been on his last visit to Berlin, in 1906. It was announced in the House of Commons that Haldane, accompanied by his brother (a distinguished physicist) and by Cassel, would travel to the German capital to study higher education for a committee which was considering the future of the University of London. This unlikely tale fooled nobody and increased the suspicion felt towards the 'Haldane Mission' in Paris and St Petersburg. But, as William himself privately admitted, only a complete shift in British policy, abandoning the ententes and lapsing into neutral isolation, could have brought Haldane any success. On the day on which he left London (7 February), the Kaiser opened the new session of the Reichstag and, in the speech from the throne, let it be known that the deputies would be asked to approve both an army bill and a navy bill in the months ahead.[33] There was too much mistrust of Germany in Westminster, and of the English Liberals in Berlin for there to be any real prospect of political understanding.

On 9 February Haldane held long conversations with the Kaiser and with Tirpitz. That evening, in Glasgow, Churchill made his first important speech since going to the Admiralty, a reasoned argument justifying the British case for naval supremacy: 'The British Navy is to us a necessity and, from some points of view, the German Navy is to them more in the nature of a luxury', he declared. It was an unfortunate remark, exploited by the German press: the word 'luxury' in English implied something superfluous; it was translated '*Luxus*', which suggested a self-indulgent pleasure. Until now William had treated Churchill amiably: he knew, and liked, his mother; and he had graciously received an inscribed first edition of *Lord Randolph Churchill* (which may still be seen today on the bookshelves at Doorn). But the 'luxury fleet' speech rankled, and he began to complain of Churchill's arrogant manner.[34] Nor did it help the unfortunate Haldane. He returned to London with a slim chance of an agreement, but no more. Ballin travelled to England a few weeks later and was so cheered by his conversations with Haldane and Churchill that he hurried back to Berlin and on 17 March announced dramatically, 'Majesty, I bring you the alliance with England.' The good news was, as William suspected, more a wish than a reality. Later that same afternoon telegrams from London left William in no doubt that the British ministers were not prepared to compromise, so long as Germany continued to build up her fleet of dreadnoughts.[35] By the end of May, army and navy bills had been ratified by the Reichstag and approval given for an extraordinary property tax to pay for this massive armament programme.

Bethmann-Hollweg was worried by the trend of German policy. It seemed to him that, by the spring of 1912, William was listening to only two advisers: his wife, who disliked Ballin and found it hard to restrain her Anglophobia; and Tirpitz, who was obsessed with the need to build up the battle fleet until the English would not risk a naval encounter. In March Dona and Tirpitz combined to put pressure on Bethmann, who suspected a plot to replace him as chancellor by the admiral. There was some truth in Dona's warning, made on a personal visit to Bethmann, that William was once more faced by a crisis of nerves: he had convinced himself that Grey ('a sanctimonious ass') was as untrustworthy as Lord Salisbury had been in the last years of the old century. The British ministers, so he maintained, presumed on his goodwill and liking for English ways: '*They* dictate and *we* are to accept', he wrote in the margin of a despatch from London. He saw no reason for halting the construction of battleships in return for an offer of British support for a German colonial empire in Central Africa, 'consisting of lands owned by foreign nations and not English property'. The 'hypocrisy' and intrigues of 'perfidious Albion' were enough to drive one mad, he complained.[36] As it was, they drove him to Corfu instead.

The Ionian skies and sunshine brought some tranquillity of mind: but this year he found the archaeological discoveries less exciting. Moreover, the peace of the islands appeared at risk. His terrace on the Achilleion looked out towards the crested amphitheatre of Albanian mountains, barely twenty miles away across the straits; and, in the evening air, the clear light picked out their summits so sharply above the sea that they seemed to bring the problems of the Balkans into the villa itself. For despite the settlement of 1909 there was still unrest in the peninsula. Albania, in that spring of 1912, was the last outpost of Turkey's north-west frontier, a region threatened by the southern Slavs of Serbia and Montenegro, anxious for access to the sea. Nor was the threat to peace entirely Slavonic in origin. Even while William was staying on Corfu, the Turks were at war with one of Germany's allies, Italy. Balkan uncertainties posed problems Germany could no longer ignore. Ever since his visit to the Sultan fourteen years before, William had encouraged German trade links with Turkey: how far was it in his interest to permit the Ottoman Empire to be weakened? If Turkey-in-Europe collapsed, would his Austrian ally allow the southern Slavs to increase their territories or would Austria-Hungary risk a war in order to secure the coastline of the southern Adriatic and stifle the Panslav feelings in the annexed provinces of Bosnia-Herzegovina? And, finally, would the Austrians – as their chief-of-staff recommended – chance a sudden war with Italy for control of the Adriatic, thereby making nonsense of the German-sponsored Triple Alliance? The Balkan danger was more acute than the chronic tensions of naval rivalry. When, in October 1912, Russian agents encouraged the Balkan states – Serbia, Montenegro, Greece and Bulgaria – to forget their differences and take the offensive against Turkey, it seemed to William (and, indeed, to Francis Joseph in Vienna) that the intricate machinery of great-power diplomacy had ceased to function. Within three weeks the Balkan League had gained victories in Macedonia, Thrace and northern Albania, and Constantinople itself was in danger. Hurriedly William arranged to meet Archduke Francis Ferdinand to discuss the Balkan power structure.[37]

William met Francis Ferdinand on 22 November. He was extravagant with offers of support in any contest with Russia over Balkan affairs.[38] At the same time he sought from his ambassadors in Paris and

London information on the reactions of the French and the British to the worsening relations between the great powers. In particular he wished to discover 'whose side Britain would take' if the Balkan quarrels proved impossible to localize. But he did not rely entirely on the diplomats. On William's instructions, his brother Henry crossed to England and visited George v at Sandringham on Friday, 6 December. Henry asked the King 'whether, in the event of Germany and Austria going to war with Russia and France, England would come to the assistance of the two latter Powers'. The King gave him an affirmative answer, though qualifying it with the phrase 'under certain circumstances', and adding that even if ententes lacked the binding commitments of a signed alliance they carried obligations of honour which could not be ignored. On the previous Tuesday the German ambassador had reported a similar statement from Haldane, a warning that Britain would not allow Germany to defeat France should a Russo-Austrian conflict in the Balkans spread to western Europe.[39]

There followed, on the morning of Sunday, 8 December, 1912 a meeting in the Neues Palais at Potsdam which has been, in retrospect, over-dramatized. Some have even called it a 'war council'.[40] It was a select gathering: Tirpitz, Moltke, Vice-Admiral von Heeringen (from the Naval Staff) and Admiral Müller (chief of the Kaiser's naval secretariat). Significantly the Kaiser did not call in the chancellor, the state secretary for foreign affairs, or the minister of war. William, referring to the telegram from London, remarked bitterly that Haldane had shown how little faith could be placed on England's friendship. He predicted that if the Austrians did not now face up to the Serbian menace, they would have considerable trouble from the Slav minorities within the Austro-Hungarian monarchy: the fleet must henceforth look on England as an enemy. Moltke regarded war as unavoidable, 'the sooner the better': Tirpitz still wanted another eighteen months before the navy was ready. The meeting, so Müller noted in his diary, achieved 'almost nothing'. Moltke subsequently told the representatives of the Bavarian and Saxon armies in Berlin that he favoured an early war against France and that the Kaiser wished the naval and military staffs to 'prepare an invasion of England on a grand scale'. But there is reason to think that William was, once more, in a flamboyant mood which he soon abandoned. Prince Henry's report of his talks with George v reached Potsdam after the Sunday morning meeting. Henry – habitually the most muddle-headed of emissaries –

misrepresented the King's views, leaving his brother with the impression that, while England would not side with Germany, she might remain neutral although at the moment she would 'probably throw her weight on the weaker side'. The Kaiser accordingly adjusted his policy so as to seek British neutrality: he even collaborated with Grey in order to settle Balkan problems through a conference of ambassadors in London. From the Sunday meeting Moltke gained, not the early war which he thought militarily advantageous to Germany, but the largest army bill the Reich had known, providing for expenditure of ninety million pounds, almost four times as much as in the last year of Bismarck's chancellorship and more than twice as high as the French army estimates. And Tirpitz secured, yet again, a reprieve to get the fleet clear of the danger zone.[41]

Yet though Europe was spared an all-engulfing conflict in the winter of 1912–13, there was a feeling in Berlin that war was 'postponed' rather than banished. William remained as inconsistent as ever. He still peppered letters and memoranda with excited comments. Sometimes they were constructive: more often childishly expletive ('Do not hold me to my marginalia', he once begged Tirpitz). But he was depressed by the prevalent war psychosis around him. His chief fear was of Austrian pretensions in south-eastern Europe, and he told his ministers that his conscience would not permit him to go to war for a cause of no concern 'to my people'.[42] He was irritated, too, by lesser considerations: 'The damned Balkan muddle has depried (sic) me of the possibility of being at my heavenly paradise Corfu', he wrote to Nicholas II on 18 March 1913.[43] Hopefully he retained confidence in dynastic diplomacy, trusting in the good sense of 'Georgie' and 'Nicky' to help check the demagogic drift to disaster. He invited the royal families of Britain and Russia to Berlin for the marriage of his favourite child, the twenty-year-old Princess Victoria Louise, to the grandson of the last King of Hanover, for whom he revived the lapsed title of Duke of Brunswick. There were absentees from the wedding: neither the Tsar's mother nor his consort felt able to suffer the pleasures of a Hohenzollern festival; nor indeed, did the widowed Queen Alexandra. George V, Queen Mary and Tsar Nicholas accepted invitations, however, and arrived in Berlin at the end of the third week in May.

This gathering of royal cousins was 'a purely family affair'. No ministers were in attendance, and Georgie and Nicky tried (not entirely successfully) to keep Willy off high politics. The marriage festivities

were spectacular: a gala at the Opera, consisting of one act of *Lohengrin*
and *Kerkyra*, a rhapsody on Ionian themes, for William's personal
satisfaction; several banquets, at one of which there were 1,200 guests;
and the famous torch-dance, traditional to German royal weddings, a
stately progression around the ballroom, begun by bride and bridegroom, preceded by pages carrying lighted candles in silver candelabra,
with the sovereigns and royal princes gradually brought into the defile
two by two. There was a parade at Potsdam, for which William wore
the uniform of a British Field-Marshal. George v lunched with officers
of 'Queen Victoria's Cuirassiers', of which he was colonel-in-chief,
while Nicholas ii was entertained by the Guards regiment named in
honour of Tsar Alexander i. Never before was there such emphasis on
monarchical kinship at any social event in Berlin: never before, for that
matter, such abundance of goodwill between the reigning dynasties.
'Took leave of them all after charming visit', wrote Queen Mary in her
diary on 27 May as the train headed westwards for the Dutch frontier
and Flushing.[44] It was a final leave-taking. European rivalries inex-
orably intruded on the game of royal happy families; and Nicky,
Georgie and Willy never met again.

11. Now or Never

The summer of 1913 was celebrated throughout Germany as a festive climax to William's reign. Sunday, 15 June, marked the twenty-fifth anniversary of his accession. Inevitably this moment for private thanksgiving was turned into a public avowal of dynastic loyalty. Berlin was in holiday mood that weekend, with streets beflagged and spanned by jubilee arches on which the imperial cypher proliferated in a delirium of heraldic ingenuity. William, so a younger member of the Household wrote, was becoming 'increasingly conscious of the soul solitude brought by advancing years' – he was fifty-four – but passing moments of lassitude and dejection did not prevent him from striking the attitudes which had, for so long, ensured him star-billing on Europe's stage. Although time was mellowing his speeches, they remained unpredictable and expectant reporters followed his progress through the German cities. The jubilee celebrations ran concurrently with the centenary of the war of liberation, and on 18 October William, invoking once again the memory of his never-to-be-forgotten grandfather, commemorated the victory of Leipzig by unveiling a massive monument on the 'battlefield of the nations'. The air remained heavy with national fervour from midsummer until late autumn.[1]

Yet throughout these four months William succeeded in keeping his patriotic emotions in check. His restraint irritated the right-wing Pan-Germans, many of whom began to transfer their hopes to the future emperor, his eldest son. The Crown Prince, for his part, hardly troubled to conceal his impatience with his father and the chancellor, Bethmann-Hollweg, and smarting under an alleged rebuff absented himself from the Leipzig commemoration. There was indeed a strange echo of past conflicts. Just as William himself had once looked to Alfred von Waldersee, so now the Crown Price had a political soldier as his champion, Baron Konstantin von Gebsattel, from Bavaria. But whereas on William's accession Waldersee was reaching the peak of his career, Gebsattel was already a retired general with a restless pen. He bombarded the Crown Prince with memoranda calling for 'courage' in foreign policy, strict control of liberal and socialist newspapers, and the proclamation of a state of siege pending the introduction of anti-Jewish laws. ('May the man soon be found who will lead us along this path', Gebsattel apostrophized ominously.) Early in November the Crown Prince forwarded one of these memoranda to his father, and to the chancellor. William, in reply, admitted he was displeased with the 'weakness' of some members of the government but he rejected Gebsattel's anti-Jewish outburst as 'utterly childish'. If the Jews were forced to leave the Reich, William explained to his son, 'they would take with them their vast riches'. There was, he conceded, a case for controlling 'the filthy search for scandal' in newspapers under 'Jewish influence', but to expel the Jews wholesale would force Germany to 'leave the ranks of the cultured nations'.[2] William distrusted the racialism of the Pan-Germans and was far from pleased to find his son associating himself politically with the Bavarian lunatic fringe.

The French ambassador, Jules Cambon, nevertheless believed William was gradually succumbing to 'the reactionary sentiment of the Court'. In a letter written in the last week of November, Cambon shrewdly observed that the Kaiser might well be jealous 'of the popularity of his son, who flatters the Pan-Germans and does not think the position of the Empire in the world is equal to its power'.[3] This comment was made at a time when the newspapers, both in Paris and Berlin, were reporting at length the series of disturbances at Zabern (Saverne), at the foot of the Vosges, where the Alsatian population had been roused by provocative and abusive remarks from some officers in the garrison. As the disturbances grew more serious, the local commander ordered his troops to raid the offices of the Zabern newspaper. The Kaiser, who was at the time enjoying his annual visit to Donaueschingen, came down heavily on the side of the military authorities, even though the civilian governor of Alsace-Lorraine had condemned their actions as high-handed. The affair was raised in the Reichstag in the first days of December, and Bethmann felt it his duty, as the emperor's servant, 'to defend the authority of the army with all energy and in all directions', although he told William confidentially he was convinced the army commanders were seriously violating the law. Bethmann's loyalty – in such contrast to Bülow's behaviour four years before – helps to explain the Kaiser's determination to retain him in office, despite his unpopularity at court. But the chancellor's behaviour heightened, rather than lessened, political tension: a motion of no confidence in Bethmann was carried by a majority of well over two hundred votes in the chamber. The prominent socialist deputy, Scheedemann, pointed to British constitutional custom and argued that, after such a defeat, the chancellor was obliged to resign. Bethmann, however, resisted this attempt to import the parliamentary practices of Westminster and turned on the Reichstag with the fire and fury of a Bismarck. The deputies, he declared, were seeking to infuse the army with revolutionary democracy: this was alien to Prussia's traditions for the army remained an instrument of the imperial prerogative, dependent solely on the will of the Supreme War Lord. It is ironical that such a powerful defence of the army as an estate independent of parliament should have been made by the first genuinely civilian chancellor of the Reich. In Germany as a whole it was assumed that William personally, and Bethmann-Hollweg's administration with him, was moving rapidly to the Right. As the year ended some commentators predicted a succession of constitutional conflicts as divisive as the dispute over the Prussian army bills of the 1860s or the more recent controversy over the 'People's Budget' in Britain.[4]

These parallels, however, ignored the true complexities of the moment. William was certainly aware that the emotional celebrations of the previous summer concealed deep divisions among his subjects. There were more classes, more gradations within a class, and more class consciousness in Wilhelmine Germany than in any other European country; for, though the range of distinctions may have been as wide in Austria-Hungary and Russia, only in Germany was there a large, concentrated, articulate and organized proletariat, unsettled by the incredibly rapid economic growth of the past thirty years. The political structure of the Reich, designed to perpetuate the privileges of the Junkers and the military élite, never possessed any mechanism of social adjustment. Theoretically there was thus a greater threat of red revolution in Germany than in either autocratic neighbour. This situation had long been familiar to the Kaiser, but its dangers were accentuated for him after the 1912 elections by the increased strength of the progressive and socialist parties and by the belated growth of a trade-union movement. Moreover the constitutional crisis over the Zabern affair coincided with the first economic recession for many years, with rising costs of food, rents and basic commodities as well as growing unemployment. Bethmann was afraid that, in this situation, if he did not appear tough enough to satisfy William, a detachment of Guards would descend on the Reichstag and send the deputies about their business, arresting the noisier dissidents and shutting down the opposition newspapers. A military *coup* in Berlin would, he thought, unleash civil war and tempt the French to cross the frontier, using the plight of the people of Alsace as an excuse for their war of revenge. William did not share his chancellor's apprehension: he spoke with increasing scorn of the parliamentary 'mad house' and of the need to 'lock up' dangerous agitators; but, as earlier in his reign, he kept the possibility of an anti-parliamentary *coup* in reserve.[5] Significantly he shirked the mental effort of considering what, constitutionally, should follow a dramatic move against the deputies and the opposition press.

An influential group of General Staff officers favoured a more drastic course. They believed the internal problems of Germany could be resolved by a victorious campaign against the French or the Russians. War, they claimed, would rally the mass of the population behind the dynasty. William rejected this cynical approach to the gravest issue in high politics. He had encouraged patriotic associations which glorified feats of arms on land and sea, believing their propaganda helped integrate the differing social classes, but he repeatedly made it clear he would only order his soldiers and seamen into battle for a worthwhile cause. Yet there were other arguments put forward by Moltke and by his own military secretariat in the winter of 1913–14 which he could hardly ignore: they pointed to the surprising recuperative power of Russia's armies; to the work on fortresses along Russia's western frontiers; to the French decision to strengthen the army by introducing three years of military service; to the growing intimacy of staff talks between the French and the Russians and, indeed, between the French and their entente partner across the Channel. And they contrasted this intensified nightmare of encirclement with uncertainties over the future of Germany's principal ally, Austria-Hungary, a multi-national empire threatened with disintegration. If, as Moltke consistently sought to convince William, a continental war against France and Russia was inevitable, then it would be as well for it to come at a time when the advantages were with Germany and over an issue which ensured the military participation of Austria-Hungary rather than at a moment chosen by Germany's adversaries. From September 1913 until May

1914 the Kaiser was confronted again and again with advice recommending preventive war. Each time the question was raised he evaded a decision, never coming down wholeheartedly on the side of the generals but letting them see he accepted many of their premises. Gradually over these winter months his attitude hardened. A flood of scaremongering information sheets from the General Staff, backed sometimes by newspaper reports, undermined his morale until he began to echo Moltke, commenting with resignation on the inevitability of war. He was obsessed by a fear of being held in contempt for 'cowardice', blamed for bringing Germany to the brink of hostilities only to shy away from reality. This, he knew, was said of him during the Moroccan crises and, earlier, over the Transvaal. In such a mood it required only a pang of his old craving for action to swing him behind the advocates of preventive war.[6]

There is no evidence to suggest William accepted the need for a preventive campaign against Germany's power rivals at a specific date. But he was inconsistent. In September 1913 he favoured extreme measures by the Austrians to curb the growing Serbian agitation against Habsburg dominance in Bosnia-Herzegovina: 'For once things down there must be put right and calm restored', he commented on a despatch from Vienna, adding a favourite injunction, 'now or never'.[7] The Austrians were puzzled, however, and during a visit to Vienna in the last week of October William assured the foreign minister, Berchthold, that he did not think a move against Serbia would provoke Russia since the Tsar's armies would not be ready for war for another six years. He wished Austria-Hungary to settle differences with Serbia soon since Germany did not want the army of her principal ally engaged in a Balkan sideshow when the 'inevitable war' with Russia broke out in the east. Berchthold was treated to an hour and a quarter of the Kaiser's somewhat one-sided conversation, but he was delighted at William's attachment to the Austro-German alliance, now thirty-four years old: 'Whatever comes from the Vienna Foreign Ministry has for me the nature of a command', William declared.[8] That was hardly Bismarck's intention when the alliance was concluded.

At no time did William suggest to Berchthold that a general war was imminent. Yet only eleven days later he was in an astonishingly different mood. On 6 November he entertained the thirty-eight year old King Albert of the Belgians at Potsdam. Suddenly, while showing Albert the curiosities of Sans Souci, the Kaiser remarked that 'the inevitable war' with France was close at hand. At dinner that evening William himself and Moltke sought to find how Belgium would react to a Franco-German war. Albert had already met William on three occasions since his accession in December 1909 but never had he found him so obsessed with military detail. The Belgian Minister, who was present at the Potsdam dinner, was convinced German war plans envisaged a march on Paris through his homeland. King Albert, refusing to be intimidated, told his hosts firmly that Belgium would remain neutral unless attacked; but he was so depressed that he made certain President Poincaré and the French government were informed of the alarming twist given to what he had anticipated as a friendly conversation.[9]

But did William really believe war was imminent? He was, during these same weeks, completing long-term plans for German penetration into south-eastern Europe and Asia Minor. He sought, in the first instance, economic concessions: the Turkish Empire had attracted German businessmen ever since the Kaiser's famous visit to the Holy Places; and in the summer of 1913 the British had indicated that they were prepared to allow Germany a free hand to develop railways in Asia Minor provided neither the Turks nor the Germans threatened British interests on the Persian Gulf. But the Kaiser, though pleased that the Baghdad railway would no longer disturb relations with England, also had a military motive in patronizing Turkey at this time. At the end of June 1913 he appointed General Otto Liman von Sanders, one of the ablest divisional commanders in his army, to head a new military mission to Constantinople. William showed an intensive concern with the Liman mission which he had not shown towards any foreign enterprise since Waldersee's over-publicized expedition set out for Peking in 1900. During the autumn of 1913, before Liman finally took up his post, the duties of the military mission were expanded until it became, in William's words, an instrument to complete 'the Germanization of the Turkish army'.[10]

In later years, when Turkey became Germany's wartime ally, commentators in London assumed the Kaiser had intended Liman's mission to rock the established British and French positions in the Near East. But William's purpose was primarily anti-Russian. On 9 December 1913 William entertained the senior officers of the Liman mission at Potsdam and gave them farewell instructions: they were, he said, to create for him in Turkey 'a new strong army which obeys my orders' and provide 'a counter balance for Russia's aggressive intentions' on the Straits and in Asia Minor. He had, however, a further motive: a German military presence on the Bosphorus would, he thought, be welcome to the British as a counter to Russian designs. His marginal comments on diplomatic reports show he was so convinced of mounting tension between Britain and Russia over Persian affairs that he dreamt, not only of dissolving the Anglo-Russian Entente, but of coaxing the British into the Triple Alliance.[11] The Turks, smarting from defeat in the First Balkan War, were glad to accommodate themselves to German plans. On 20 December Liman von Sanders took command of the principal army corps at Constantinople.

William's assumptions were sound, up to a point. The Russians could not ignore the challenge: they had, indeed, been protesting to the German Foreign Ministry ever since the first rumours of Liman's appointment became current, early in September. But in making a snap judgement William exaggerated the degree of mutual suspicion within the Anglo-Russian relationship. The British were no longer sufficiently interested in Russia and the Straits to use the question as an excuse for weakening the Entente, let alone for making common cause with the Triple Alliance. Moreover no one in Berlin shared William's readiness to risk a midwinter war over Liman's appointment. 'What is at stake is our world reputation, which is maligned by one and all. Let us stiffen our backs and put our hands on the sword', he wrote at the foot of a despatch from St Petersburg in the second week of December.[12] But in the Wilhelmstrasse not a back stiffened: hands reached speedily for pens rather than for the sword. A compromise was reached by which Liman von Sanders was created a Turkish field-marshal and inspector-general of the Turkish army, dignities which saved Germany's face and went some way to satisfy the Russians by making Liman too senior to serve as an army corps commander, at Constantinople or anywhere else. The Kaiser was far from satisfied; and when Liman returned to Berlin and reported to him in the third week of February, William declared: 'Either the German flag will soon fly over the fortifications on the Bosphorus or I shall share the sad fate of the great exile on St Helena'.[13]

The Liman von Sanders crisis was as much a consequence of William's diplomacy as Agadir had been of Kiderlen's or Tangier of Holstein and Bülow's. Outwardly it was less disastrous. But it provided material for the staff officers who believed in a Russian threat to Germany. For, understandably, the German build-up on the Straits convinced the Russians of their need to increase their armies in Europe and their fleet in the Black Sea. Several German newspapers began to print alarmist articles depicting the reckless mood of a headstrong war party in St Petersburg. By early spring in 1914 Russian military preparations were receiving press treatment reminiscent of the German attitude to the British naval estimates during the peak period of battleship construction.[14] A short and sudden continental war seemed probable. Nobody in Berlin – least of all the Kaiser – thought hostilities would last as long as a calendar year. Every European conflict over the past century had been brief: the greater the destructive power of weapons, the sooner would come decisive victory; or so it was believed.

The 'younger Moltke' – as the sixty-six year old chief of the Great General Staff was called to distinguish him from his famous uncle – thought a war might last three months. He was not an original strategist. On becoming Chief of Staff in January 1906 he accepted the principal war directive of his predecessor, the 'Schlieffen Plan': the main German offensive would be mounted in the West, with an enveloping movement through Holland and Belgium against France, while the Russians would be checked in East Prussia and Poland by holding operations until France was defeated, when Germany would concentrate all armies in the East and destroy the Russian menace for all time. Moltke subsequently made two amendments to Schlieffen's directive: he gave up the proposed advance through Holland, though retaining the planned march into Luxemburg and Belgium; and he strengthened the forces left to defend Germany from an invasion. But Moltke, like Schlieffen, assumed that Austria-Hungary would resist the numerically superior Russian forces for six weeks, giving Germany a chance to gain the decisive victory in the West. The Austrians, however, were far from enthusiastic over the role cast for them in these plans. Despite William's generous remarks in the past, he seemed now to be treating Austria-Hungary as a junior partner rather than as an ally.[15]

In order to reassure the Austrians, William visited Vienna on his way to Corfu at the end of March 1914. William found Emperor Francis Joseph much aged, pathetically hoping 'that everything would continue as peaceable as ever'. The only man who impressed the Kaiser during his short visit was Istvan Tisza, the prime minister of Hungary.[16] But it was an unfortunate meeting. For William had one other social and political engagement before sailing down the Adriatic to

Corfu. From Vienna he travelled south to Miramare, the white lime-stone castle in terraced gardens above the sea, three miles from Trieste. There, in this loveliest and saddest of Habsburg palaces, William brought the full strength of his personality to bear on the heir to the throne, the Archduke Francis Ferdinand, whom the German General Staff persistently considered 'unreliable' as a future ally. Unfortunately William – who, on slender grounds, prided himself on understanding the morose and taciturn archduke – committed a major political sole-cism: he praised Tisza in conversation, commending his statesmanlike attitude to the problems of the Habsburg Monarchy and of Europe as a whole. To Francis Ferdinand Tisza's dedicated Hungarian patriotism had long seemed close to treason and he was resolved to remove Tisza from office as soon as he came to the throne. He listened coldly to his guest's comments on the political situation, saying so little that William assumed he had won the archduke over to his ideas. But, while William was on Corfu, the German embassy in Vienna discovered the Mira-mare visit had been a disaster, leaving the heir to the throne convinced that the Germans, in return for their continued support, intended to force 'Tisza's policy upon him'. Throughout May there was, accord-ingly, a hurried and embarrassed campaign by the German diplomats to arrange another meeting between Kaiser and archduke to clear up the Miramare misunderstanding.[17]

Hence, at the end of the second week in June, William duly travelled to Bohemia and visited Francis Ferdinand at Konopischt, his hunting lodge some thirty miles south-east of Prague. Francis Ferdinand was always at his happiest and most relaxed while staying at Konopischt: he had spent his honeymoon there, after his morganatic marriage to Countess Sophie Chotek in 1900; and William had already visited Konopischt in October, 1913, delighted to find there the sociable family atmosphere he regarded as an essential background for a congenial shoot. Kaiser and archduke talked amiably over the weekend of 12–14 June: the Tisza remarks were explained away, William declaring that, although he thought the Hungarian prime minister a person of rare energy, he quite understood that such men needed to be controlled with a fist of iron; and the conversation then turned to Balkan problems. By now the Austrians had become seriously alarmed at the growth of revolutionary feeling in Bosnia-Herzegovina, which they blamed on Pan-Serb organizations in Belgrade. At Francis Joseph's request, the archduke tried to discover whether the Kaiser was still prepared to give

Austria-Hungary unconditional support in destroying the Serbian 'hornets' nest', as his grandiose assurances to Berchthold in the previous October had indicated. But William was now less forthcoming: it would be as well for Austria to do something before the general situation deteriorated, he observed obliquely, and there was no reason to fear Russian intervention since the Tsar's armies were not yet ready for a war; action of this type would certainly have Germany's full support. William made himself agreeable to the archduke's wife and family, admired the Konopischt rosarium, and left for Berlin. A courtesy telegram thanked the archduke for his hospitality and let him know that by now the roses were blooming at Potsdam, too. It was the last communication between the two men.[18]

William left Potsdam on Thursday, 18 June, only four days after his return from Bohemia. His immediate programme of events was as full as ever: the Hanover agricultural fair; inspection of the Eilweise wireless station; a day at the Uhlan manoeuvres on Lüneberg Heath; and so, by the following Tuesday, to the annual Elbe Regatta where his yacht, *Meteor*, gained an early success. Next day, 24 June, he sailed in the *Hohenzollern* through the Kiel Canal, which had recently been widened so that it could now take dreadnought-class battleships; there was a ceremony at Holtenau, the village at the northern end of the canal, when the Kaiser formally declared the widened canal open. At Kiel a courtesy squadron of British warships, including four battleships and three cruisers, was moored alongside the Imperial High Seas Fleet. There followed four days of hospitable exchanges, yacht races, garden parties and dances. Lichnowsky – whose services to Anglo-German friendship had recently been recognized by an honorary doctorate at Oxford, a distinction never previously bestowed on a German ambassador – had come over from London for the occasion. The British ambassador and many members of his staff were also present.[19] On Friday afternoon the Kaiser was received aboard the super-dreadnought, *King George V*. He wore the uniform of a British Admiral of the Fleet and was thus technically the senior Royal Navy officer present. For the last time the 'giddiness' of wearing the uniform of St Vincent and Nelson went to his head, and there was an absurd incident. Sir Horace Rumbold, counsellor at the British embassy in Berlin, was invited aboard *King George V*, and since he knew he would meet the Kaiser on the quarter-deck he wore a morning coat and top hat. But the 'Admiral of the Fleet' decided Rumbold was inappropriately dressed:

'If I see that again I will smash it in', William declared, pointing to the top hat. 'One doesn't wear tall hats on board ship.' Apart from this extraordinarily discourteous outburst, Rumbold remembered the 'great cordiality' between the seamen (officers and ratings) in the two fleets.[20]

The festivities ended abruptly. In mid-afternoon on Sunday, 28 June, a telegram reached the *Hohenzollern* from the German consul in Sarajevo with news of the assassination of Archduke Francis Ferdinand and his wife as they drove through the Bosnian capital. William was racing in his yacht *Meteor* that afternoon and Admiral Müller, as chief of his naval secretariat, put to sea in a launch with the telegram. He caught up with the *Meteor* well out into Kiel Bay and, on the Kaiser's insistence, called out the bad news as the boats drew level. William cancelled the race, returned to the *Hohenzollern*, and next morning set out on the seven-hour journey back to Potsdam. He was personally distressed that the archduke and his wife, his hosts only a fortnight ago, should have been shot, apparently by agents of the Pan-Serbs in Belgrade. The poignancy of this terrible news was intensified by the recollection that, a year before, Francis Ferdinand had been the Kaiser's guest at Kiel and stood beside him watching the manoeuvres of those same warships whose ensigns now hung at half-mast.[21]

William had no doubt Serbia was responsible for the Sarajevo crime. The aggressive tone of his marginal notes show how deeply his emotions were stirred. 'The Serbs must be disposed of, and that very soon', he wrote on a despatch from his ambassador in Vienna on 2 July: it was, he wrote, a question of 'now or never'.[22] Not everyone in Berlin was agreed on the best way of handling the sudden crisis: the Foreign Ministry wished to restrain Austria-Hungary, but the General Staff argued that the assassination afforded a pretext for war at a time when Germany was, militarily, better prepared for a lightning campaign than her potential adversaries. The navy was still not ready to go into battle – Tirpitz had told Admiral von Müller nine weeks previously that he needed at least another six to eight years – but both Tirpitz and Müller were disturbed by intelligence reports of a proposed Anglo-Russian convention for increased naval collaboration, and they were inclined to favour any policy which would weaken Russia before this agreement became effective. William himself sided with the advocates of vigorous action against Serbia, even at the risk of a continental war. When the Austro-Hungarian ambassador came out to Potsdam about noon on 5 July with a personal letter from Francis Joseph, he found the Kaiser readily receptive to war talk. Although insisting he must discuss such questions with Bethmann, William told the ambassador he thought it certain that Germany would give 'full support' to her 'old and faithful ally'. He thought it unlikely the Tsar would fight to save Serbia, but 'should war between Austria-Hungary and Russia prove unavoidable' then Germany would stand at Austria's side: 'the present moment is all in our favour', the ambassador reported him as having said.[23] Later that afternoon William received Bethmann-Hollweg and the Prussian war minister, Falkenhayn, in audience. It is clear from the record of these conversations that William assumed the Austrians were planning to invade Serbia: he only hoped the invasion would begin while Europe was still shocked by the double murder in Sarajevo. There was not, as Allied propagandists later claimed, a war council in Potsdam that Sunday, for too many key figures were far away. The chief of the Great General Staff had gone to Carlsbad on the very day of the assassinations in order to seek a cure for the chronic kidney trouble which had racked him for several months, and did not take up his duties again until 26 July; Tirpitz was on holiday in the Engadine; and the foreign secretary, Jagow, was in the last days of his honeymoon. But William consulted senior members of the Foreign Ministry and the service departments that Sunday evening and early on Monday morning. From General Falkenhayn he received an assurance that the army was ready for any emergency.[24]

Soon after breakfast on Monday, 6 July, William set out once more by train for Kiel. In the evening he entertained his friend, the industrialist Gustav Krupp von Bohlen: he told Krupp that the Austrians were intending to wipe out Serbia, that Germany would support them even at the cost of war with Russia and that 'This time I shall not give in', a point he made on three occasions in the conversation, as though willing himself to remain resolute.[25] That night he embarked in the *Hohenzollern* for his annual cruise in northern waters and he remained at sea for the next twenty days, with occasional expeditions on foot in the Norwegian coastal towns. The Kaiser's absence from Berlin saved his ministers from those sudden switches of policy which had frequently proved exasperating in earlier crises. Moreover Bethmann and Jagow could be more selective in the information they passed on to their sovereign than had he remained in Potsdam. Important messages were telegraphed directly to the *Hohenzollern*, though long analytical despatches were frequently retained in the Wilhelmstrasse. William did not therefore see all of Lichnowsky's reports from London. It is unlikely any of these despatches would have deflected him. His comments during the cruise show impatience with the Austrians for not bringing the crisis sooner to the boil, rather than any wish for them to turn off the heat: why delay their ultimatum to Serbia until the harvest was in, and why wait until the French president had concluded his state visit to St Petersburg?[26] The 'now or never' mood persisted. Only once was William perplexed: should he, or should he not, send the customary congratulations to King Peter of Serbia on his birthday, he asked Jagow? It seemed hypocritical at a time when he knew an Austrian invasion was imminent. But Jagow was anxious not to arouse suspicion by neglecting the usual courtesies, and a telegram of greeting was wired directly from the *Hohenzollern* to Belgrade on 11 July.[27]

Most of the summer cruise was spent in the Kaiser's favourite Norwegian waters, the coast and inlets immediately north of Bergen and, in particular, the Sognefjord. A squadron of battleships and cruisers sailed from Wilhelmshaven on 10 July and remained in close touch with the *Hohenzollern*, manoeuvring off the Norwegian coast, while the flagship sailed up the Sognefjord itself as the crisis intensified in the third week of July. In Berlin Bethmann and Jagow knew by 18 July of Austria's intention to present Serbia with a forty-eight-hour ultimatum on the evening of 23 July; they knew, too, how the Austrians planned to phrase their demands so stiffly that the Serbs could hardly accept them; and they made certain that William was kept informed of these developments.[28] In a diary entry, written on 19 July, Admiral Müller describes the Kaiser as being 'extremely excited about the ultimatum which is to be presented by the Austrians to Serbia'.[29] In Berlin the diplomats were still confident a war could be localized; William himself does not appear to have realized Russia would back up the Serbs until news-agency reports of the excitement in St Petersburg reached him as he was setting out for a morning's sailing in the fjord on Saturday, 25 July. That evening the *Hohenzollern* headed for the open sea and set a course for Kiel, six hundred miles to the south. By Monday afternoon the Kaiser was back at Potsdam. He was met at Wildpark railway station by the chancellor, and Müller noted a coolness between the two men. Bethmann, Jagow and the generals would have preferred William to carry on with his cruise, although Jagow had already suggested confidentially that the *Hohenzollern* might steam south from the fjords into more secure waters. The only person on record as declaring 'glad you are back' to William was Nicholas II, in a telegram from Peterhof.[39]

There followed a week of intensive drama in which it seems at times as if the soldiers, infatuated by the detail of war plans, were throwing every safety switch on the diplomatic machine. Moltke arrived back from Carlsbad on Saturday, rather more than forty-eight hours ahead of his emperor. That weekend, in William's absence, Moltke drafted for the Foreign Ministry a message which he wished sent, in due course, to Brussels, justifying a German march into Belgium in order to forestall an alleged invasion by the French. At the same time, in the Reich Ministry of the Interior, officials drew up emergency decrees providing for mobilization and internal security, and requiring only the signatures of Kaiser and chancellor to become effective.[31] Already, by the time William's train reached Wildpark, the Austrians had broken off diplomatic relations with Serbia and resolved finally on action; and while Bethmann was talking to William at Potsdam, Jagow was explaining to the French ambassador that he could not support a British proposal to settle the dispute with Serbia at an ambassadorial conference in London since that would imply recognition of Austro-Hungarian, as well as Serbian, responsibility for tension in the Balkans. At precisely the same hour, in the British Admiralty, the First Sea Lord was sending a signal to the commander-in-chief of the Grand Fleet ordering him to concentrate his battle squadrons at Scapa Flow, sailing northwards through the Straits of Dover under cover of night and without lights. Although Jagow told the French ambassador Germany was still confident of Britain's neutrality, time was running out for those who, like William and Bethmann, thought Britain must be kept out of a continental war if Germany was to gain a speedy victory.

Yet it is not clear what precisely William did believe on his return to Potsdam. Despite his remarks to Krupp von Bohlen three weeks before, he seemed irresolute, far from convinced war was necessary or inevitable. Early on Tuesday morning (28 July) he received a copy of the Serbian reply to Austria's ultimatum. He realized the Serbs had conceded almost every Austrian demand: the suppression of all anti-Austrian publications, propaganda and organizations; the arrest and punishment of anyone connected with the Sarajevo conspiracy; and even the collaboration of Habsburg officials in stamping out subversive movements. 'This is more than one could have expected', William commented. 'A great moral victory for Vienna, and with it every reason for war disappears.' This last phrase the Kaiser repeated twice, and underlined, in a handwritten message to Jagow sent from the Neues Palais at Potsdam at ten o'clock on Tuesday morning: he proposed that outstanding differences between the Austrians and Serbs should be settled by negotiation and that military operations should be limited to the temporary occupation of Belgrade. A telegram embodying the Kaiser's proposals was not sent to the German ambassador for another twelve hours, and even then in a form which seemed to be urging the Austrians on, rather than holding them back, for nothing was said of William's assertion that the pretexts for war had vanished.[32] That evening William sent a telegram to Nicholas II – in English, as was customary in their personal exchanges – asking the Tsar, in the name of 'the hearty and tender friendship which binds us both from long ago with firm ties', for help in smoothing 'over difficulties that may still arise'. This vaguely phrased telegram crossed a more precise one from Nicholas asking William 'to stop your allies from going too far'.[33] But it was too late. Already Austria-Hungary had declared war on Serbia. While William was reading Nicholas's telegram on Wednesday morning, two monitors from the Austro-Hungarian flotilla on the Danube were lobbing shells at the fortress of Belgrade, the smoke from their guns marking the opening shots of a world war.

William was therefore in a totally different mood on Wednesday morning from Tuesday evening. Then he had wired a conciliatory message to Peterhof; now he commented testily in the margin of Nicholas's telegram, complaining it was 'a confession of weakness' and contained a veiled threat. With the 'halt in Belgrade' proposal already a curiosity of yesterday – not least because the Austrians had no intention of making a frontal assault on the Serbian capital – William became once more an advocate of a war which would remove the potential threat to Germany from the East. His ambassador in St Petersburg was ordered to warn the Russian foreign minister that Russian mobilization would be followed by German mobilization, and that it would then be difficult to prevent the outbreak of a general European war. To William, and to Bethmann, it was essential for Russia to appear the aggressor: nothing would so unite the Reich as a call to resist Russian tyranny; even the socialists, whose 'anti-military demonstrations in the streets' were infuriating the Kaiser that Wednesday morning, would rally to a crusade against the dark forces of Tsardom. 'In all events

Russia must ruthlessly be put into the wrong', Bethmann reminded the Kaiser.[34]

For another three days William and Nicholas continued to exchange messages. In St Petersburg there was a faint hope the Kaiser would mediate. At Potsdam, William occasionally wavered, suggesting to Bethmann that, if it was impracticable to 'halt in Belgrade' then the Austrians might seize some other strategic position to hold as a security for Serbia's good behaviour. But the wording of William's telegrams, and his confidential minutes, show that he was seeking more and more with each day that passed to place the blame for a continental war upon the Russians. Since Russia, vast in size and hampered by slow communications, needed longer than any other European empire to prepare for war, it was inevitable she should fulfil the role William cast for her. A partial mobilization was decreed in St Petersburg on 29 July: it was followed by general mobilization on Friday, 31 July. News of Russia's full mobilization reached Berlin at noon on Friday. An hour later the Kaiser proclaimed a state of 'imminent war' and an ultimatum was drawn up which required Russia to halt all military preparations. The Russians could not check their mobilization plans, nor indeed had they any desire to do so, and at seven in the evening of Saturday 1 August the German ambassador in St Petersburg delivered a declaration of war. Three hours later William sent Nicholas a final message: only immediate orders to begin demobilization and to prevent Russian troops committing 'the slightest act of trespassing over our frontiers' would 'avoid endless misery', it said. On this extraordinary document the Tsar wrote, laconically, 'Received after war declared'.[35]

Although William accepted the fact that the localized Austro-Serbian dispute had spread into a continental war, he still hoped it could be contained both in extent and in duration. It was therefore essential to keep Britain out of the war in its opening phase, for British participation would carry the conflict to Africa and the Far East as well as impose an intolerable strain on Germany's maritime commerce. Bethmann was optimistic, at least until the night of 29–30 July, when telegrams from London began to alarm him. Only a few hours earlier, at a Crown Council in Potsdam on Wednesday afternoon, William declared he was convinced Britain would remain neutral: his brother, Prince Henry (who had been yachting at Cowes while William was cruising in the fjords) had called on his cousin George v in Buckingham Palace after breakfast on Sunday and, on arriving back at Kiel on

Tuesday, had quoted the King as saying 'We shall try all we can to keep out of this and shall remain neutral.' Although Henry had already shown he was an inaccurate reporter of his English relatives' remarks – probably through a failure to understand linguistic subtleties – the Kaiser gave more attention to this message than to any other reports from London or the assessments of his naval intelligence department. When Admiral Tirpitz doubted if the British would stay out of the conflict, William replied haughtily, 'I have the word of a King, and that is good enough for me.'[36] After the council Bethmann offered the British ambassador a neutrality agreement, guaranteeing the territorial integrity of France and Belgium within Europe in any post-war settlement, provided the British did not enter the conflict. When this proposal reached the British Foreign Office at nine o'clock on Thursday (30 July) it was immediately interpreted as a sign that Germany was determined on war and had every intention of violating Belgian neutrality. The proposal therefore hardened the British attitude rather than eased the tension, for successive British governments had invariably accepted the obligation to uphold Belgian independence, first guaranteed in 1839 and reaffirmed in 1870. Schlieffen, in drawing up his plan in 1905; had assumed a German violation of Belgian territory would automatically bring the British into a war against Germany. This point was emphasized by Jagow in a conversation with Schlieffen's successor, Moltke, early in 1913, and it is strange that neither the Kaiser nor his chancellor seem to have been prepared to accept the wider diplomatic and strategic implications of invading Belgium. Both men wrongly believed they 'understood the English'.[37]

This assumption, at least on William's part, was shattered by the telegrams and despatches he found awaiting him on Thursday morning, 30 July. He realized at last that the British would probably enter the war ranged alongside Germany's enemies. His most frequently quoted marginal notes – abusing the English as 'that mean crew of shopkeepers', Sir Edward Grey as 'a common cur' . . . 'mean and Mephistophelian', and George v as 'a liar' – were all written in a nervous explosion of wild scribbling that morning, So, too, was his complaint that the Triple Entente was seeking 'totally to ruin us' and that 'Edward vii is stronger after his death than am I who am still alive.'[38] But William was still eager to clutch at any straw holding a prospect of British neutrality. At five o'clock on the afternoon of Saturday, 1 August, the Kaiser signed the order for general mobilization and

Moltke left the Berlin palace to drive back to the General Staff building in the Königsplatz, a mile and a half away. Before Moltke's car completed the journey it was intercepted by an outrider: the Kaiser wanted him to return to the palace urgently. There, Moltke found William exuberant: a telegram newly arrived from Lichnowsky held out a hope that Britain would remain neutral, and would guarantee French neutrality in a Russo-German war, provided Germany did not take the initiative and attack in the West. 'So now we need only wage war against Russia', William told Moltke, 'We simply advance with the whole army in the east'.

Moltke could not believe that a Supreme War Lord who had prided himself on his knowledge of military science could be so naïve. Patiently he explained that military plans could not be improvised, that a million men could not be redeployed without reducing a disciplined force to rabble. William was angry: 'Your uncle would have given me a different answer', he snapped. Tempers rose. German patrols were already infiltrating Luxemburg, across the Moselle, and a division alerted at Trier (Trèves) was about to seize the Luxemburg railway system, as a key point in the advance westwards. The Kaiser, ignoring Moltke's protests, ordered his principal adjutant to send a signal to Trier halting all operations. Moltke retired, white-faced and in tears, to his room. But at eleven at night he was summoned yet again to the palace. A further telegram from London made it clear there could be no pledge of neutrality in the West. There was no need for the strategic timetable to be dislocated any more. 'Now you can do what you like', William remarked, turning bleakly on his heel in dismissal.[39]

It was by then almost midnight. William, emotionally strained, was near the end of his tether. In dismissing Moltke and retiring to bed he was acknowledging his own inability to influence events. Throughout Sunday young men in France and Germany bade their families farewell and donned uniforms to fight in a war they had long expected, even though it was not clear for what precisely they were fighting. The division from Trier secured the Luxemburg railways, not desperately inconvenienced by six hours of confused orders. At eight o'clock on Sunday evening an ultimatum was presented in Brussels, seeking the passage through Belgium of German troops. Germany declared war on France on 3 August and the first German units entered Belgium in the small hours of 4 August. The British ultimatum to Germany was despatched that Tuesday afternoon.[40]

In the evening some of the Berlin crowd, having cheered the Kaiser on the palace balcony, stoned the windows of the British embassy for half an hour. Next morning an aide-de-camp from the palace expressed official regret at the incident. But the aide-de-camp had a supplementary mission to perform. On instructions from William he explained to the ambassador that the behaviour of the mob showed the Berliners' anger that England should have forgotten 'how we had fought shoulder to shoulder at Waterloo'. The Kaiser, the aide declared, had been proud of his rank as Field-Marshal in the British army and Admiral of the Fleet in the Royal Navy, but he would now shed these honours. 'Not a gentleman', commented the Counsellor of Embassy, whose top-hat had caused the *ci-devant* Admiral of the Fleet such pain at Kiel forty days, and a lifetime, away.[41]

12. War Lord on Sufferance

Germany, like France and Britain, went to war in 1914 confident the nation was fighting for a righteous cause which would be vindicated by speedy victory. Russia, it was assumed, had ignited the tinder of Europe for the sake of the Panslavs and Serbia: the French, eager to avenge their defeat in 1870–71, and the English, envious of Germany's stature as a world power, completed the encirclement of the Fatherland. All good patriots – conservative, liberal, radical, centrist, or social democrat – rallied round the Kaiser, who assured them from the palace balcony that henceforth he knew no political parties but only Germans. 'It is not love of conquest that inspires us', he told Reichstag deputies. 'We draw the sword with a clear conscience and with clean hands.'[1] The mood in Berlin was hardly distinguishable from the mood in London, Paris or St Petersburg. Popular enthusiasm burst into loyal songs; the parliamentary leaders accepted a political truce; and war credits were voted unanimously in the Reichstag.

To those closest to him William seemed 'much aged' by these events. Dona insisted he should be permitted to rest for as long as possible, his sleep interrupted only for unresolved matters of great urgency. As early as the third day of war his principal adjutant, General Hans von Plessen, was emphasizing to members of the suite that they must 'at all costs keep the Kaiser in good spirits'. Outwardly William displayed before his troops all the confidence and dignity expected from a Supreme War Lord. 'You will be home before the leaves have fallen from the trees', he told them; and when, on 11 August, the First Foot Guards paraded at Potsdam on the eve of departure for the Western Front, he swore never to sheathe the sword until he was able to dictate the peace. That afternoon he went riding in the Grunewald; the officers in attendance found him unusually silent and deep in thought.[2]

Prussian tradition required the sovereign to leave his capital in time of war and establish field headquarters close to the battle zone. The Kaiser's grandfather had set out for Bohemia fifteen days after the outbreak of hostilities in 1866, and for the Rhine front a mere twelve days after France's declaration of war in 1870. The army automatically assumed in 1914 that William would follow precedent. Yet to many people in Berlin, and especially to the naval chiefs, there seemed few parallels between Bismarck's wars and the complexities of twentieth-century military science. In 1870 there had been no threat from the East, no concern over colonial defence, and no High Seas Fleet, for that matter. Now it was essential to retain responsible authorities in the capital in order to handle political and diplomatic problems, maintaining links with Germany's Austrian ally, consolidating gains made by the Liman mission in Turkey, and placating the spokesmen of powerful neutral governments. There was, too, a particularly controversial matter, in which William had indicated that he was especially interested: should Germany foment revolution within the enemy camp? William had in mind Ireland and India: 'If we are to be bled to death, at least England shall lose India', he wrote in a marginal note on the eve of war. But there were also the more delicate problems of subject nationalities within the Russian Empire and (as proposed originally by the Austrians) of using Russian revolutionary exiles in Switzerland to strike at the Tsar's throne – a suggestion William strongly resisted. All these questions, and the military difficulties of a war to be fought on many fronts, made it undesirable for the Kaiser and his chief ministers to isolate themselves in distant towns behind armies engaged in a particular campaign. William, however, did not see the force of these arguments.He thought the war would be brief, and a decision reached in the West within weeks. By 12 August he had made up his mind to leave for Coblenz at the weekend. Once victory was assured in the West, he would travel across to eastern Prussia or Silesia for the final phases of the Russian campaign. The naval leaders, who had not prepared any precise strategic war plan, were ordered to wait: either they would be required to repel a British attack; or they would help impose a settlement on 'England' should she continue the war after Germany gained her decisive land victories in the West and the East. Then, too, would be soon enough to inflame Ireland and 'the whole Mohammedan world' against the 'conscienceless' tyranny of London.[3]

William accordingly set up headquarters at Coblenz on Monday, 17 August. He was housed in the official residency of the Lord-Lieutenant of the Rhineland while Bethmann-Hollweg, Tirpitz, members of the civil, military and naval administrations and the whole apparatus of the General Staff were somehow accommodated within the over-crowded city. Throughout the week good news arrived from war zones in the West: a French thrust into Lorraine was thrown back, and Nancy threatened; and from Liège the maps showed the German line advancing systematically and on schedule towards Brussels, Namur and Charleroi, wheeling left towards Mons where a trap was set to envelop the British Expeditionary Force. Reports from the East, on the other hand, were alarming: Russian weight of numbers was forcing General Prittwitz's Eighth Army to contemplate a withdrawal behind the Vistula. The news that large tracts of East Prussia were thus being abandoned to the Russians left the Kaiser a prey to his own uncertainties. His military suite were worried by the sudden switches in his temperament. There was an odd incident on the first Friday he was in Coblenz: two senior officers, walking with him in the residency grounds, fetched a second bench rather than sit with him on a seat too short for three, but he asked petulantly, 'Am I already such a figure of contempt that no one wants to sit next to me?' Yet next morning there were such encouraging reports from Lorraine that he became jubilantly optimistic. Within four days he was so 'radiant' that he insisted on telling recruits whom he saw training near Coblenz that final victory was in sight in the West.[4] This alternation between dark, suspicious moments of frustration and confident assertions of imminent triumph remained the most marked characteristic of the Kaiser's personality throughout the years of war.

His suite soon realized the professional inadequacy of their Supreme War Lord. Some officers had, indeed, perceived his weaknesses long ago, amid the deceptive showmanship of annual manoeuvres. For William, though once rated the best cavalry commander in his army, had no deeper understanding of strategic operations than his sailor cousin George of England or Tsar Nicholas in Russia. His basically cyclothymic temperament denied him three essentials of top command: decisiveness of judgement; nerves of steel, hardened by inner self-assurance; and the will to apply the mind to detail. Every assessment of people and events was intuitive, not necessarily unsound and sometimes shrewdly far-sighted, but never based on the sober appraisal of reality favoured by military and naval academies. If, as Moltke believed, the merits of his modified Schlieffen Plan guaranteed rapid victory, the facile inconsistencies which he deplored in William's character were of no immediate danger. But should it prove impossible, after all, to annihilate the enemy's power of resistance Moltke had no confidence his sovereign could give to Germany any resolute continuity in leadership. The war machine, as constructed by Schlieffen and lubricated by Moltke, could carry an emperor as passenger, but it was a vehicle with no room for backseat drivers.

Moltke resolved the first crisis of the war – the threat to Prittwitz and the Eighth Army in East Prussia – without placing too much strain on the Supreme War Lord's powers of decision. General Erich Ludendorff, who had worked closely with Moltke on the General Staff from 1908 to 1912, had distinguished himself by capturing the citadel of Liège in the second week of war. On 22 August Ludendorff was summoned from Wavre to Coblenz and told he must leave at once for the Eastern Front, where he would take over as chief of staff in the Eighth Army. But he was not to serve under Prittwitz. That morning General Paul von Beneckendorff-und-Hindenburg, sixty-six year old retired veteran of Bismarck's wars, received two telegrams at his home in Hanover. The first asked if he was ready for service. The second appointed him, by order of the All Highest War Lord, successor of General Prittwitz. He was commanded to meet Ludendorff that night at Hanover Station. The two men would then proceed immediately to Eighth Army headquarters in Marienburg.[5] Thus was forged the most important partnership in German history since Bismarck was befriended by Roon. The genius of Ludendorff was readily acknowledged by Moltke, and William willingly conferred on him the first *Pour le Merité* cross of the war after his exploits at Liège; but neither Moltke nor the Kaiser bothered much over the 'retired Excellency' they had found at Hanover. He was, they assumed, a figure-head.

The Russians were routed within four days of Hindenburg's arrival in East Prussia. Their defeat owed much to the enterprise and ingenuity of the senior general staff officer under Prittwitz, Colonel Max Hoffmann, but credit for this greatest single disaster in Russia's military history was accorded to the two generals whom Moltke had conjured up in a critical hour. The Kaiser received news of Hindenburg's success as he was on his way to the garrison church in Coblenz on Sunday morning, 30 August, although he did not at first appreciate the magnitude of Germany's victory. Little things loomed disproportionately large at imperial headquarters. What should the battle be called in the war communiqués? Maps showed it as fought between the railway junction of Ortelsburg and Soldau, but Hindenburg requested the battle should be named Tannenberg, after the village where he established his headquarters on 28 August and in order to avenge the defeat of the Teutonic Knights by Poland on the same battlefield in 1422. Since Germany was at this moment bidding for Polish national support against Russia, Hindenburg's request lacked political tact, as a senior officer at Coblenz pointed out. But William, believing he recognized in Hindenburg a general who shared his acute romantic association with the past, ignored all objections; and the Tannenberg Legend was thus assured of imperial patronage at its inception. Only after meeting Hindenburg and Ludendorff together for the first time, in the closing days of November, did William sense the limits of Hindenburg's imagination, whether historical or contemporary. Still more months were to pass before William realized that the Hindenburg cult, which he was encouraging, threatened to become the gravest restraint on his authority since the political elimination of the Bismarcks.[6]

All this, however, lay well in the future during those late-summer days of 1914. Soon after receiving Hindenburg's first report on the Tannenberg victory the Kaiser left Coblenz and crossed into Luxemburg, where he took up residence in the German legation. Moltke's headquarters were some distance across the city: the General Staff had commandeered a commercial hotel opposite the railway station and a nearby lycée, so cramped that the Operations Branch was installed in the girls' cloakroom. It was from here that Moltke sought to control the movement of 760,000 men, wheeling to invest Paris; and everyone waited for the great news expected in September from the West. Such was the air of confidence that Moltke felt bound to remind several members of the Kaiser's suite that the French, though driven back, were not yet defeated; but, as he was known for his caution and modesty, nobody gave too much attention to his warning. Bethmann-Hollweg began to prepare a memorandum on Germany's war aims, and his chief assistant drafted a proclamation which the Kaiser would make to the French people after Joffre had sued for an armistice: the Kaiser would explain that, although victory had settled the issues separating France and Germany, it would be necessary for German armies to occupy northern France so long as 'your allies, and especially England, continue the war.[7] The proclamation was ready for signature on 6 September, a little prematurely. That Sunday William returned from Metz, where he was elated to see, for the first time, artillery firing on an enemy position, six miles away. In the evening he ordered preparations for a visit next day to Third Army headquarters at Châlons-sur-Marne, nearly 120 miles away. He hoped to cross the Marne and see in action the Guards to whom he had bidden farewell at Potsdam four weeks before.

The Kaiser and his escort left Luxemburg city at seven on Monday morning. They skirted Longwy and Montmédy, followed a hilly road down to the Meuse at Stenay, and then through dense woods to the upper Aisne at Vouziers. It was stifling weather, the roads were dusty, especially when they reached the chalk plateau around Suippes, and the stench of putrefying horse flesh came in through the car windows. Beyond Suippes the staff officers could hear the thunder of guns distinctly. To their consternation the noise was coming from three directions. The cars halted and a colonel was sent ahead to Châlons, now little more than a dozen miles away. After an hour and a half of waiting, the Kaiser saw the colonel coming back. He did not think the cars could get through safely; the Guards were heavily engaged against General Foch's Ninth Army on the edge of the St Gond marshes, twenty-five miles away to their right; but, in the colonel's opinion, there was a risk of a cavalry patrol breaking through in a quieter sector of the line and capturing the Kaiser. The cars turned back to Luxemburg.[8] It was less than twelve months since this same General Foch had been a guest observer at the Kaiser's autumn manoeuvres.*

The events of this Monday, 7 September, began to tear the modified Schlieffen Plan into shreds, and with it Moltke's military reputation. For, while the Kaiser's car was halted that afternoon on the Suippes-Châlons road, the legendary shuttle service of taxis was bringing fresh troops to aid the French defenders north of Paris. These 'taxis of the Marne' did not in themselves save Paris, for the decisive sector of the battle lay farther east, but they symbolized the resilience of France, the refusal of Generals Joffre and Gallieni to be stunned by the knock-out punches Moltke threw at them. By 7 September the invading armies were running into difficulties: they had been advancing for three weeks

---

* There were justifiable grounds for concern that afternoon. The following evening General von Kluck, the commander of the German First Army, had to leap out of his staff car and help fight off a surprise attack by French dragoons, ranging well behind the recognized front line (although some distance from the Suippes-Châlons road).

under a blazing sun and in heat of almost tropical intensity; individual army commanders were out of touch with headquarters in Luxemburg and were, in consequence, showing an independence which Schlieffen would never have permitted and which would have brought them a thunderous reprimand from the elder Moltke. But the great man's nephew was not equal to the demands of so exhausting a campaign: his doctor had warned him twelve months before that he was suffering from cardiac irregularities and that his heart was getting bigger. He was, moreover, a person of strong feelings, his conscience troubled by the conflict between his sense of humanity and his fatalistic acceptance of war as an inevitable episode in 'world evolution'. Physical strain, emotional doubts, and panic rumours of 80,000 Russians landed by the British in Belgium all contributed to reducing Moltke to the irresolution and inconsistency he had condemned in his sovereign. During the Kaiser's ten-hour absence from Luxemburg that Monday, Moltke's nerves began to crumble: he wrote a letter of abject misery to his wife; and a staff officer found him sitting, hunched over a table, his face tense and stained with tears. Next day he delegated to his chief of intelligence, Lieutenant-Colonel Hentsch, the responsibility of visiting each of the army headquarters in France. Should disaster appear imminent, Hentsch – a Saxon and not a Prussian – was authorized to order a general retreat to defensive positions along the river Aisne. There is no evidence that over this vital decision, which ruled out all prospects of an early peace, the Supreme War Lord was once consulted. William, as he complained a few weeks later, had become a mere spectator, told nothing by the General Staff nor asked for his advice. In the afternoon of 9 September Colonel Hentsch, finding the Second Army already pulling back, fulfilled his mission. By 10 September William could see from his maps that the armies were in full retreat.[9]

The Supreme War Lord was not, however, entirely a cipher. Senior appointments remained his prerogative and he watched, with anxiety, the rapid decline of Moltke's health. On 14 September he decided to order Moltke to hand over the functions of chief of the General Staff to Falkenhayn, the Prussian Minister of War; the change was not officially announced for another seven weeks for everyone was agreed that the nation – and its enemies – must be shielded from knowledge of the demoralization at headquarters that autumn.[10] General Falkenhayn's advancement was determined by the Kaiser personally and against the wishes of some close advisers. By reputation Falkenhayn was a court

favourite, but if William hoped the new chief would allow him more
influence on the conduct of operations, he was soon disappointed.
When Falkenhayn moved his headquarters from Luxemburg to
Mézières at the end of September, William and the whole of the
imperial suite followed him. A local industrialist's home at Charleville,
across the Meuse, was commandeered for the Kaiser's use and he
stayed there intermittently over the following thirteen months, until it
was felt that the villa's proximity to the railway station made it an easily
identifiable target for bombing planes. But Falkenhayn had no intention of encouraging William to come south of the river and see for
himself the day-to-day conduct of the battles in Flanders and northern
France. Gradually Charleville became spiritually as remote from operations as Luxemburg, or indeed Berlin.

At first, however, William found Charleville a convenient centre for
visits to his troops in the front line. Sometimes he travelled by car and
sometimes in the imperial train, whose blue, cream and gold coaches
were painted green as a concession to wartime security. These visits
were not always popular with his personal staff or with the field
commanders, for his behaviour was unpredictable. Naïvely bellicose
speeches embarrassingly exposed a gap between his concept of war and
the experience of troops fresh from the trenches. Occasionally he made
gestures which were thoughtless, and misunderstood: thus a visit to
Warneton, south of Ypres, on 31 October created a 'bad impression' on
a predominantly Bavarian division who saw their emperor speaking
amiably, in English, to a group of British prisoners whom they were
escorting back from the salient.[11] Soon these day excursions to the war
zone became rarer and William found life at Charleville increasingly
tedious. He sawed wood in the parkland; he inspected past battlefields,
like Sedan twelve miles away; he sat long over his dinner table, talking
interminably and often inconsequentially; he played skat, the three-
handed card game he had popularized aboard the *Hohenzollern*. On 25
November he sent a private letter from Charleville to Houston Stewart
Chamberlain, who was now a naturalized German citizen: 'It is my
unshakeable conviction', William wrote, 'that the country to which
God gave Luther, Goethe, Bach, Wagner, Moltke, Bismarck and my
grandfather will yet be called upon to fulfil great tasks for the benefit of
mankind.'[12] It is not clear if this curious and selective incantation of the
illustrious dead was for the sake of the recipient or of the writer's
morale.

The failure to gain a rapid victory raised new questions, over which the chancellor and the Foreign Ministry representatives consulted the Kaiser. Was the war to continue in the East and the West, or should an attempt be made to reach a separate peace with Russia? Was the fleet to risk that 'twentieth-century Trafalgar' for which so much money had been screwed from a reluctant Reichstag? How much support should Germany give to Austria-Hungary and to the new ally, Turkey, whose warships under German command had bombarded Russia's Black Sea bases at the end of October? William had clear answers to all these questions: he hoped the armies in the West would advance back to the Marne, and beyond; he favoured an early separate peace with Russia, irrespective of Austrian and Turkish susceptibilities; and he remained steadfastly opposed to any naval engagement between German and British capital ships. Above all he emphasized the need to ensure that the war was ended on acceptable terms speedily, for he feared the consequences of heavy casualty lists and sustained blockade on the internal structure of the Reich. On 21 January 1915 the prominent Turcophile professor, Ernst Jäckh, dined at Charleville and alarmed the Kaiser by predicting the future successes of Liman von Sanders' military mission: by the autumn, Jäckh declared, Prussian officers in their spiked helmets would be looking out on the Suez Canal. 'You must be mad', snorted the Kaiser. 'My troops are not there (in Turkey) for that purpose'; and Admiral von Müller, who was present, noted that William seemed depressed and 'obviously terrified by the thought of a long war'.[13]

He was convinced he knew how the fighting should be ended. War and peace, William had always thought, were conditions of existence determined by emperors and kings. He had little use for the repeated offers of mediation from the President of the United States. 'I and my cousins George and Nicholas shall make peace when the proper time has come', he told Colonel House, Woodrow Wilson's special adviser, who came on two missions to Europe in the hope of halting the war.[14] William's faith in dynastic solidarity remained unshaken so long as Nicholas II was on the throne, and in policy discussions he regularly voiced his scruples over challenging the authority of the Tsar, either as Russia's emperor or as Grand Duke of Finland. He exploited the dynastic links of the Bavarian and Belgian royal houses to seek a settlement with King Albert and he urged the Grand Duke of Hesse to try and establish contact with his sister, the Empress of Russia, in the hope she would encourage Nicholas to conclude a separate peace.

The most promising contact with Russia was, however, by way of Copenhagen. In the fourth week of November 1914 Albert Ballin privately informed William at Charleville of an offer originating from King Christian x of Denmark, who suggested he might send the Danish shipping-magnate, Hans Niels Andersen, on missions to England and Russia as a preliminary to a mediated peace. Neither William nor his chancellor were interested in contacts with London at this stage, but the Kaiser intimated he might respond to peace overtures from Petrograd (as St Petersburg had been re-named early in September). Andersen duly visited Petrograd in the first week of March 1915 and found Nicholas cautious but not unsympathetic to peace talks. A fortnight later Andersen was in Berlin and Bethmann escorted him to Charleville where, on 20 March, he was able to give the Kaiser his impressions of the Russian court. William was interested: he explained to Andersen that Germany had not begun the fighting in the East; he added that he personally set high value on his old friendship with Nicholas and therefore he welcomed King Christian's attempts to secure peace between the two empires. The King sent a letter from Copenhagen early in April suggesting that a Russian emissary be sent to Denmark for negotiations with a German representative, but this was the spring in which British and Russians had high hopes of victory at Gallipoli, and the prospect of securing Constantinople was a guarantee that Russia would stay in the war. Nicholas remained silent for many weeks after receiving the Danish proposal, finally returning a clear-cut 'No' at the beginning of August, on the first anniversary of the outbreak of war. William remained convinced 'Nicky' would soon change his mind.[15]

Meanwhile William was faced by a mounting threat to his authority. The German navy possessed no unified command, nor had it ever accepted the primacy of the chief of the Admiralty Staff. The Kaiser always looked upon himself as central and supreme commander. In peacetime he was arbiter of ship construction, of training schedules, of cadet admissions and of officer promotion; and he assumed that responsibility for the disposition of the fleet in time of war remained in his hands. This supremacy of the Kaiser had been nurtured and preserved by Grand Admiral Tirpitz, partly to keep out possible rivals but also to make certain that, in war, the 'non-professional' emperor would leave naval matters to the person whose vision conjured up a High Seas Fleet in the first place.[16] The Kaiser, however, no longer listened solely to Tirpitz. The influence of his brother, Grand Admiral Prince Henry, was greater than Henry's limited gifts warranted, and in recent years William had paid increasing attention to the opinions of his third son, Adalbert, a lieutenant-commander serving aboard one of the newest battleships. The captain of any vessel in the fleet had a right of direct access to the Kaiser: if his mood inclined towards naval matters he gave close attention to such representations, and there are in the marine archives unexpected instances of imperial concern with petty questions; but if his thoughts, serious or frivolous, were elsewhere, then he complained at being badgered with details instead of treated as a distant and omnipotent commander. Such temperamental vac-illations did not incline Tirpitz to accept uncritically William's direc-tives for the fleet 'at a time when Germany is engaged in a struggle for her very existence'. There was, moreover, enough truth in William's suspicion that the desk-bound grand admiral was out of touch with naval actuality to make the quarrel between the two men deep, bitter and personal.[17]

Basically there were three causes of dispute: the Kaiser's reluctance to risk the main body of the fleet in a premature naval battle; the hostility of both Kaiser and chancellor to U-boat attacks on merchant vessels; and the restraints which William and Bethmann wished to impose on naval Zeppelin attacks on English cities, especially London. William's position was weakened by his inconsistencies: he allowed cruiser raids on the English coast one month, and then clamped down on them again as soon as the *Blücher* was caught and sunk near the Dogger Bank; he permitted the announcement that merchantmen would be sunk without warning in British waters, and then banned the sinking of passenger vessels after the *Lusitania* was torpedoed on 7 May 1915; he authorized naval Zeppelins to raid English coastal towns in January 1915, and then forbade attacks on London for another two months.* Tirpitz's sense of frustration made him offer his resignation as State Secretary of the Navy Office at the beginning of June 1915 and

* The first Zeppelin raid on London (31 May/1 June 1915) was carried out by a military airship rather than a naval one. But the naval Zeppelin L.8 appears to have been heading for London when she was shot down off the Belgian coast on the previous 5 March. The Kaiser repeatedly emphasized that raids were to be limited to the docks and industrial targets and was opposed to 'terror' bombing.

again eleven weeks later, but on both occasions it was rejected by William. At the same time William was determined to assert his authority over naval matters: 'I have created and trained the fleet', he commented petulantly in the margin of Tirpitz's second letter of resignation. 'Where, when, and how I wish to use it is *exclusively* the supreme commander's business. Everybody else will have to remain silent on this matter and obey.'[18]

William also complained, privately, that Tirpitz was a 'downright' conspirator. The charge was not unfounded. Tirpitz had little regard for Falkenhayn, Bethmann or any of the principal figures at Charleville-Mézières, whom he collectively damned as 'the Hydra'; but he became an early acolyte of the Hindenburg cult. In March and April 1915 Tirpitz toyed with the possibility of inducing the Kaiser to retire on sick leave 'for eight weeks or more' while Hindenburg would take over the joint responsibilities of the chancellor and chief of the General Staff, backed by the Crown Prince as Regent. For this plan to succeed Tirpitz needed the support of the medical officers at Charleville as well as the collaboration of the Empress and the Crown Prince. Dona was genuinely concerned over her husband's vulnerability of temperament and consistently favoured his return to Germany from field headquarters. She also appreciated, as William did not, that the nation looked to Tirpitz and Hindenburg for leadership rather than to the unpopular Bethmann and the unknown Falkenhayn. More than once, William regretted that Dona should appear a partisan of the Hindenburg-Ludendorff combination. The Crown Prince declared himself 'grateful that Heaven has given us two such men as Hindenburg and Ludendorff', thought that his father needed relief from the pressures of Charleville, but remained 'politely uncommunicative' in his talks with Tirpitz. The doctors were the chief stumbling block: to suggest any curtailment of the Kaiser's authority on medical grounds seemed to Niedner, William's chief physician, unethical and a dangerous cheapening of the concept of monarchy. Nothing therefore came of Tirpitz's intrigue, and it is not clear how much William suspected. But from the spring of 1915 onwards he treated Tirpitz coolly, distrusting any policy he championed.[19]

In mid-December 1915 Tirpitz formally proposed the Kaiser should appoint him supreme commander of the fleet. William refused. For two more months Tirpitz pressed for unrestricted submarine warfare as a means of 'bringing England to her knees'. The chancellor, afraid of the effect of U-boat activity on American opinion, opposed Tirpitz; but the Kaiser wavered. 'Were I the captain of a U-boat I would never torpedo a ship if I knew that women and children were aboard', William told his admirals at Wilhelmshaven on 23 February 1916.[20] Yet six days later he allowed the attacks to begin, and it seemed as if Tirpitz was triumphant. But William was uneasy; within a week he changed his mind, accepting Bethmann's warnings of repercussions across the Atlantic. He ordered that only 'armed merchantmen' might be attacked. This wavering was too much for Tirpitz. On 8 March he submitted his resignation for the third time in nine months, and William accepted it. Admiral von Capelle was appointed to succeed Tirpitz on the understanding he would seek to accommodate his policies with the ideas of the Kaiser and the chancellor. From the Crown Prince's headquarters in the field there came a protest: 'The resignation of Tirpitz is a national disaster', he declared to Admiral von Müller, asking him to pass this comment on to his father.[21] But William cared little for his son's indignation. To a man who had dropped the pilot at the height of his fame, dropping the Grand Admiral seemed to cause scarcely a ripple.

Tirpitz's resignation coincided with a crucial moment in the struggle on land. For most of the year 1915 Germany had stood on the defensive in the West, successfully withstanding French and British attacks, but making little progress in any sector compared with the steady eastwards advance in Lithuania, Poland, Byelo-Russia and Galicia. Significantly throughout the summer of 1915 and the early winter the Kaiser's headquarters were at the castle of Pless in Upper Silesia, close to the Austrian frontier. But Falkenhayn was a convinced 'westerner', believing victory would come only by knocking out France and depriving 'England of her hold on the continent'. Shortly before Christmas 1915 Falkenhayn visited the Kaiser at Potsdam and persuaded him that a concentrated assault on the salient of Verdun 'would bleed the forces of France to death', since reasons of national sentiment would 'compel the French General Staff to throw in every man they have' rather than lose a historic citadel on the route to Paris. William accepted Falkenhayn's reasoning and on 21 February the German Fifth Army – nominally commanded by the Crown Prince – began a devastating bombardment of French positions on the hills north-east of Verdun.[22] Three days later the Kaiser's headquarters returned to Charleville, although William personally moved into a new and more comfortable residence, the Villa Belleaire, outside the town. There he confidently awaited news of a breakthrough at Verdun, fifty miles higher up the Meuse.

His optimism was unjustified. Verdun became a disaster, bleeding white defenders and assailants alike. For the first five weeks of battle – and there were forty-three weeks in all – German soldiers perished at the rate of one every forty-five seconds. French casualties were greater still, but Verdun (like Ypres) never fell. Ultimately on this one sector of the Western Front the Germans suffered a third of a million casualties in occupying a cratered wasteland half the size of metropolitan Berlin. As early as 10 March the Kaiser was despairing of victory. Falkenhayn told him nothing; he complained: 'I might as well be living in Germany', he added. He remained at Charleville for another two months and then trailed off to Homburg, to join Dona for a week's sick leave. By now he was thinking less and less about the war: 'I never wanted this', he was heard to murmur from time to time.[23]

Even in naval affairs, he was now no more than a war lord on sufferance. Admiral von Capelle consulted him, but largely as a routine gesture. It was therefore the naval staff and the commander-in-chief of the High Seas Fleet, Admiral von Scheer, who evolved the strategy which turned an intended raid on the English coast into the great naval action off Jutland, which the Germans called the battle of the Skagerrak. The Kaiser was informed of this first and last engagement between rival dreadnoughts as he was returning from the Eastern Front. His reactions afford a significant contrast to his pre-war style of behaviour. He heard at breakfast on Friday, 2 June that his admirals were claiming a tactical victory in the North Sea* and that the fleet was anchored safely in the roadstead off Wilhelmshaven. But, instead of hurrying to Wilhelmshaven or enjoying the sight of his capital with streets be-flagged for a naval triumph, he went to Cadinen in East Prussia to visit the Hohenzollern home farm. 'His thoughts are no longer with the war', commented Admiral von Müller that night. Only on Monday did William travel to the coast, inspecting the damaged ships in pouring rain and assuring the crew of the flagship, 'The spell of Trafalgar is

---

* The battle of Jutland (Skagerrak) was claimed as a victory by both sides. 151 British vessels were engaged: 3 battlecruisers, 3 cruisers and 8 destroyers were sunk, with 6,000 casualties. 99 German vessels were engaged: 1 battleship, 1 battlecruiser, 4 light cruisers and 5 destroyers were lost, with 2,500 casualties. The 44 dreadnoughts were in action against each other for only twenty minutes, 6.15 to 6.35 on the evening of 31 May.

broken'. By then, as the shrewder officers and ratings perceived, Admiral Scheer was interpreting Jutland as evidence that his fleet was not strong enough to inflict decisive losses on the Royal Navy, however well individual commanders may have fought their vessels: 'A fleet action will not *force* England to make peace', Scheer told his master. William accepted the admiral's verdict, but he still held out against the naval pressure group which argued that the only way of humbling the British was by giving the U-boat captains a free hand. Jutland intensified rather than resolved his naval dilemma: no surface action for fear the High Seas Fleet would be annihilated by a greater concentration of vessels; no unrestricted submarine action for fear of bringing the United States into the war.[24]

William's bearing impressed the ratings at Wilhelmshaven. Seaman Stumpf aboard the battleship *Helgoland* wrote in his diary that the Kaiser, so far from looking 'aged since I had last seen him here' in 1914, seemed ten years younger, delighting at the success of the navy 'which he considered his very own creation'. He came aboard, 'a riding crop in his hand', with 'vigorous, confident step'.[25] But William's sea-going bluster concealed inner worries. He knew there was discontent in Berlin over high prices and an intensifying food shortage, and he was painfully conscious of the lengthening casualty lists from Verdun. Yet he was out of touch with public opinion; he read only selected digests from censored newspapers and spent little time in the capital or any of the more populated areas of the Reich. He underestimated the depth of feeling against his chancellor, who was known to oppose an intensified U-boat campaign, and he minimized the enthusiasm for the legendary father-figure from the East. William thought Hindenburg lacked initiative and suspected the old man's imperturbability was as much a sign of limited comprehension as of iron nerve. Nor could William forget his antipathy towards Ludendorff, whose brusque ungraciousness contrasted with the sycophantic manners of more aristocratic officers in the court circle. 'I will never make Ludendorff chief of staff', William had told Bethmann in January 1915. 'He is a dubious character, fired by personal ambition.'[26] And after eighteen months the Kaiser saw no reason to modify this opinion. The Eastern Front commander whom he most admired was August von Mackensen, an epitome of the traditional cavalry officer corps, who was only two years younger than Hindenburg and, like him, a veteran of 1870. At heart William wanted no radical changes: he still had confidence in his protégé, Falkenhayn, even if, for much of the time, he treated his Supreme War Lord as an encumbrance.

Yet by midsummer in 1916 Falkenhayn had few supporters at headquarters or in Berlin. Hindenburg and Ludendorff consistently opposed his general strategy; Bethmann-Hollweg resented his attempts to tighten censorship; and the Austrian representatives blamed his concentration on Verdun for encouraging Russia to launch powerful attacks in the East, especially successful in Galicia. In July the Anglo-French offensive on the Somme led Falkenhayn to divert men and munitions from the Verdun sector, and thereby further discredited his strategy. His fall, however, was precipitated by an event in eastern Europe which he had anticipated, but not so soon. The Russian victories in Galicia tempted Roumania to enter the war on the side of the Entente powers. Falkenhayn had told the Kaiser that, if the Roumanians moved, they would not do so until after the harvest was in. But the declaration of war came on 27 August 1916, a month too soon for German calculations. Briefly there seemed a risk of Russian and Roumanian troops seeping through the Carpathian passes and reaching the vital granary of Hungary. This surprise development threw William off balance. For the first time he was heard to remark, 'The war is lost'.[27]

Supreme Headquarters was, at that moment, in Pless. Both William and his generals were therefore more responsive to what was happening in south-eastern Europe than had they been at Charleville or Berlin, or indeed with Hindenburg in Brest-Litovsk. Nobody else saw the situation quite so gloomily as William, but Falkenhayn's opponents were ready to exploit the Kaiser's mood. His military secretariat proposed he should dismiss Falkenhayn and call Hindenburg in as Germany's saviour. Similar advice had come to him from Bethmann three days before. The empress, who was visiting Pless, added her plea too. William gave way: an urgent telephone call to Brest-Litovsk in the early afternoon of 28 August asked Hindenburg and Ludendorff to set off for Pless at once; and Falkenhayn, on hearing that the Kaiser was seeking advice from his powerful rivals, offered his resignation.[28]

Next morning Hindenburg and Ludendorff were told they were to be, respectively, chief and deputy chief of the General Staff. But they did not meekly accept the greatness thrust upon them. Ludendorff saw himself as no man's deputy: he was created 'First Quartermaster General', an innovation in the military hierarchy. Titles, however, were of small importance. What mattered was the style in which the two men fulfilled their responsibilities. In effect, during those hours of needless panic at Pless, the Kaiser had given the Reich a duo-dictatorship of military men unknown in Europe since the counter-revolution of 1848–9. It is ironic that, after twenty-eight years as a sovereign, William II should have found himself fettered by his generals as closely as Francis Joseph on his accession as a young man of eighteen. In 1912 Major Ludendorff of the operational division of the General Staff had told his superior, Moltke, that the easiest way to handle the Kaiser when war came was to ask him nothing.[29] That cynical advice the First Quartermaster General could now follow as a principle of policy.

13. Nemesis

The crisis which brought Hindenburg and Ludendorff to supreme command was soon resolved. The Roumanians were weak in artillery, munitions and aircraft and had anticipated more assistance from their allies than the Entente could give. It was therefore an easy task for the Germans and Austrians to counter the tentative Roumanian probes into Transylvania, responding with a formidable pincer movement in which Mackensen attacked from the south and the demoted Falkenhayn from the west. On 6 December 1916 Mackensen entered Bucharest, the Kaiser celebrating with champagne and a proposal to name the next battlecruiser in Mackensen's honour. By Christmas all the fertile plain was under German occupation. With the food shortage in Germany grimmer that winter than in either of its predecessors, this acquisition of grain land was of greater value than captured towns listed in war communiqués; but place-names were given due prominence in the press, for it was good for morale to pin little flags in an advancing line on the wall maps. From the Western Front there was no such heartening news. On their first visit to France Hindenburg and Ludendorff were horrified by the 'lunar landscape' of the Somme and the 'hell' around Verdun: 'The battles there exhausted our troops like an open wound', Hindenburg declared. Ludendorff proposed a defensive policy in the West until shortages of men and equipment were made good: then, and only then, a decisive thrust would be made on Paris.[1]

William was not consulted over the general strategic plan. For four days in October his presence was tolerated on the Western Front, but he spent most of the autumn and much of the winter at Pless, with journeys to Potsdam and also to Vienna for the funeral of Francis Joseph, who died on 21 November aged eighty-six. Yet although the Kaiser took little part in purely military discussions, he remained the final political authority. The decision to set up a puppet Prussian-sponsored king-dom of Poland (proclaimed on 5 November) was ultimately his own, even though it was taken with misgivings: he feared patronage of the Polish cause might make it harder to secure peace with Russia, but he accepted Ludendorff's plea that the army required an enthusiastic cadre of Polish troops for the coming decisive battle. William was also closely consulted over the chancellor's desire to make a public peace-offer once Bucharest had fallen to Mackensen's army. He was interested in the possibilities of a general peace settlement, provided the German proposal was seen to come from a position of strength and not interpreted as a sign of weakness. On 12 December Bethmann accord-ingly told the Reichstag that Germany was prepared to discuss a peace settlement around a conference table in one of the neutral countries: he set out no detailed terms, but his speech mentioned 'reparation', 'resto-ration', and the need for military and economic guarantees. The Ger-man front line, Bethmann claimed, was 'indestructible' and he gave a warning that Germany had it in her power to use submarines in order to starve a persistent enemy into surrender. As if to emphasize Germany's military potential William himself delivered a warlike speech on that same Tuesday to troops parading at Mulhouse, the second city in Alsace, and his words received equal press coverage with the barbed-wire olive branch waved so aggressively by Bethmann in the chamber.[2] There was never much likelihood of a favourable response by the Entente powers to a peace initiative of this character, and the Germans for their part turned down President Wilson's subsequent offer to 'take soundings' towards a mediated peace. William privately told his suite he was 'amazed' at the Entente's lack of enthusiasm towards Bethmann's speech. Germany, he declared, would now have to extend her war aims against France and Belgium: 'King Albert . . . could not be allowed to return to Belgium', he remarked on 2 January 1917, 'and the coast of Flanders must be ours'.[3]

The enemy's reluctance to negotiate peace on Germany's terms strengthened the advocates of a tougher U-boat campaign. On three occasions in the last five months of 1916 William assured Bethmann of his continued opposition to unrestricted submarine warfare. But he was less resolute than in the earlier phases of the war: no one else backed the chancellor, and when the naval and military leaders appealed to the Kaiser again early in January 1917, he gave way. In a Crown Council at Pless on 9 January the supreme command assured William that submarine warfare would force the enemy to sue for peace before American aid in men or material could reach Europe. The Kaiser, 'pale and distraught', listened impatiently to Bethmann's objections; when the chancellor admitted he could not ask his sovereign to reject the unanimous recommendations of his military advisers, the issue was decided.[4] It was announced that unrestricted submarine warfare would commence on 1 February 1917. The tempo of the war quickened, but not as Hindenburg and Ludendorff predicted. On 3 February the United States broke off diplomatic relations: on 6 April, after American merchant vessels had been sunk by German submarines, Congress in Washington passed a joint resolution declaring war on Germany; on 2 July the Kaiser was told the first American troops had landed in France. There were still no peace feelers from London.

The Kaiser's suite had expected Bethmann to resign (or be dismissed) after the Crown Council at Pless. But who would take his place? Hindenburg said he did not feel able to face the Reichstag: the Kaiser ignored hints that Tirpitz might ably fulfil the duties of chancellor; and he reacted with positive hostility to suggestions that Bülow be recalled, even though he was the favourite candidate both of the empress and the supreme command. Bethmann decided against submitting his resignation: he told a close colleague that he hoped he might apply a brake to the irresponsible policies which the military chiefs were seeking to foist on the Kaiser. This third hard winter of war was draining away the spirit of the nation, and Bethmann argued that if the people were to recover their vitality they should be promised a share in the government of the Reich as soon as victory brought a secure peace. Twice during February and March he spoke of his faith in political reform and on 2 April he travelled to Homburg, where William was recovering from a hernia operation. Bethmann suggested the Kaiser might give his people 'assurance of his liberal sentiments' at a time of political doubt and upheaval. William welcomed the proposal. At the end of the week it would be Easter: what could be more appropriate than an Easter Gift to his people? On Easter Day – 8 April – the newspapers carried a decree in William's name promising post-war franchise reform to bring democracy to Prussia and revision of the whole constitutional structure of the Empire. The Grand Duke of Hesse telephoned William personally at Homburg to let him know of the jubilation aroused in Darmstadt by the Easter Message. Yet William's suite shared none of this enthusiasm. 'Only soldiers know how to deal with democrats', General von Plessen told the empress.[5] The remark so pleased Dona that she passed it on to her husband – to whom, no doubt, it came as a distant and unwelcome echo from his own past.

This flirtation with democracy annoyed Hindenburg and Ludendorff: talk of future domestic reform during a war emergency was controversial, divisive and demoralizing. Their hostility to Bethmann increased early in July when they suspected he was in favour of a negotiated and, in their eyes, 'weak' peace: on 29 June Bethmann reported to the Kaiser on talks he had held three days earlier with the new papal nuncio, Monsignor Eugenio Pacelli (later Pope Pius XII), on the possibilities of peace. William himself received the nuncio after lunch, discussing with him at length the Church's attitude towards a general peace settlement. At the same time the two supreme commanders disapproved of the way Bethmann was handling a Reichstag 'peace resolution', sponsored by the leading figure in the Roman Catholic Centre Party, Matthias Erzberger. All this talk of franchise reform and ending the war was too much for Hindenburg and Ludendorff. Since they were confident of the Empress and the Crown Prince, they presented William with a virtual ultimatum: either he dropped Bethmann-Hollweg, or they resigned. To strengthen their position, Ludendorff let his supporters in the Reichstag know 'what the Field Marshal and I' proposed, and he made certain the Kaiser's personal advisers were aware that the Pan-German deputies were in his confidence. Privately William complained that Prussian generals had never before resorted to such crude political blackmail, but he did not resist the pressure. Bethmann fell on 13 July, William showing little interest in the whole affair and having no successor in mind.[6] A scheme for dividing the Centre Party by appointing Erzberger's superior, the seventy three year old Bavarian prime minister Count von Hertling, broke down when the count declined the post because of his age. A minor official sponsored the candidature of George Michaelis, the sixty year old controller of food supplies for the Kingdom of Prussia. Ludendorff took up the proposal, apparently because the generals had been impressed by Michaelis's turn of phrase on his visits to headquarters. The Kaiser did not know him, but Hindenburg assured William he was a God-fearing Prussian.[7] With this testimonial Michaelis became the sixth chancellor of the German Empire.

The chancellorship of Michaelis lasted a mere 111 days. He was a man of no ambition who, as he picturesquely remarked, had been 'content to run beside the carriage of politics' for many years.[8] It was soon clear that, as coachman, he held the reins too lightly. On 2 August 1917 there was a political demonstration by the crew of the battleship *Prinzregent Luitpold* at Wilhelmshaven which was regarded as an act of mutiny by the naval authorities.* Michaelis, though agreeing on the need to strengthen discipline in the fleet, failed to satisfy his military patrons by taking severe measures against socialist agitators in general, and he cut a poor figure in the Reichstag debates. By the end of October there was another 'chancellor crisis', with William – who had still only met Michaelis on a dozen occasions – complaining he had hardly had the opportunity of getting to know the fellow. The coachman clambered down again on 1 November, and Count Hertling was induced to accept the post for which he had regarded himself as too old three months before.[9] The government of the Reich was thus nominally entrusted to a Bavarian Roman Catholic, as in the days of Hohenlohe. Hertling's change of mind was in part prompted by the fact that by now a Bavarian Roman Catholic was also in charge of the Foreign Ministry; for, early in August, the Kaiser had appointed as State Secretary for Foreign Affairs, Richard von Kühlmann, the young diplomat whose adroitness on a heaving rope ladder at Tangier had impressed his emperor twelve years before. If the Hertling-Kühlmann partnership was to stand up to the Hindenburg-Ludendorff combination it would need a suppleness of mind to match the agility of that unforgettable morning in Morocco.

William, however, was rarely present nowadays to watch the confrontation of military and civil authority. After the fall of Bethmann-Hollweg in July, Hindenburg and Ludendorff encouraged the Kaiser to undertake extensive journeys: to Tarnopol in eastern Galicia and then north to Vilna in Lithuania; out to Heligoland; to the Flanders front; and back to Riga in the north-east. There were, too, visits to strengthen the morale of Germany's allies. The Kaiser travelled by train to the Roumanian front, where there was a dramatic meeting with King Ferdinand of Bulgaria and his two sons at sunset beside the Cernavoda Bridge over the Danube. Another journey took him through Serbia into

---

* A stoker from the *Prinzregent Luipold* and a seaman from the flagship, *Friedrich der Grosse*, were executed by an army firing-squad at Cologne on 5 September 1917 for having incited mutiny in the fleet. Sentences on the two men, imposed by courts-martial, were confirmed by Admiral Scheer who (as he wrote later) did not think it right to place the responsibility for such matters on the Kaiser as Supreme War Lord.

the heart of Bulgaria and over the former Greek frontier so as to inspect a crack Bulgarian regiment in the rain-swept ruins of the amphitheatre at Philippi. He then spent a few days in Constantinople, driving in great state along the shore of the Bosphorus to the Yildiz Palace, as nineteen years before when first he rehearsed his role as Islam's supreme protector. A film was made of this latest visit to the Sultan, and on his return to Berlin William abandoned the customary evening game of skat in favour of a 'home movie' show. To his exhausted suite it appeared as though William was constantly seeking distraction from pressing realities.[10] He had become, yet again, the *Reise-Kaiser*, 'the emperor on the move', whose restlessness once prompted Berliners to joke that 'his young majesty has no time to rule'. The wry asides of 1889–90 were, by 1917, ominous reflections on the quality of wartime leadership.

In the late autumn of 1917 the success of the joint Austro-German offensive on the river Isonzo, which led to the Italian disaster at Caporetto, brought William hurrying to the southern front. On 11 November he travelled to Trieste – but not, this time, to Miramare, with its ghosts of a recent past – and he went on by train to Pula, a base for U-boat operations in the Mediterranean. This journey gave him the opportunity to meet the new ruler of Austria-Hungary, Charles, and his consort, Zita, both of whom were eager for an early end to the war. William's exuberance over the recent triumph on the Isonzo made their inner hopes of a speedy, negotiated peace appear so defeatist that they limited conversation to generalities. For differing reasons both emperors seemed to be escaping from the problems of the moment.[11]

Those closest to William were troubled by this constant retreat into a fantasy world. At first Bethmann-Hollweg's fall left him deep in gloom, but at the end of July his chronic depression gave way to an artificially elated optimism: for the remainder of the year he noticed and remembered only victories and successes. Frustration at Ypres, defeat on the Aisne, five Zeppelins lost in a single raid on England, declining morale in a fleet that rarely put to sea – none of these questions held his attention. He bothered himself with trivialities, such as the cut of a new jacket for naval officers. In spare moments he redrew the post-war map of Europe to accommodate ambitions as megalomaniac as anything held by Napoleon I at his zenith. Toying with thrones became a pleasant pastime: vacancies in Roumania and Belgium?; Courland?;

Poland?; Finland?; Lithuania?. Although in conference he continued to show more sense and moderation than the generals, his table talk was bombastic. There was nothing new in such a contradiction in character, but it puzzled Hindenburg and Ludendorff who had only known the All Highest briefly, and for the most part from a distance.[12]

The reality giving passing substance to these dreams was the disintegration of the Russian state. To William the overthrow of the Tsar in March 1917 seemed an inevitable consequence of weak rule: Nicholas had compromised the sacred traditions of autocracy and allowed himself to be led into a disastrous war by rash counsellors. The establishment of the Provisional Government and the growth of republicanism in Russia removed William's inhibitions on the use of extreme revolutionaries. On 11 April he learnt that, in conjunction with the supreme command, the chancellor had begun to assist Russian revolutionaries to return home, since they would help disrupt the war effort of the Provisional Government and hasten a general collapse on the Eastern Front. William suggested certain conditions which should be imposed on the returning radicals – including the presentation to them of copies of his 'Easter Message' – but by that time Lenin's famous 'sealed train' had completed its journey from Berne to the Baltic and the Bolshevik time-bomb was being primed in southern Sweden.[13] After receiving assurances that all his precautionary instructions had been anticipated (which was not strictly true), the Kaiser lost interest in the matter, until early December when he received a detailed report from Kühlmann on Germany's success in financing *Pravda* and other Bolshevik sources of propaganda. Meanwhile William had shown genuine concern for Nicholas II and his family: there is strong evidence he sent a warning message to Petrograd, through Copenhagen, that the Provisional Government were responsible for the Romanovs' welfare and that, should the family wish to seek refuge in the west, German vessels would not attack a warship carrying them through the Baltic (where, of course, the Russian Empress's brother-in-law, Prince Henry, was commander-in-chief of all naval forces).[14] This relatively simple method of ensuring the safety of the imperial family was ruled out in mid-August when the Romanovs were removed to the inner heart of Russia in order, as Kerensky told Nicholas, to protect them from the mounting fury of the Bolshevik mob in Petrograd. Lenin's promised 'world-wide Socialist revolution' was already stripping away the decencies of dynastic solidarity.

The 'October Revolution', which brought the Soviets to power in Petrograd, held out an immediate prospect of peace and ultimately of German dominance over the rich farmland of the Ukraine. On 26 November Trotsky formally requested an armistice: Ludendorff told the Kaiser he wished for a speedy settlement in the East in order to release troops for a great spring offensive which would take Paris and end the war in the West. William agreed with this general policy, but he clearly had little idea of the character of the new regime in Petrograd, for on 29 November he proposed to Kühlmann that, provided peace negotiations made good progress, Germany should 'enter into a sort of relationship of alliance or friendship with Russia'. Patiently Kühlmann sought to explain the extraordinary nature of events in Petrograd.[15] It was accepted that Germany should wait and see whether this strange Congress of Soviets was one of the 'new political combinations agreeable to us'.

Peace talks opened at Brest-Litovsk on 22 December, with Kühlmann heading the civil delegation and Major-General Max Hoffman the military. At first William firmly backed Kühlmann, supporting him whenever Ludendorff tried to rush through a settlement: 'The Kaiser is the only sensible man in the whole of Germany', Kühlmann remarked to the Austrian foreign minister on 28 December.[16] But there were limits to William's defiance of the supreme command. Five days later a serious clash occurred between the Kaiser and Ludendorff at a conference in the small Bellevue Palace at Berlin when William proposed a frontier line in Poland on which, as he explained, he had decided after talks with 'that excellent and competent expert, General Hoffman'. Ludendorff, losing all self-control, demanded to know by what right the Kaiser was seeking the opinion of a subordinate general without reference to the supreme command? Not even Bismarck had addressed William in such terms at a conference table. But instead of asserting himself and prompting the resignation of the chief of the General Staff as well as the First Quartermaster General, the Kaiser merely remarked coldly that he would await a report from the supreme command on the whole problem. Next day Ludendorff repeated the tactic he had used in the chancellor crisis: he let the Pan-German newspapers know he was about to resign because of differences with the Kaiser. At once telegrams began to arrive at the royal palace begging William to retain Ludendorff, and he bowed before the threatened storm of public wrath. But one astute critic,

Crown Prince Rupert of Bavaria, the highly competent commander of the northern army group on the Western Front, was dismayed to find the All Highest War Lord a puppet of the supreme command: he had been surprised when, on 22 December, the Kaiser inspected troops in the Cambrai-Le Cateau sector and brought them greetings and praise 'from the Field Marshal' (Hindenburg). It worried Rupert that a sovereign should thus appear the mouthpiece of a subject before his troops: 'In the old days it would have been impossible', Rupert commented.[17]

There was another scene in the second week of January 1918 when Hindenburg sought the dismissal of Rudolf von Valentini, who had been head of the Kaiser's civil secretariat for the past ten years.[18] Valentini was suspected by the supreme command of sympathizing with Bethmann's plans for post-war reform. William was angered by Hindenburg's 'fatherly advice' to drop a loyal servant and stalked out of the room, slamming the door. But the war situation was too critical to risk the loss of Hindenburg and Ludendorff: if the talks at Brest-Litovsk failed, the eastern armies, already cut drastically in size, would have to march on Petrograd; moreover, Ludendorff's staff had already been working for two months in preparation for the great spring offensive, due to begin on the Western Front in eight or nine weeks' time. To lose Ludendorff would imperil the intricate timetable of successive attacks: if Hindenburg, the legendary idol, went too, then there could well be a palace revolution ending in William's abdication in favour of his eldest son. After his angry scene with Hindenburg, William retired to bed, allegedly with a bad cold, leaving the problem of Valentini's future for others to settle. The Empress and the Crown Prince were as opposed to Valentini as the supreme commanders; and when Valentini eased William's difficulties by tendering his own resignation, it was largely on Dona's insistence that the Kaiser appointed the arch-conservative Baron von Berg as his successor.

This tussle with the supreme command, and the clear evidence that his family backed the generals, emphasized once more William's social and political isolation. The ousting of Valentini rankled. Around the conference table he became fidgety, morose and discursive. He celebrated his fifty-ninth birthday, with dignified restraint, in Berlin on 27 January but set out that evening for Homburg, in the Taunus mountains, eleven miles north of Frankfurt-am-Main. Apart from two days in Munich, he remained there for six weeks, seeking benefit from the saline springs, occasionally rattling a sabre to remind his suite he was sovereign of an empire at war, but still hoping the Almighty would soon will Germany to bring peace to Europe. 'War is a disciplinary action by God to educate mankind', he explained to a deputation of Homburgers in a speech from the balcony of the schloss on Sunday, 10 February, 'Our Lord God means us to have peace, but a peace in which the world seeks to do what is right and good'.[19]

Yet this old-fashioned Protestant doctrine of obligation was at variance with popular sentiment. Five weeks previously Woodrow Wilson had delivered his 'Fourteen Points' address to Congress: already some German liberals were turning for inspiration to the prophet in Washington. Significantly the Kaiser's household had ceased taking the principal Rhenish newspaper, the *Frankfurter Zeitung*, considering it too democratic in sentiment; but William picked up some notion of what 'Wilson-ism' implied. In a rambling address to a war council at Homburg on 13 February he complained that the American president had the removal of the Hohenzollern dynasty as one of his war aims: the Entente as a whole wanted no peace with the Hohenzollerns, he maintained; a strike movement in Germany was financed by radicals in Paris; and a massive conspiracy stalked the world, with the Bolsheviks backed by Wilson, by 'international Jewry' and by the Grand Orient Lodge of the Freemasons. It was only ten weeks since Kühlmann (who was present at this war council) had told William of the Foreign Ministry funds which subsidized *Pravda*, but in his paranoic mood William conveniently forgot such embarrassing details. He now declared that if Trotsky continued to procrastinate at Brest-Litovsk, the German army must march on Petrograd and wipe out Bolshevism before it brought revolution to Germany: only a week ago a German-language broadcast from Tsarskoe Selo (of all places) had called on German troops to rise in revolt, murder the Kaiser and his chief military advisers and conclude a fraternal peace with their Russian comrades.[20]

William absented himself from the afternoon sessions of the war council: the supreme command had been told what he wanted, and he left matters in their hands. German troops resumed their advance eastwards at dawn on 18 February, pushing the line forward at thirty miles a day, like 'a victorious express train', as General Hoffmann wrote. After a week it halted, at Narva, still a hundred miles west of Petrograd. Five days later Russian delegates at Brest-Litovsk signed a treaty which cost Russia a third of her pre-war population, a third of her arable land, and nine-tenths of her coalfields. At Homburg the Kaiser celebrated with champagne, ordered flags to be flown in every German city and gave children throughout his empire a day off school.[21] With the Russian bear dead, there no longer seemed any pressing need to bury Bolshevism.

The Kaiser left Homburg on 11 March, spent three days in Berlin and then travelled to Spa, in Belgium, where headquarters were established for the offensive on the Western Front. The town was commandeered *in toto* by the German military authorities. Hindenburg and Ludendorff took over the Grand-Hotel Britannique (now a boarding school) in the Rue de la Sauvenière, but left within a few days for advanced headquarters at Avesnes, in northern France fifteen miles over the frontier. Since there was as yet no accommodation ready for William at Spa, he lived in the imperial train for over a month, visiting Avesnes and other sectors of the front in Artois and Flanders, although using Spa as a base. The tranquillity of Spa helped calm his nerves which, as he admitted, were strained by the horrors of the battlefields with their endless vista of scarred wasteland. Spa evoked a recollection of childhood, for none of the twelve thousand annual peacetime visitors to the town had left so great a mark as the British: William and his suite attended services held in the Anglican church of St Peter and St Paul on the Boulevard des Anglais; and at the end of the tramway, up in the woodland and beyond the lakes, there was even a cluster of houses marked on the Kaiser's maps with the placename 'Balmoral'. He found Spa far more attractive than Charleville.

The first wave of the great German offensive broke on 21 March 1918. Sixty-two divisions attacked along a seventy-mile front on either side of St Quentin. In the following week the Germans advanced forty miles, and William considered 'the battle won, the English utterly defeated'. The German newspapers, taking their cue from the war communiqués, called the offensive 'The Kaiser's Battle', thus encouraging the belief that William personally was directing military operations.[22] This impression, although initially bolstering the falling prestige of the monarch, rebounded against him once the prospect of imminent victory receded. The Allied armies suffered appalling casualties and photographs showed the German people streams of prisoners and captured material; but German losses were also heavy, and within three weeks both the initial offensive and the second attack (which captured Armentières) had come to a halt. At the end of May the third wave of assault took Soissons from the French, reached the Marne again and brought the Germans within forty miles of the centre of Paris. In June and July the fourth and fifth waves broke violently against defences which had been strengthened to hold back the flood. On 16 July the tide turned, and two days later Marshal Foch launched his counterstroke against the road from Soissons to Château-Thierry. The German army never again bid for victory.

Until the second week in June the Kaiser remained convinced of success. At times he seemed intoxicated by the triumph of his armies, whom he visited on more days than at any other period in the war. Often in conversation he assumed a tone of brutality calculated to convince his listeners of their master's iron resolve to crush the enemy, but his sense of humanity occasionally asserted itself: thus he insisted on having wounded English prisoners-of-war, whom he encountered in southern Flanders, properly bandaged and carried by German medical orderlies down the line. It would seem, too, as if it was in this period that he belatedly sponsored attempts to have the Russian imperial family entrusted to German care, a possibility ignored during the Brest-Litovsk talks when Germany was militarily in a far stronger position to enforce demands in the East than in the early summer of 1918.*[23] But although, in June, the Crown Princess represented her father-in-law as spending 'sleepless nights mourning over the Romanovs' fate', he seems primarily to have been worried over the evident desire of his Austrian ally for a separate peace. The absence of any convincing news from the West meant there was nothing to hearten the Emperor Charles and keep the Habsburg armies actively engaged in Italy and the Balkans. Although Kühlmann established unofficial contact with the British in The Hague, William consistently refused to interest himself in peace negotiations so long as the supreme commanders were optimistic. As late as 18 June Ludendorff was

---

* On 26 December 1917 Adolf Joffe, one of the principal Russian delegates at the Brest-Litovsk conference, gave the Austro-Hungarian foreign minister private assurances on the condition of the Tsar and his family (Czernin, *In the World War*, p. 227) but otherwise the topic did not come up during the talks. For conflicting evidence on the Kaiser's attitude to the fallen Tsar, see Summers and Mangold, *The File on the Tsar*, pp. 272–90 and pp. 386–8. The assassination of the German ambassador in Moscow, Count Mirbach, on 4 July must have hampered direct negotiations over the fate of the Romanovs at a crucial moment and may explain the confused activities of freelance would-be rescuers later in the month (ibid., pp. 286–9).

maintaining that a French collapse would come soon; but by the middle of July uneasy doubts had begun to assail Ludendorff's staunchest admirers.

Not all the public figures bubbled with Spa optimism. On 24 June Kühlmann reviewed the diplomatic situation for the benefit of Reichstag deputies: he told them not to expect 'any definite end to the war from a military decision alone'.[24] His remarks provoked an outcry at headquarters, echoing protests in the Pan-German press. Only a few months previously William considered Kühlmann a likely contender for the chancellorship when Hertling finally doddered into senility, but now William hurriedly dissociated himself from Kühlmann's alleged defeatism. When the twin paladins of the supreme command asked for his dismissal, the Kaiser gave way to them without a fight: and Künlmann was discarded under pressure, as Falkenhayn, Bethmann and Valentini had been before him. On 8 July he surrendered the Foreign Ministry to Rear-Admiral Paul von Hintze, a naval officer entrusted for many years with diplomatic responsibilities, and a one-time confidant of the fallen Tsar.

The silencing of a frank political observer like Kühlmann could not in itself bring a military decision nearer. On 22 July William drove to Hindenburg's advanced headquarters at Avesnes and there heard the field marshal admit the offensive was a failure. After dinner that evening William was sunk in deep depression: 'I am a defeated War Lord to whom you must show consideration', he told his companions at table. It was just two days since the first reports of Nicholas II's death reached the West; the awful tidings from Russia and the burden of defeat combined to rob William of repose. That night it was as if all his English and Russian relatives, every minister and general of his reign, passed before him, holding him up to scorn: only Queen Maud of Norway, the youngest sister of George v, showed any sign of goodwill. So vivid was the nightmare that William insisted next day on telling his luncheon companions about it in the prosaic surroundings of a Belgian railway station: but who among them could comprehend the confused loyalties and affections, the dismay of soul, opened up by such a night of torment? To a sensitive mind it was especially terrifying to find, not only ghosts from the past in this cavalcade, but mocking figures who were still alive. Their presence suggested he was an outcast among the kings, a crowned reprobate spurned with revulsion by those whose friendship he had once enjoyed. Already he knew that

Allied propagandists represented the hideous conflict as 'the Kaiser's war', that he stood condemned from pulpits as well as from political platforms. Now he felt the blast of anathema. The nightmare warned him that, at best, in defeat he might expect a life of solitude. On no other occasion during these months of strain did he confide his dreams to his companions; but there were at least three separate days when he seemed so wrapt in black despondency that his doctors recalled the nervous collapse after the *Daily Telegraph* affair ten years before. Did he still possess the mental vitality to force himself towards recovery, they wondered?[25]

When the allied counter-offensive freed Amiens on 8 August William accepted there was no longer hope of victory in the West. 'We have reached the limits of our capacity', he told Ludendorff. 'The war must be ended'; but not in a hurry. At a council held in Spa on 14 August he proposed that an approach should be made at a moment of German recovery, rather than of weakness; it should ensure the realization of a minimum programme of German 'war aims', notably at the expense of the Belgians. Victory had receded: but defeat was not imminent. Soon the Allied counter-offensive would lose momentum, just as Ludendorff's waves of attack had done earlier in the summer.[26] Meanwhile William determined to get away from the tension of headquarters. He travelled down to Wilhelmshohe, near Kassel, where he remained from 19 August until 9 September.

The ostensible reason for this long absence from Spa was the Empress's health, for Dona's doctors were alarmed by her cardiac condition. William insisted he had a duty to remain with his wife at such a time. In fact his own health was precarious. Continuing bad news from the Western Front so depressed him that on 2 September he took to his bed. There he remained in a state of apathetic collapse until Dona herself coaxed him up again three days later. On that Thursday (5 September) his friend Albert Ballin arrived at Wilhelmshohe hoping he could persuade William to approach President Wilson for peace talks before public opinion in America hardened against the Hohenzollern dynasty. For much of the war Ballin had been kept away from the Kaiser because his alleged Anglophilism was unacceptable to many prominent figures at court, including the Empress. The two men had not met for a private conversation since May 1917; but now Ballin came to Wilhelmshohe at the request of an emissary from Ludendorff, who believed a personal friend of the Kaiser might achieve more with him than a straight talk from his military commanders.* Ballin, however, was unsuccessful. He was asked by the Empress to make certain he treated William 'gently' and the two men were accompanied on their walk in the palace grounds by Baron von Berg, who distrusted Ballin's influence. William told Ballin he was confident that Hindenburg would stabilize the front: then, and only then, would be the moment for peace talks. Already an offer of mediation had come from Queen Wilhelmina of the Netherlands: William assured Ballin that, at the right moment, he would accept the Queen's proposed peace appeal. Ballin returned to Kassel convinced that Berg and the Empress between them were keeping William out of touch with reality.[27]

Four days later William left Wilhelmshohe and travelled to Essen. There, on 10 September, he made what he considered a fighting speech to the Krupps' workers: the present, he told them, was no time for party politics since the 'parties have failed in this war'; Germany needed cohesion and unity; and anyone spreading false rumours or circulating anti-war leaflets deserved to go to the gallows. Some members of the Kaiser's entourage were impressed, but the workers gave the speech a cool reception. A fortnight later he travelled to Kiel for a couple of days, addressing the crew of a minelayer and summoning four hundred U-boat officers to hear a fiery 'traitors to the wall' speech. It was his last attempt to fan the flame of patriotic resistance. A few hours later that Wednesday (25 September) news reached him that the Balkan front was collapsing: British troops had entered Bulgaria, red flags were out in several Bulgarian towns and King Ferdinand was sending plenipotentiaries to seek an armistice. William was left with few illusions: Bulgaria's defection would be followed by Turkey's; and Turkey's collapse by the disintegration of Austria-Hungary. Wretchedly miserable once more, he ordered his train back from Kiel to Kassel, and spent three days cosseted by the empress at Wilhelmshohe. On Saturday night (28 September) he travelled by train to Spa, where next morning Hindenburg and Ludendorff at last insisted that peace must

---

* Ludendorff sent Colonel Max Bauer to Berlin on 20 August in the hope that he could meet Ballin, but in the end contact was made by Major von Harbou through the industrialist Hugo Stinnes on 2 September (Lamar Cecil, *Albert Ballin* pp. 333–4). It is significant that the strongly anti-semitic Ludendorff should have sought the intervention on this occasion of the Kaiser's principal Jewish friend. Had Ballin succeeded in inducing William to seek peace, it would have been simple in later years for the former army leaders to place all responsibility for an armistice on 'Jews who betrayed the fighting man'.

be sought urgently.[28] But would Woodrow Wilson negotiate with an unregenerately militaristic government?

There followed a fortnight of re-adjustment, superficially a revolution from above. By 2 October the Kaiser was back in Berlin. Hertling resigned as chancellor, and William turned to the one prominent royalist liberal in the empire, Prince Max of Baden, his second cousin.[29] Reluctantly Prince Max accepted office on 3 October, thus becoming (at fifty-one) the only chancellor of William II's reign younger than the sovereign. Max insisted on constitutional changes making all ministers responsible to the Reichstag, giving the two parliamentary chambers the sole right to declare war or conclude peace, and removing the last formal vestiges of personal control by the Kaiser over the army and the navy. While this 'modernization' of the constitution was being completed, Prince Max authorized an approach to Woodrow Wilson for an armistice and for peace terms based upon his Fourteen Points speech of 8 January 1918.

By now, however, the 'Allied and Associated Powers' were unwilling to conclude any peace which fell short of full victory. In a succession of notes sent, through Swiss intermediaries, to the German Government, the Secretary of State sought to clarify President Wilson's attitude: the second note, sent on 14 October and received in Berlin a day later, reminded Prince Max that Wilson had stated in a speech at Mount Vernon on 4 July that 'the destruction of arbitrary power' was a pre-condition of peace.[30] William was incensed at this message: 'Don't you see?' he asked one of his aides-de-camp, 'The object of this is to bring down my house, to set the Monarchy aside'; and Dona, who had come back from Wilhelmshohe to join her husband in Potsdam, was righteously indignant over 'the audacity of that parvenu over the seas who has dared to humiliate a princely house in such a way'. The Kaiser assumed this was a specifically American reaction, an unwelcome gesture of democratic republicanism. He still did not understand that his tenure of the throne was imperilled by the years in which he had boasted of his personal mastery of the Reich: it was now a misfortune to possess the face that had launched a thousand bitter caricatures.[31] So ignorant was William of world opinion that, on 14 October, the day the Secretary of State despatched the second American note, he prepared a detailed memorandum, more than a thousand words long, in which he outlined for his Foreign Ministry the arguments favouring close union between Germany and Austria once the fighting was over. Although

William had written off the old Austro-Hungarian monarchy, the memorandum shows he assumed Habsburgs would still rule the new states in central Europe and that he personally would remain on the throne in Berlin.[32] Max of Baden hoped William would have the good sense to abdicate of his own volition, and the chancellor encouraged members of the Kaiser's secretariat who believed the cause of monarchy would best be served by William's departure. But although he had talked of abdication during the 'Kaiser Crisis' of 1908 and at less dramatic moments in his reign, William now rejected the idea out and out. He could not shirk his duty, he claimed. 'A successor of Frederick the Great does not abdicate', he told one of Prince Max's intermediaries on 19 October.

Some fanatics believed he had an obligation, not to abdicate, but 'to go to the front at the head of a regiment', as Admiral Scheer suggested. There was sound Hohenzollern precedent for such a gesture: 'Won't some accursed bullet finish me off?', the great Frederick had been heard to cry as his army fled towards the Oder bridges at Kunersdorf in 1759. But modern warfare was ill-suited to dynastic heroics, and William believed it was irresponsible to ask officers and men to follow him in some death-or-glory venture on the battlefield. Meanwhile at Wilhelmshaven the naval staff was preparing 'Operation-Plan 19', a project calling for a sortie by the High Seas Fleet in order to bring the British to battle off the island of Terschelling; and on 22 October the naval commanders met in conference to consider whether the Kaiser should be invited aboard the flagship for this great naval engagement.[34] Details of this conference are not known, but no invitation reached William, nor indeed was he consulted over an operational plan of which he would hardly have approved. The mere rumour of the proposed sortie led to such unrest among the ratings that the plan was abandoned on 29 October, a few hours before the battle cruisers were to have put to sea. Two days later the proposed fleet commander, Admiral von Hipper, wrote in his journal, 'Our men have rebelled. I could not have carried out the operation even if weather conditions had permitted it.'[35]

At Potsdam the Kaiser became rapidly disenchanted with Max of Baden. The chancellor was determined to show that responsibility for ending the war rested now with the government, not with the supreme command. On 26 October William agreed to the chancellor's request that Ludendorff should go: he was succeeded as First Quartermaster

General by Wilhelm Groener, a Württemberger who had shown himself to be an imaginative genius in the strategic use of railways and who knew and understood many prominent Social Democrats. But throughout the weekend of 25–27 October the Empress was at William's side, begging him to accept no more demands from Prince Max or his government. Max himself was suffering from influenza, and William refused to receive him in audience for fear of infection. In reality, the Kaiser was coming increasingly under the influence of Dona and Baron von Berg, both of whom urged him to get away from the pernicious politicking in Berlin and seek support from his field army. When, on 29 October, a message arrived from Hindenburg suggesting William should visit front-line troops, the Kaiser made up his mind. He spoke briefly to Prince Max on the telephone, declined to see him, and at eleven that night left Potsdam in the imperial train, never to return.[36]

Next morning, at Spa, he told Hindenburg, 'Prince Max's government is trying to throw me out'. Traditional loyalty continued to bind serving officers to their falling War Lord; and when, on 1 November, an emissary from the chancellor arrived at headquarters with a plea for the Kaiser to abdicate, he received a cool reception from Hindenburg and Groener. 'I wouldn't dream of abandoning the throne because of a few hundred Jews and a thousand workers', William declared. 'Tell that to your masters in Berlin.'[37] More calmly, Groener visited the capital on 5–6 November, saw Prince Max and other members of the government, and insisted that there could be no abdication while the army was in action, for he did not wish discipline to break as it had in Russia. At midday on Wednesday, 6 November, Groener met the moderate socialist leader, Ebert, and a group of trade unionists in the chancellery. Ebert proposed that William should abdicate 'today or, at the latest, by tomorrow', and entrust a Regency to one of his sons, although not the Crown Prince who was 'hated by the masses' and therefore 'impossible' in this emergency.[38] But Groener was as obdurate as his royal master. Perhaps it was too late: a telephone call from Kiel declared that mutinous sailors were on the march and prepared to take over the government. They were not a Bolshevik rabble, but no one was sure of their mood. Some, indeed, did not stay to find out: for, as William was to learn a few hours later, Grand Admiral Prince Henry had already escaped from Kiel, by the simple device of putting a red armband over his greatcoat sleeve, a red banner on his car, and driving his wife and son at high speed through a picket line of sailors.[39] Should revolution come to Spa there was no guarantee Henry's brother would be so fortunate, even if he agreed to place good sense and safety before dynastic dignity.

When Groener returned to Spa he found William favoured the drastic solution of leading his field army back into Germany and putting down mutiny and revolution wherever it raised its head. With armistice talks beginning in the forest of Compiègne and with increasing doubts over the loyalty of many units, the calmer members of the Kaiser's suite soon saw this proposal was nonsensical. Groener sounded opinion among the commanders of the forward troops, and by the morning of Saturday, 9 November, he was convinced that, for his own safety, the Kaiser should abdicate and go into exile. Hindenburg accepted the logic of Groener's arguments, but was so deeply set in feudal loyalty to his 'Most Gracious Kaiser, King and Lord' that he hesitated to advise abdication. By now, too, a deep division was noticeable between the officers of the General Staff in the Grand Hotel Brittanique and the aides and adjutants of the emperor, a mile and a half away, in the wooded parkland of the Château de la Fraineuse, where William had gone into residence. The General Staff officers were realists; the Kaiser's aides remained courtiers, still believing in their hearts that their master should hear only what it was good for him to know. It was left to Groener to tell William the truth that Saturday morning at La Fraineuse: 'The army will march home in peace and order under its leaders and commanding generals, but not under the command of Your Majesty, for it no longer stands behind Your Majesty.'[40]

Even now, the Kaiser failed to understand the situation. Groener's devastatingly calm assessment left him perplexed. He dismissed his attendants and went out into the gardens of the château, damp with an autumn mist slow to lift. Someone noticed it was still only eleven in the morning, and was surprised it was not later. The Kaiser paced up and down for nearly an hour, talking sometimes to Hindenburg, sometimes to Hintze, sometimes to one of the generals. Soon after midday the Crown Prince arrived, to strengthen – as he believed – his father's resolve. The party returned to the comparative warmth of the château. A staff-colonel, sent earlier in the morning to consult regimental commanders, confirmed Groener's gloomy predictions: Bolshevik notions were spreading rapidly through the troops. General von der Schulenburg, chief of staff to the Crown Prince, deplored such defeatist talk: all good soldiers would stand by their oath to the colours, he declared. But Groener had no patience with this make-believe optimism: 'Today oaths of loyalty have no substance' (*'Der Fahneneid ist jetzt nur eine Idee'*), Groener remarked grimly.[41]

At half-past one Kaiser and Crown Prince lunched privately. They were given no time to digest the meal. A telephone message came from Berlin: Prince Max, faced by imminent revolution, had on his own initiative announced the abdication of the Kaiser and the renunciation of the succession by his eldest son. 'Treason, gentlemen, barefaced treason', William raged, and asked Schulenburg for advice. 'Your Majesty must not yield to such an act of violence', the general replied. William reached, not for his sword, but for the weapon he used more often and more disastrously than any other monarch – the telegraph form. Reprimands, reproaches, denials and orders sped ineffectually along the wires to Berlin and Potsdam: nothing happened. Hindenburg returned to the château: he could not, he said, guarantee the Kaiser's safety, and he advised him to abdicate and proceed at once to Holland.[42] At this point, as in the last act of a drama, Admiral von Scheer came on the stage. The Kaiser suffered the bitterness of hearing that the fleet, on which he had lavished the love of a parent, could no longer be counted loyal. 'My dear admiral, the navy has left me in the lurch very nicely', William replied. But Scheer could only support Hindenburg. By five in the afternoon, William had decided to abdicate as Kaiser but not as King of Prussia, and to cross into Holland for safety.[43]

At five o'clock next morning – Sunday, 10 November – the Kaiser's train pulled out of Spa station, heading towards the Dutch frontier forty miles away. After ten minutes the train stopped at a wayside halt: William himself and seven officers of his suite clambered down and got into two large cars, leaving the train to go ahead without them, since it had to travel through Liège, where the army was said to be mutinous. The cars drove, largely along by-ways, to the Belgian-Dutch frontier north of Vise, which they reached soon after seven o'clock. Young Bavarian militiamen manned the frontier post: the senior officer in the leading car called out, 'General von Franckenberg with some officers on important business to Holland.' The guard saluted, the post was raised, and in total anonymity Kaiser William II passed into exile.[44]

14. Amerongen and Doorn

The high drama of William's final days at Spa was followed by anti-climax. No one expected the fugitives at the Dutch frontier post of Eysden, and it was eight o'clock before the first officials arrived from Maastricht, six miles away, surprised to be fetched out so early on a November Sunday. The two German cars remained at the frontier all the morning. William said little at first: he smoked an occasional cigarette and paced up and down, seeking to stimulate his circulation, for the weather was raw and it was mid-morning before a pale sun began to break the mist around the leafless trees. Across the fields church bells summoned Dutch Catholics to Mass. Otherwise everything was peaceful, a marked contrast to the frenetic bustle of the past three days.[1]

Soon after midday a Dutch major allowed the Kaiser and his escort to continue up the road to Eysden station where he was able to rejoin the imperial train which had passed through Liège and other 'mutinous' areas without any serious incidents. William lunched and dined in his restaurant car, still unsure of his destination. As the initial shock of exile receded, he became talkative: he spoke of his grandfather, of his father, and of the difficulties facing a young ruler called to manage a living institution like Bismarck. It is odd that, at such a moment, William should have talked of the statesman who had created the Reich, but he seems to have found past conflicts more congenial than his present state of limbo, for at least they had come to a definite conclusion. Not until nearly midnight was he able to relax, with news from the German minister at The Hague that Queen Wilhelmina would give him sanctuary.

Although a Dutch general had visited Spa in the previous week, there is no evidence that the authorities in the Netherlands had prepared in any way for William's coming. At two o'clock on Sunday afternoon –

while the fugitives were lunching at Eysden – Count Godard Bentinck was asked on the telephone if he could accommodate the Kaiser and his suite for three days in his seventeenth-century moated house at Amerongen. The two men had never met, although the Kaiser stayed briefly with Count Bentinck's brother while visiting the Netherlands in 1909. The count was a widower, two years older than his prospective guest, and the father of three sons and a daughter, who lived with him. He recognized that Amerongen had advantages as a place of refuge: the countryside around the small town was attractive but so off-track that the region was totally ignored in the Baedeker handbooks; and the house itself was isolated behind double moats, a natural deterrent to journalists or other unwelcome intruders. The count had no particular sympathy with the Hohenzollern dynasty but he took seriously his obligations as a Knight of St John of Jerusalem, an order of which the Kaiser was a titular commander, and it was therefore natural he should offer protection to the fallen monarch.

The imperial train left Eysden at twenty minutes past nine on Monday morning, 11 November, steaming slowly to Maastricht and on through Roermond northwards. At eleven o'clock – the mystic 'eleventh hour of the eleventh day of the eleventh month', when the Armistice brought silence to the Western Front – William was somewhere between Venlo and Nijmegen. News of the journey had become public, and curious onlookers stared from platforms, occasionally making a hostile gesture as the carriages went by. At twenty past three in the afternoon the train stopped at the small station of Maarn, twenty-five miles west of Arnhem. There, for the last time, William stepped down from his saloon coach and was received by the provincial governor of Utrecht and by Count Bentinck. From Maarn to Amerongen was a half-hour drive, and William said scarcely a word. He was tired and confused, uncertain of his standing with this Dutch nobleman, some of whose close relations by marriage had fought with the British army. The journey to Amerongen, much of it through pleasant woodland, may well have reminded William of a similar November afternoon eleven years before, when he was driven through the New Forest to stay as guest of another host he had never met, at Highcliffe; for, as the car pulled off the cobbles of Amerongen and crossed the moat, he turned contentedly to Count Bentinck and gave his first request, 'Now please, a cup of really good English tea'. With typically Dutch hospitality he was treated to flapjacks as well.[2] A few hours later, at eight o'clock, the

German party were surprised to find a full formal dinner set out for them: 'many courses and the best wine', the youngest of William's aides, Captain Sigurd von Ilsemann, recorded in his diary. Soon William was writing to Dona, in Potsdam, letting her know how much he was benefiting from the 'exquisitely kind and sympathetic' attitude of Bentinck.[3]

About the same time that the exiles were enjoying their first meal in Holland, another diarist was attending a much smaller dinner-party at 10 Downing Street, given by the British prime minister, Lloyd George. General Sir Henry Wilson found that his fellow guests were Winston Churchill and F.E.Smith, the Attorney General: they talked of the coming general election but also of the fate of Germany and its monarch; and that night Sir Henry noted in his journal, 'L.G. wants to shoot the Kaiser. Winston does not . . .'.[4] This question 'What do we do with the ex-Kaiser?' figured prominently on election platforms over the next four weeks, serving partly as a distraction from more pressing issues. Popular prejudice favoured 'hanging', with 'shooting' a minority taste. Feeling, whipped up by a sensationalist press, ran so high that even responsible statesmen such as Lord Curzon and Lord Robert Cecil believed the Kaiser should, at least, be placed on trial for war crimes. But there were some calmer voices. The foreign secretary, Balfour, and most of the diplomatic service disliked any notion of retributive justice; the American Secretary of State, the secretary to the Imperial War Cabinet, and several leading statesmen from the British overseas empire opposed any trial of vanquished by victors; and Lloyd George himself became less vindictive once polling had taken place on 14 December. Eventually, however, provision for the trial of 'the former German emperor' was included in the terms of the Treaty of Versailles: Article 227 arraigned William II 'for a supreme offence against international morality and the sanctity of treaties', and announced he would be tried by a commission of five judges, one each from France, the United Kingdom, the United States, Italy and Japan; this commission would 'fix the punishment which it considers should be imposed'. Most delegates to the Peace Conference knew this article was a dead-letter as soon as it was drafted: it was a gesture to popular indignation, to a hatred of the Kaiser fanned by four years of propaganda. Even before the end of December 1918 the Dutch Government made it clear it had no intention of handing over a ruler who had sought asylum; and the Dutch did not change their stand on this issue. Since the Dutch were not signatories of the Treaty of Versailles they had every right to refuse extradition. All they asked of William was an undertaking he would abstain from active politics so long as he remained in the Netherlands. This pledge he gave and observed.

William himself was puzzled and distressed by the intensity of hatred shown towards him: he continued to believe that in 1914 Germany was forced to go to war because of the threat from Russia; and he knew that during the war he had restrained the advocates of unrestricted U-boat attacks and had sought to define and limit the targets chosen for aerial bombardment by aircraft and Zeppelins. If he were brought to trial, he did not doubt he could defend his actions, none of which ran counter to the basic political concepts of the past two centuries. He was not alarmed by all the talk of hanging and shooting, especially during an election campaign: he had himself indulged in this type of irresponsible posturing during the earlier years of the reign. But the accusations seriously worried the Empress, who joined William at Amerongen on 28 November 1918 (the day on which he regularized the German constitutional question by formally signing an act of abdication both as Kaiser and as King of Prussia). The events of the previous two months imposed an additional strain on Dona's heart, destroying the benefits acquired from her weeks at Wilhelmshohe. Dona never liked or trusted Englishmen, Frenchmen, Italians or Americans, and she insisted that her husband's life was in danger. Momentarily, on 5 January 1920, it seemed as though her fears were justified: two American officers, on their own initiative, arrived at Amerongen that evening and claimed they had authority to escort the Kaiser to Paris. This inept and embarrassing attempt to hustle William out of the country was easily foiled by the Bentinck family, and the intruders never even reached the Kaiser's apartments. Four weeks later an American stoker, from a ship docked at Antwerp, turned up at Amerongen and demanded to see the Kaiser, or at least to speak to him on the telephone. Once more the Bentinck family handled the problem with tact. The local burgomaster and the Dutch police made certain William was adequately protected, not only from such reckless adventurers and cranks, but from the press out for a good story or a photographic scoop. But, however assured William might appear, Dona's world had tumbled, and she could find no footing on the one that took its place. Privately she was convinced that, sooner or later, 'they' would come for William, to carry him off to England or to Paris, or even to the fate that had struck down Nicholas in Russia.[5]

The Kaiser's nerves were under better control during the months he spent at Amerongen than they had been for many years. Over the winter of 1918–19 he ceased to act the autocrat: moustaches, no longer waxed or given an upward thrust by a court barber, were allowed to turn grey, and did not dominate the face; a trim beard, and white hair brushed back, softened his features. He became a more natural person, giving free rein to a charm which, in earlier years, rarely revealed itself to the public at large. Count Bentinck's good sense and tact helped defuse his belligerency. Host and guest liked each other. What had been planned as a three-day temporary asylum lengthened into an eighteen-months' visit. The Kaiser – improbable though it sounds – was a descendant of William the Silent and his third and favourite wife, Charlotte of Bourbon. So, too, was Count Bentinck; and, on his sixtieth birthday, the count presented his guest with a portrait of their common ancestor. Increasingly William emphasized the Dutch connections of his family and he was well disposed towards the people of Amerongen, who behaved with admirable discretion. Before leaving Amerongen in the spring of 1920 he presented the small town with a cottage hospital, financed out of his personal funds.

During these eighteen months at Amerongen, William began to prepare a couple of books, with assistance from visiting specialists. Partly as a reinsurance against sudden accusations, he compiled a collection of 'comparative tables', summarizing the history of Europe between 1878 and 1914 in a highly selective fashion: extracts were leaked to newspapers in The Hague and the tables appeared, in book form, in 1921. At the same time William wrote a book about Corfu, which included an account of the archaeological discoveries of 1910–11. Professor Dörpfeld was entertained at Amerongen in April 1919 and some prominent Dutch archaeologists were invited to meet him: 'The word "Gorgon" comes up in conversation about fifty times a day', noted Ilsemann in his diary on 17 April.[6] But William was not entirely escaping from the present. He followed events in Germany closely, complaining from time to time of the 'softness' with which the republican government handled left-wing opposition. In March 1920 he convinced himself, momentarily, that a restoration of the monarchy was imminent: Count Bentinck came into the garden at Amerongen on Saturday, 13 March, and told him there had been a right-wing putsch in Berlin, led by Wolfgang Kapp and General von Lüttwitz. 'The Kaiser was completely surprised and, in his excitement and joy, grasped my hand', wrote Ilsemann a couple of days later. 'He said, "Tonight we shall have champagne", just as in the war, when news arrived of a victory.' But the Kapp Putsch was a senseless premature episode: few members of the officer corps supported it; and the government of President Ebert answered the Berlin *coup* by fleeing to Stuttgart and calling a general strike. Within a week the right-wing movement collapsed and Kapp took refuge in Sweden. At Amerongen the Kaiser's companions tried to convince him of the need for patience, but he remained personally optimistic.[7] The voluntary exile of his grandfather in 1848 had lasted for only three months; and William found it hard to believe the German people would wish him to continue to live in Holland indefinitely. Yet he would not join in any conspiracy: a restoration must be at the express wish of the government in Berlin. He deplored the two abortive bids of Emperor-King Charles to recover his throne in Hungary.

Early in 1920 William purchased the moated country-house at Doorn, five miles west of Amerongen and twelve miles to the east of Utrecht. Originally 'Huis Doorn' was a fourteenth-century castle built by the Bishops of Utrecht to defend their possessions, but it was demilitarized and rebuilt in 1780 to mirror the neatly classical lucidity of the time.[8] The house lay in parkland, south of the village of Doorn, and, like Amerongen, was secure from intruders. The main entrance to the park was removed from the Utrecht-Arnhem road to the quieter Langbroekerweg, and an impressive gatehouse, traditionally Dutch in character, was built for the guards. William and Dona moved into Doorn on 15 May 1920. They were visited six days later by the Crown Prince, who had fled to the Netherlands at the time of the Armistice and was interned on an island in the Zuyder Zee as an officer serving in a belligerent army. The Crown Prince remained at Doorn for Whitsun and was joined by his youngest brother, Joachim. Unfortunately it was far from being a happy family reunion: their father was irritated by the behaviour of both sons, especially of Joachim who was by now gambling heavily. The thirty year old Prince was, like so many former officers of his generation, disillusioned by the war and its aftermath, and he felt unable to face the future with confidence. From Doorn he returned to Germany. Three weeks later he shot himself at a hunting lodge near Potsdam.[9]

The suicide of her youngest son speeded the deterioration in the Empress's health. Even before leaving Amerongen, she had been unable to walk unaided across a room. Soon she was forced to take to a wheelchair. It was (as Ilsemann writes) 'against all expectation' that she survived Christmas and the New Year and quietly celebrated her fortieth wedding anniversary in February 1921. Seven weeks later she died, with a last request she should be laid to rest 'in the homeland'.

Her body was taken by train to Germany for burial at Potsdam, but William was not permitted near the frontier – Charles's recent escapade in Hungary made the authorities sensitive over the movements of exiled emperors – and he could accompany the coffin no farther than the station at Maarn. His grief, marked by a characteristically Coburg sentimentality over material objects, deeply moved his companions and made them fear for his mental health. He had, however, been preparing his mind for Dona's death ever since the late summer of 1918 and he seemed to recover his spirits rapidly, helped by the presence of his brother Henry and his wife and by a succession of visits from his daughter, the Duchess of Brunswick. It was rare for William to be alone at Doorn for any length of time, and additional accommodation was soon constructed for the benefit of guests. Furniture, relics and books arrived from Potsdam and other palaces in Germany. He had much with which to occupy himself. A study was fitted out in the tower, with a high desk at which he would write while seated on a saddle, a practice he had followed at the Achilleion on Corfu (where visitors are still shown the Kaiser's saddle-seat). He was now working at his memoirs, a political apologia which threw the blame for disaster impartially on everyone except himself and Admiral Tirpitz, whom he regarded as the most reliable monarchist within Germany at this time.[10]

William also sought to deal with a considerable correspondence, not all of it gratifying to its recipient. Among the letters which reached him on his sixty-third birthday was an artless and respectful tribute from a German boy, the son of Prince Schoenaich-Garolath who had been killed in the war. The boy's maternal grandfather was Prince Henry XXII of Reuss, a vassal sovereign of William as King of Prussia for the first fourteen years of his reign. William knew the family, and its background. He invited the boy to come with his mother, Princess Hermine, to visit him. The Princess (who had been one of Dona's many godchildren) was dark, vivacious and strong-willed, a thirty-four year old mother of five. She arrived at Doorn, without her son, on 9 June 1922. The Kaiser enjoyed her company and found her attractive.

By the end of the summer he was resolved to marry her, even if the more conservative monarchists and some of his children disapproved. The marriage took place on 5 November 1922, with journalists and photographers jostling in every village from Utrecht to Amerongen. 'Hermo', as William called his second wife, was totally different in character from the placid Dona. She seemed to some members of the exiled court a disruptive influence, although by now they had become so set in their ways that they would have resented any intruder. She was sufficiently young and active to create a home for the Kaiser, not merely a museum. As William himself wrote in a private letter that winter, Hermine brought 'sunshine into this house of darkness, sorrow and mourning'.[11]

He was acquiring, if not serenity, then at least patience. Hermine shared his enthusiasm for the gardens at Doorn, for roses and rhododendrons: a 'rosarium' was completed in 1928; a 'pinetum', with an extensive and unusual collection of conifers, followed six years later. William enjoyed drives in the wooded countryside around Doorn, although he rarely ventured far from home. In May 1923 he made a fifty-mile round trip to admire the fruit blossom in the Betuwe district, but he would not go to the tulip fields at Haarlem. There was always a risk of hostile demonstrations should he be recognized by tourists visiting Holland, and he did not wish to embarrass the Dutch authorities by seeking permission to drive into other provinces, where his presence would pose new problems of policing and security.[12] Hermine, on the other hand, could still move freely in the Netherlands and in Germany as well. She stayed in Berlin, visited Crown Prince Rupert of Bavaria at Berchtesgaden and, in October 1924, was a guest of Hindenburg in Hanover. This call on the seventy-seven year old field marshal was seen by the Kaiser's six military adjutants at Doorn as a mission of reconciliation. William was convinced he had been hustled into exile in 1918 by Hindenburg in order to avoid civil war and he resented the way in which the field marshal then made his peace with the German Republic. As Spa faded into the background, William forgot the concern of the staff officers that he might fall into the hands of mutinous troops or suffer the fate of the Tsar; and he treated the field marshal coldly. Hermine's visit to Hanover eased the tension, but William remained jealous of the old man's legendary reputation. When Hindenburg was elected German President in the spring of 1925 and received in triumph by the people of Berlin, the Kaiser pointedly remained silent in front of his military suite. He preferred, at that moment, to busy himself with a first draft of memoirs from his earliest days. The army, which had despised the republic, now had as president a supreme commander whom it could respect both for his wartime victories and for keeping the troops together in November 1918. So long as Hindenburg was in office there was no likelihood of a joint monarchist and militarist putsch against the republic.[13]

To many writers and political commentators, the Kaiser's Germany lay in the past; and William had the curious experience of observing historians passing judgement on him, as though he were already in the grave. Official collections of diplomatic documents, histories, memoirs were read and annotated by him, and he provided several writers with material for their detailed studies. His prejudices remained unchanged, although in retrospect he judged Bismarck less harshly than in earlier years. He could find little to the credit of Kiderlen-Waechter, Bülow or Holstein; he still insisted that Edward VII sought 'encirclement' and that Sir Edward Grey had 'engineered the war'; his great regret was the rejection of the Björkö Treaty which would (so he wrote) have enabled Germany to lead the continent 'as a guardian of peace with no wish for conquest'. Attempts to explain his behaviour in psychological terms did not impress him. 'It is only possible to interpret the impulses of this wayward and intelligent monarch by referring them to the strange psychic abscess produced by his love–hate for England', wrote Harold Nicolson. 'Hand the gentleman a glass of water!' William commented wryly in the margin. 'He would prove to England that she owed her continued existence solely to his own Imperial chivalry and love' (Nicolson): 'Such elementary nonsense, thank Heaven, never entered my mind!' (William).[14] Like most monarchs hustled into exile, he remained disinclined to acknowledge publicly faults in his character or in his past actions. On the other hand his religious convictions were strengthened rather than diminished by misfortune. He read a form of morning prayer each day to his household, assembled in the entrance hall of Huis Doorn, and he spent more and more time in private prayer and meditation. No one can tell if he thus gained an inner tranquillity.

These last ten years of his life were, however, overshadowed not by the symbols of traditional faith but by the crooked cross of Nazism. William's attitude towards Hitler's movement was clear, if not always consistent. He approved of its basically patriotic enthusiasm: he was disgusted by racial persecution, and deplored the pagan nihilism of

Hitler's pseudo-philosophy. At first it was the nationalistic element in
the movement that attracted his attention and he appears to have
believed, with the Crown Prince, that a Nazi triumph would bring him
back to the throne. This was certainly the impression given, both to
William and to Hermine, by Hermann Goering, who was invited to
stay at Doorn in January 1931 and again in May 1932. The Kaiser liked
Goering, whom he had decorated with the *Pour le Merité* as an air ace
during the war. It is probable that Goering's patronage of the monarchy was prompted by the knowledge that Heinrich Brüning (German
chancellor from March 1930 until June 1932) favoured the re-
establishment of the empire, with Hindenburg proclaimed Regent for a
grandson of the Kaiser. Both William and the Crown Prince believed
their personal prospects were better with Goering than with Brüning
and the ageing Hindenburg. This was the greatest error of judgement
committed by the Kaiser during his years of exile: the Nazis were
radical revolutionaries of the Right, not conservatives. Once in power
Hitler had no use for the monarchists, while William himself had to
behave circumspectly, since his former guest, Goering, controlled the
amount of annual allowance permitted to leave Germany from the
revenue of the old royal domains in Prussia; and Goering's generous
nature seemed, nowadays, readily to take offence.[15]

On 1 August 1934 President Hindenburg died. The Nazis acted
quickly, settling the problem of the headship of state while the monarchists within the officers corps were still discussing ways of bringing
about a restoration. Hitler proclaimed the amalgamation of the presidency and the chancellorship. Less than twenty-four hours after Hindenburg's death, Hitler received oaths of allegiance from the commanding officers of the armed forces. At last William recognized he
would probably end his days in exile. The prospect troubled him much
less than in the early twenties. He was happy enough at Doorn: the
villagers treated their mildly eccentric squire with amiable tolerance,
doffing hats to him as he strolled through the parkland on a summer
evening, straw boater sloping gently to the right, white spats showing
beneath narrow trousers and carrying an ebony cane which he would
hook over his left arm if he stopped for a few moments of conversation.
In winter months he was patron of the *Doorner Arbeitsgemeinschaft*
('Doorn Study Circle') to whom he gave erudite papers on archaeology,
primitive forms of transport, and kindred subjects. Once, in 1934, he
spoke on eastern symbolism: the swastika, so he told his audience,

could have its upper beam pointing to the right and representing 'summer, fame, fortune, or wealth', but if it pointed to the left (as in Hitler's flag) it stood for 'darkness, death and misfortune'.[16] He was also, by now, reading lighter books: he enjoyed P. G. Wodehouse, and his library shelves include such unexpected works as a collection of short stories by Dorothy Sayers and an early Ellery Queen. Throughout the thirties he particularly delighted in private film shows, many of which tended to feature historical epics: he admired Herbert Wilcox's *Victoria the Great* so much that he ordered one of his suite to send a message of congratulation to the director on the convincing manner in which Anna Neagle had brought his grandmother to life on a cinema screen.[17] More and more he inclined to bitter-sweet recollections of childhood and youth: there were around him at Doorn so many treasured trophies from the past – an ornate ink-stand from his English grandmamma; the Queen's Cup he had won at Cowes; silver and snuff-boxes from Potsdam; a carpet presented by the Sultan when first he visited Constantinople; eighteenth-century dining chairs from the Marble Palace; a portrait of Queen Louise which was a favourite of her son, his grandfather, William I; and military and naval insignia accumulated in thirty years of 'fishing for uniforms''. Perhaps because he never saw Doorn until after the great crises of his life were over, memory conjured up only benign ghosts from the past: 'scoundrels' – and his table talk was peppered with them – remained imprecisely etched in some distant limbo.

Yet William's life was not to end in soft twilight. By 1938 he had come to fear that war was again imminent. He was so relieved at the Munich settlement that he wrote to George V's widow, Queen Mary, in London assuring her of his wish to 'unite my warmest sincerest thanks to the Lord with yours and those of the German and British people that He saved us from a most fearful catastrophe'.[18] A direct link was thus restored with the British royal family, who had already in 1934 welcomed his daughter, the Duchess of Brunswick, back to London and who had entertained two of the Crown Prince's sons. When George V had died, in January 1936, the Kaiser ordered his senior aide-de-camp to go to Berlin and offer his condolences to the British ambassador, at the same time asking that he should be represented at his cousin's funeral. King Edward VIII suggested that the Crown Prince might attend the funeral, but the Foreign Office thought it advisable for the House of Hohenzollern to be represented by a less controversial figure, the Crown Prince's fourth son, Prince Frederick, who had been received by George v at Cowes.[19] These, largely informal, dynastic contacts were maintained until the German invasion of the Netherlands. On the Kaiser's eightieth birthday, in January 1939, he was pleased to receive telegrams of congratulation and good wishes from King George vi and other members of the British royal family.

By now the British Foreign Office was taking an interest in the Kaiser again, although behaving with caution and circumspection. In February 1938 senior officials in Whitehall learnt, from two sources, of a plot which they reported as originating with the former Lord Mayor of Leipzig, Carl Goerdeler: there would be a naval putsch at Kiel, with a warship broadcasting a recorded message from the Kaiser in which he would call on royalists to support one of his grandsons in restoring sane government to Germany. Later in the year Major Ewald von Kleist came secretly to England, met Winston Churchill at Chartwell and told him that a group of generals were hoping to establish a new government in Berlin 'probably of a Monarchist character'.[10] It is unlikely either of these projects was known to the Kaiser in Doorn, but the old man – and his sons – were becoming increasingly hostile to the Nazi movement. William was deeply shocked by the anti-Jewish pogrom in November 1938, which he condemned privately as 'an infamous blot' on Germany's reputation. The Foreign Office was excited by an alleged interview, which appeared in an American magazine and was reported in the *Daily Telegraph* on 8 December: in it William damned the Nazi regime squarely. But two days later a statement from Doorn insisted that the interview was a fabrication and that William always observed a public silence over current political questions. It was presumably for this reason that the Foreign Office showed no enthusiasm for a proposal made by Mr John Boyd-Carpenter – whose family had been known to the Kaiser in pre-war days – that he should visit Doorn and obtain a declaration from William intended to ease the general tension in Europe.[21]

In the third week of August 1939 the Kaiser received two eminent British writers, closely connected with the Foreign Office: the former 'secret agent' in Petrograd and Moscow, Mr R. (later Sir Robert) Bruce Lockhart, and Mr J.W. (later Sir John) Wheeler-Bennett. Since Sir John was planning to write a biography of the Kaiser, conversation was mainly concerned with the past, but his guests noted with interest their host's spryness and his cautiously phrased hostility to the Nazi system.

There no longer seemed to him any possibility of avoiding a second world war for he felt Hitler was by now the slave, rather than the master, of events: 'The machine is running away with *him* as it ran away with *me*', William remarked on 27 August.[22]

War followed before the end of the following week, and soon William learnt that the eldest child of his fifth son, Prince Oscar, had been killed fighting as an infantry lieutenant in Poland. William's loyalties were divided: he felt events as a German, but he was also conscious that the war menaced the whole future of his court-in-exile at Doorn and that he owed a debt to the Netherlands, which had afforded him sanctuary. His actions reflected his uncertainty. He sent a message to Hitler, through the German ambassador at The Hague, expressing relief that the Führer had survived an alleged assassination plot in Munich on 8 November; and he also sent a telegram of condolence to Queen Wilhelmina when, ten days later, the Dutch steamer, *Simon Bolivar*, was sunk in the North Sea. Privately, between October 1939 and January 1940, William arranged for two-thirds of his personal funds to be transferred for safe keeping to Switzerland. Equally privately, in the second week of November 1939, the British ambassador in The Hague was told that, should the future of the Kaiser be raised in conversation by the Dutch authorities, he was to seek to have him transferred to Sweden or Denmark, and 'only in the last resort to the United Kingdom'.[23]

At 3.30 in the morning of Friday, 10 May 1940, the sound of gunfire was heard in Doorn, as hundreds of German planes seemed to be following the line of the river Waal, down to Rotterdam. Three and a half hours later the local Dutch commandant sent word that, as German troops had crossed the frontier, the Kaiser and his suite were to consider themselves interned. It was a day of drama. In London Churchill succeeded Chamberlain as prime minister: a message was sent on Admiralty notepaper to the Foreign Office, 'Mr Churchill wonders whether it would not be a good thing to give the ex-Kaiser a private hint that he would be received with consideration and dignity in England should he desire to seek asylum here.'[24] The Foreign Office staff were hesitant, but were told that 'Mr Churchill feels strongly on the subject'. The proposal was approved both by the foreign secretary (Lord Halifax) and by King George VI, who wondered where the Kaiser could best be accommodated. Churchill's proposal was telegraphed to the ambassador in The Hague at 5.15 pm on 11 May. Only after the offer was made were there strongly hostile reactions in Whitehall: 'I cannot for the life of me see why the old architect of evil should be allowed to come here', wrote Sir Robert Vansittart in a brief memorandum. 'Many people will object to it very strongly, and rightly.'

He need not have worried. The Kaiser was unlikely to have accepted Churchill's offer. It was conveyed to him on Sunday afternoon by the Burgomaster of Doorn, Baron van Nagell: if he accepted the offer, William would be flown out, with Princess Hermine, in an RAF plane which would land in Holland in a matter of hours. The proposal was not turned down out of hand. William asked for some time to reflect upon it, for it was a decision almost as grave as the one he had faced at Spa. He could not believe that the British regarded him as anything but an enemy, and they had indeed interned one of his grandsons. Twelve members of his family were serving with the German army: he did not wish to appear a traitor to them, even though he detested the swastika flag and all it stood for. It seemed extraordinary to involve a man of eighty-one, who had never flown in an aeroplane, in so uncertain an escapade. At 6.51 on the evening of 12 May the Foreign Office received a reply from the ambassador in The Hague: 'Offer of asylum gratefully declined.' Thirty-six hours later units of the German 207th infantry division entered Doorn.

The Kaiser told Ilsemann that the British offer of asylum was merely a ruse to involve him in a game of 'political chess' with Germany. Later, he was still more outspoken to his daughter, the Duchess of Brunswick: 'A piece of impudence, a propaganda move by Churchill', he said. 'You can imagine my answer'.[25] Yet it is difficult to assess his true reactions. He knew he was surrounded by Nazi spies and had become a hostage to Hitler's fate. Naturally he did not wish it thought he had been in contact with the British prime minister. Moreover, along with many anti-Nazi Germans that summer, he was deeply stirred by the rapid victory in France, especially since his eldest grandson was mortally wounded at Valenciennes in the first thrust towards the old battle zone in Artois and Picardy. On 17 June, three days after German troops entered Paris, the Kaiser telegraphed his congratulations directly to Hitler: he quoted the message sent by his grandfather, William I, in 1870, *Welch eine Wendung durch Gottes Fügung* ('Through God's merciful dispensation, what a change of fortune'), and the words of the great Lutheran chorale, *Nun danket alle Gott* ('Now thank we all our God').[26] This was the language of a lost generation, not of the Third Reich; but it sincerely caught William's mood. Several writers have maintained the telegram was the work of Nazi sympathizers around the exiled Kaiser, not of William himself. This, however, is improbable. Too much of his life had been spent in thinking of a 'march on Paris' for him to remain silent. These events touched deep emotions within him. 'The German war flag over Versailles', he wrote exultantly to the Duchess of Brunswick. 'Thus is the pernicious entente cordiale of Uncle Edward VII brought to nought.'[27]

For the final twelve months of William's life German troops mounted guard at Doorn and he was saluted by a generation who had been taught that the last Hohenzollern sovereign had 'meant well for Germany', but failed her at the crucial hour. To some extent, the chameleon quality of his character asserted itself yet again: the eccentric Dutch squire faded, and the fallen German war lord stood out more sharply against the campaign maps on the wall. He had pledged himself to help, if he could, the Dutch people who had befriended him; and he was photographed bare-headed and in silent prayer beside the graves of fallen soldiers from both armies. Yet there was, in reality, nothing he could do except listen and observe. He was worried next spring over the fate of his granddaughter, Crown Princess Frederika of Greece, forced to seek safety with her young children, Sophia and Constantine, from German panzer divisions sweeping down on Athens from Macedonia. Frederika's portrait was beside his bed, and yet he followed with professional interest the route of Field Marshal List's army to Thermopylae and beyond. By now, however, all realized his health was failing: the heart was erratic and, in the last week of May, his doctors suspected he was suffering from pneumonia. He rallied, but not for long. By the first days of June it was clear his thoughts were not always in the present. The Duchess of Brunswick and other members of the family gathered at Doorn. 'Without England, Germany cannot survive', his daughter heard him say.[28] But which England? And whose Germany?

He died on the morning of 4 June 1941. Nine years before, at Christmas 1933, he had prepared elaborate instructions for his burial: if he returned to Germany, he was to be interred in the mausoleum at Potsdam, but if he died in exile, he wished his body entombed within his estate at Doorn. In neither case was there to be any display of swastika flags. William's wishes were observed so far as possible, although the hated symbol appeared on a wreath from Hitler and, in miniature, on the uniforms of certain officers. On 9 June detachments from the German army and navy, and from the Luftwaffe, mounted a last parade for the war lord who had once been All-Highest. Princess Hermine, the Crown Prince and his surviving brothers, the Duchess of Brunswick, several grandsons and dignitaries from all over Germany followed a slow-moving motor hearse from Huis Doorn to a small chapel near the main entrance of the park. There his body was to rest until the construction of a mausoleum, north of the main house. It was a dignified ceremony, strangely lacking in pomp. No funeral oration; no tolling of cathedral bells; no sombre music, only a chorale and the sound of the Yorck March as the guard of honour marched away; no minute guns, only a volley fired by riflemen as a final salute.[29]

One incident that Monday remained in everyone's memory: the ninety-one-year-old Field Marshal von Mackensen, wearing orders and ribbons dating back to 1870, had travelled to Doorn to honour his imperial master for the last time. Supported by his sword, he knelt unaided beside the catafalque, silent in prayer. It was noticed he was in tears. Was he weeping for the empire he had seen created and destroyed, or for a life of promise which never expanded into greatness? There was no one else present who could remember that accession proclamation in the summer of 1888: 'We are bound to each other – I and the army – we are born for each other, and we shall hold together indissolubly whether it be God's will to send us calm or storm.' William's tragedy was to have been 'bound', not merely to an army which cast him aside, but to an inherited system of government which sought to impress the people without winning their hearts. The forced aggression of his personality hid an artificial character, cut to size and shape by Hinzpeter's style of education. He was not the inspired leader of the Reich, but a mirror of Germany's strength and weakness. Long ago Edward VII described his nephew as 'the most brilliant failure in history'. It was a cruel anticipatory epitaph. Unfortunately, for William and for Europe, it proved to be tragically apt.

The Kaiser's Europe

Frontiers of July 1914 ‗ ‗ ‗ ‗ ‗

kö
etersburg

erg

RUSSIA

ovsk

RIA-HUNGARY

RUMANIA

BLACK SEA

Bucharest

evo

Belgrade

BULGARIA

Constantinople

ZE

SERBIA

Sofia

NA

MONTENEGRO

TURKEY

LBANIA

GREECE

AEGEAN

Corfu

Athens

CYPRUS

Damascus

CRETE

Jerusalem

ERRANEAN SEA

EGYPT

LIBYA

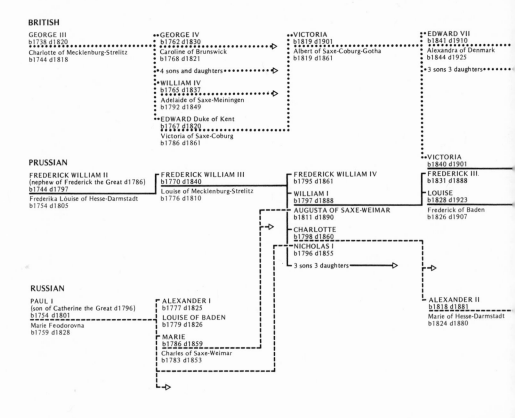

BRITISH

GEORGE III
b1738 d1820
Charlotte of Mecklenburg-Strelitz
b1744 d1818

GEORGE IV
b1762 d1830
Caroline of Brunswick
b1768 d1821

4 sons and daughters

WILLIAM IV
b1765 d1837
Adelaide of Saxe-Meiningen
b1792 d1849

EDWARD Duke of Kent
b1767 d1820
Victoria of Saxe-Coburg
b1786 d1861

VICTORIA
b1819 d1901
Albert of Saxe-Coburg-Gotha
b1819 d1861

EDWARD VII
b1841 d1910
Alexandra of Denmark
b1844 d1925

3 sons 3 daughters

VICTORIA
b1840 d1901

PRUSSIAN

FREDERICK WILLIAM II
(nephew of Frederick the Great d1786)
b1744 d1797
Frederika Lóuise of Hesse-Darmstadt
b1754 d1805

FREDERICK WILLIAM III
b1770 d1840
Louise of Mecklenburg-Strelitz
b1776 d1810

FREDERICK WILLIAM IV
b1795 d1861

WILLIAM I
b1797 d1888
AUGUSTA OF SAXE-WEIMAR
b1811 d1890

CHARLOTTE
b1798 d1860

NICHOLAS I
b1796 d1855

3 sons 3 daughters

FREDERICK III.
b1831 d1888

LOUISE
b1828 d1923
Frederick of Baden
b1826 d1907

RUSSIAN

PAUL I
(son of Catherine the Great d1796)
b1754 d1801
Marie Feodorovna
b1759 d1828

ALEXANDER I
b1777 d1825
LOUISE OF BADEN
b1779 d1826

MARIE
b1786 d1859
Charles of Saxe-Weimar
b1783 d1853

ALEXANDER II
b1818 d1881
Marie of Hesse-Darmstadt
b1824 d1880

The Kaiser's Family Tree

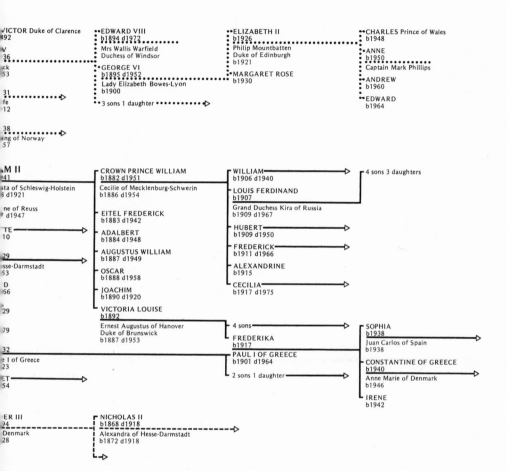

VICTOR Duke of Clarence
892

IV
36

ck
53

31
fe
12

38
ing of Norway
57

•• EDWARD VIII
b1894 d1972
Mrs Wallis Warfield
Duchess of Windsor

• GEORGE VI
b1895 d1952
Lady Elizabeth Bowes-Lyon
b1900

•• 3 sons 1 daughter

•• ELIZABETH II
b1926
Philip Mountbatten
Duke of Edinburgh
b1921

• MARGARET ROSE
b1930

•• CHARLES Prince of Wales
b1948

• ANNE
b1950
Captain Mark Phillips

•• ANDREW
b1960

•• EDWARD
b1964

M II
41

sta of Schleswig-Holstein
d1921

ne of Reuss
d1947

TE
10

29
sse-Darmstadt
53

D
66

29

79

32
e I of Greece
23

ET
54

CROWN PRINCE WILLIAM
b1882 d1951
Cecilie of Mecklenburg-Schwerin
b1886 d1954

EITEL FREDERICK
b1883 d1942

ADALBERT
b1884 d1948

AUGUSTUS WILLIAM
b1887 d1949

OSCAR
b1888 d1958

JOACHIM
b1890 d1920

VICTORIA LOUISE
b1892
Ernest Augustus of Hanover
Duke of Brunswick
b1887 d1953

WILLIAM
b1906 d1940

LOUIS FERDINAND
b1907
Grand Duchess Kira of Russia
b1909 d1967

HUBERT
b1909 d1950

FREDERICK
b1911 d1966

ALEXANDRINE
b1915

CECILIA
b1917 d1975

4 sons

FREDERIKA
b1917

PAUL I OF GREECE
b1901 d1964

2 sons 1 daughter

4 sons 3 daughters

SOPHIA
b1938
Juan Carlos of Spain
b1938

CONSTANTINE OF GREECE
b1940
Anne Marie of Denmark
b1946

IRENE
b1942

ER III
94
Denmark
28

NICHOLAS II
b1868 d1918
Alexandra of Hesse-Darmstadt
b1872 d1918

231

Reference Notes

Fuller details of books and articles in this reference section will be found in the List of Sources. I have used the following abbreviations:

AHR: *American Historical Review*

Albertini, *Origins*: L.Albertini, *The Origins of the War of 1914*

BD: *British Documents on the Origins of War*

CEH: *Central European History* (periodical)

DD: *Die Deutschen Dokumente zum Kriegsausbruch*

Eckardstein: H.von Eckardstein, *Lebenserinnerungen und politische Denkwürdigkeiten*

EL: Wilhelm II, *My Early Life*

FO: Foreign Office Correspondence

Geiss: Imanuel Geiss, *July 1914*

GP: *Die Grosse Politik der Europäischen Kabinette*

Grant, *Letters*: N.F.Grant (ed.), *The Kaiser's Letters to the Tsar*

GW: *Die Gesammelten Werke Bismarcks*

Haller: J Haller, *Philip Eulenburg, the Kaiser's Friend*

Herwig: H.H.Herwig, *The German Naval Officer Corps*

Hohenlohe, Denk.: Hohenlohe, *Denkwurdigkeiten der Reichskanzlerzeit*

HJ: *Historical Journal*

HP: *The Holstein Papers*, ed. Norman Rich and M.H.Fisher

HZ: *Historische Zeitschrift* (periodical)

Ilsemann: S. von Ilsemann, *Der Kaiser in Holland*

JCH: *Journal of Contemporary History*

K. on N.: the Kaiser's marginal comments in a copy of Harold Nicolson's *Die Verschwörung der Diplomaten*

LEF: *Letters of the Empress Frederick*, ed. Sir F.Ponsonby

MK: German Marinekabinette archives

O-UA: *Oesterreich-Ungarns Aussenpolitik von der Bosnischen Krise 1908 bis zum Kriegsausbruch 1914*

PRO: Public Record Office

REFERENCE NOTES

QVL: Queen Victoria, *Letters*
Ritter, *S and S*: G.Ritter, *The Sword and the Sceptre*
SP: Salisbury Papers
Spitzemberg: *Das Tagebuch der Baronin Spitzemberg*, ed. R. Vierhaus
Waldersee, *Denk.*: A. von Waldersee, *Denkwurdigkeiten*

Chapter 1   THUS WIN ALL MEN'S APPLAUSE

1 Details of William's birth: Wheeler-Bennett, *A Wreath to Clio*, pp. 167–8; Corti, *Wenn*, pp. 84–5; *The Times*, 28 January 1859; *The Illustrated London News*, 4 February 1859; Queen Victoria to King Leopold, 2 February 1859, *QVL*, series 1, volume III, pp. 313–14; Viktoria Luise, *Ein Leben als Tochter des Kaisers*, p. 35; Paget, *Embassies of Other Days*, pp. 109–10; Zentler, *Kaiserliche Zeiten*, p. 10; House of Commons debates, 3 February 1859: Hansard, Third Series, CLII, p. 59 and p. 71.
2 *EL*, p. 22; Daphne Bennett, *Vicky*, pp. 85–7.
3 Crown Princess to Queen Victoria, 2 May 1859, quoted from the Royal Archives by Cecil Woodham-Smith, *Queen Victoria 1819–1861*, p. 396. For further medical details, cf. Kurtz, *The Second Reich*, p. 11; Crown Princess to Queen Victoria, 12 December 1859, Fulford, *Dearest Child*, p. 224.
4 Queen Victoria to Crown Princess, 25 February 1859, ibid., p. 163; *LEF*, pp. 20–1; Corti, *Wenn*, p. 86; Queen Victoria to King Leopold, 1 March, *QVL*, series 1, volume III, p. 324.
5 Prince Consort to Crown Prince, 9 March 1859, Corti, *Wenn*, p. 86.
6 The opening sentence of William II's *My Early Life* (*EL*, p. 1) refers to Osborne. See also Woodham Smith, op. cit., p. 398; *LEF*, p. 24.
7 Queen Victoria to Crown Princess, 1 April 1865, Fulford, *Dearest Mama*, p. 189.
8 *EL*, p. 1; Queen Victoria to Crown Princess, 27 January 1865, Fulford, *Your Dear Letter*, p. 16.
9 Crown Princess to Queen Victoria, 26 January 1863, Fulford, *Dearest Mama*, p. 168.
10 *EL*, pp. 2–3.

Chapter 2   HINZPETER'S PUPIL

1 Crown Princess to Queen Victoria, 17 August 1866, Fulford, *Your Dear Letter*, p. 92; Bennett, *Vicky*, pp. 140–1.
2 The same to the same, 10 December 1866, Fulford, op. cit., pp. 111–12; Ramm, *Morier*, p. 7.
3 William on Hinzpeter, *EL*, pp. 17–24: Hinzpeter on William, Hinzpeter, *Der Kaiser*, pp. 2–14.
4 *EL*, pp. 50–1.

5 Bigelow, *Prussian Memories*, pp. 39, 45 and 48: *EL*, pp. 28–30.

6 Crown Princess to Queen Victoria, 6 January, 9, 22 and 30 April 1873, Fulford, *Darling Child*, pp. 73, 85, 88–9; *EL*, pp. 71–3.

7 For Kassel, ibid, pp. 97–115 (remark on Eton schoolboys, p. 108).

8 Queen Sophie's comments, cited by Theo Aronson, *The Kaisers*, pp. 106–7.

9 *EL*, pp. 117–18.

10 *LEF*, pp. 174–5; Fulford, *Darling Child*, pp. 237–9.

11 Corti, *Wenn*, p. 140.

12 Lee, *King Edward VII*, I, p. 424.

13 *EL*, pp. 127–41.

14 Ibid., pp. 143–4 (Ilfracombe), p. 146 (Paris), p. 209 (Disraeli) and pp. 209–10 (cricket). Comment on purchase of Suez Canal shares, Fulford, *Darling Child*, pp. 199–200.

15 Hough, *Louis and Victoria*, pp. 53 and 55; *EL*, pp. 137–8; M.Buchanan, *Queen Victoria's Relations*, pp. 13 and 94–5.

16 *LEF*, pp. 176–81; *EL*, pp. 183–5.

17 *LEF*, p. 179; Hinzpeter's comments, Dorpalem article, *AHR*, 58, p. 20; Waldersee, *Denk.*, I, p. 129.

18 *LEF*, pp. 183–4; Keller, *40 Jahre in Dienst der Kaiserin*, p. 22; Kürenberg, *War Alles Falsch?*, pp. 56–7.

Chapter 3   PRINCE OF THE MARBLE PALACE

1 Corti, *Wenn*, p. 355; *EL*, pp. 175–7.

2 *EL*, p. 201.

3 Crown Prince to Bismarck, 28 September 1886, *GW*, xv, pp. 455–6.

4 *EL*, pp. 211 and 308–13.

5 Ibid., pp. 245–52 and 310–25: Prince William to Tsar Alexander III, 25 May and 19 June, 1884, *Krasny Arkhiv*, II, pp. 120 and 124.

6 Corti, *Alexander of Battenberg*, pp. 263, 265, 278–9, 286–8 and 292.

7 Crown Princess to Queen Victoria, 22 April 1887, *LEF*, p. 215.

8 *EL*, pp. 189–96; on Chelius, see also William's high praise of him to Tsar Nicholas II, 26 February 1914, Grant, *Letters*, pp. 280–8.

9 The most judicious assessment of Eulenburg's personality and influence is contained in the introduction to Dr Röhl's splendidly edited *Philipp Eulenburgs Politische Korrespondenz*, I, pp. 9–52.

10 Herbert Bismarck to Eulenburg, 11 August 1886, Haller, I, p. 31. The Englishwoman who remembered Eulenburg's 'quiet, soft, subtle voice' was one of Princess Victoria Louise's governesses, Miss Anne Topham: see her *Memories of the Kaiser's Court*, pp. 195–6.

11 Harden, *Köpfe*, pp. 169–70: Röhl, op. cit., pp. 194–5.

12 Holstein's diary, *HP*, II, p. 343.

13 Ibid., I, pp. 137–9: Waldersee, *Denk.*, I, pp. 339, 343–6, 348, 353–4: Palmer, *Bismarck*, p. 237.

14 Lucius von Ballhausen, *Bismarck-Erinnerungen*, p. 413; Crown Princess to Queen Victoria, 2 June 1887, *LEF*, p. 238

15 *EL*, pp. 213–17 (quotation taken from p. 217); *QVL*, series 3, volume I, pp. 320–3; letter to Holstein from one of the Crown Princess's ladies-in-waiting, 26 July 1897, *HP*, III, p. 219.

16 Crown Princess to Queen Victoria, 14 September 1887, *LEF*, p. 245.

17 The same to the same, 15 and 21 November, 1887, ibid, pp. 256–7 and 262–3: A. Ponsonby, *Henry Ponsonby*, p. 291; *EL*, pp. 281–3 and 326.

18 Corti, *Wenn*, p. 478; *EL*, pp. 295–6.

19 Palmer, op. cit., pp. 240–2.

20 Bennett, *Vicky*, pp. 262–6; Corti, *Wenn*, pp. 480–2 and 529–39; *LEF*, pp. 314–21; Waldersee, *Denk.*, I, p. 404; Kürenberg, op. cit., p. 88.

Chapter 4   CHANCELLOR AND KAISER

1 William II, *Speeches*, p. 5: Waldersee, *Denk.*, I, p. 405; Paget, *Embassies of Other Days*, II, p. 452; Spitzemberg, p. 253.

2 Nichols, *Germany after Bismarck*, p. 31: Palmer, *Bismarck*, pp. 242–3.

3 Kiderlen-Waechter to Holstein, 19 July, 1888, *HP*, III, p. 282.

4 Magnus, *Edward VII*, p. 211, quoting Queen Victoria to Salisbury, 15 October 1888: Gwendolen Cecil, *Salisbury*, IV, pp. 366–7.

5 William II to Malet (forwarded to the Queen), 14 June 1889, *QVL*, series 3, volume I, p. 504. For William's subsequent visit to Cowes, see ibid, pp. 520–2.

6 William II to Queen Victoria, 17 August, 9 and 30 October, 1889, ibid., pp. 526, 530, 532–3; Magnus, op. cit., pp. 215–16; Marder, *British Naval Policy*, p. 149.

7 Queen's Journal, 9 August 1889, *QVL*, series 3, volume I, p. 523: Rich, *Holstein*, I, p. 246: Holstein to Radolin, 28 November 1889, *HP*, III, p. 323.

8 Eulenburg to William II, 24 September 1889, Röhl, *Eulenburgs Politische Korrespondenz*, I, no. 234, p. 350: Haller, I, p. 201.

9 Palmer, op. cit., pp. 245–6.

10 Ibid., p. 247: Nichols, *Germany after Bismarck*, p. 13: Lucius, *Bismarck-Errinerungen*, p. 496.

11 Rich, *Holstein*, I, pp. 250–4: Röhl, *Germany without Bismarck*, p. 33.

12 Röhl article on the Disintegration of the *Kartell*, HJ, IX, pp. 81–6.

13 *GW*, XV, pp. 491–4: Palmer, op. cit., pp. 251–2.

14 Röhl, *Germany without Bismarck*, pp. 41–2; Holstein to Eulenburg, 27 January 1890, Röhl, *Eulenburgs Politische Korrespondenz*, no. 293, pp. 421–3. Holstein's advice was forwarded by Eulenburg to William II on 30 January, ibid., no. 296, p. 426: Rich, op. cit., I, p. 268.

15 Ibid., p. 260: Holstein to Eulenburg, 26 December 1889, Röhl, *Eulenburgs Politische Korrespondenz*, no. 270, pp. 393–5.

16 *GW*, xv, pp. 512–15: Eulenburg, *Aus 50 Jahre*, pp. 223–35: Stern, *Gold and Iron*, pp. 451–3.

17 Holstein to Eulenburg, 11 March 1890, Röhl, *Eulenburgs Politische Korrespondenz*, no. 345, pp. 489–90; Marschall to Eulenburg, 12 March, ibid., no. 349, pp. 493–4; Eulenburg to Grand Duke of Baden, 13 March, ibid., no. 350, pp. 494–6; Eulenburg to William II, 14 March, ibid., no. 351, pp. 496–8.

18 Eulenburg, op. cit., p. 235.

Chapter 5 OFFICER OF THE WATCH

1 Nichols, *Germany after Bismarck*, p. 46.

2 Ibid., p. 68.

3 Ibid., pp. 33 and 40–1.

4 Rich, *Holstein*, I, pp. 301–2; Spitzemberg, pp. 487–8; Waldersee, *Denk.*, II, p. 138.

5 Kitchen, *German Officer Corps*, p. 87; Waldersee journal entry for 21 September 1890, *Denk.*, ii, pp. 145–6.

6 'Simplicity of a child' comment, private letter from unspecified source in Berlin, forwarded to Lord Salisbury, April 1891, SP 60/no. 57; Nichols, op. cit., p. 111.

7 Ibid., pp. 130–2; *LEF*, pp. 130–3: Haller, I, pp. 202–4; Spitzemberg, p. 296.

8 The five sermons preached between 12 July and 9 August 1891 are printed in William II, *The Word of the Lord upon the Waters*. For the Kaiser's comment to the Dean of Windsor on 'dogmatic trash', see Bell, *Randall Davidson*, I, p. 240.

9 Kiderlen-Waechter to Holstein, 3 August 1891, *HP*, III, p. 383.

10 Waldersee journal, 21 February 1892, *Denk.*, II, p. 232; William's address to the Brandenburg Provincial Assembly, 24 February, *German Emperor's Speeches*, p. 293.

11 Nichols, op. cit., pp. 178–80; Haller, I, p. 205; Empress Frederick to Queen Victoria, 27 February 1892, *LEF*, p. 434; *Punch*, 5 March 1892 (cf. *Punch* special supplement to issue of 16 September 1914, p. 5).

12 Nichols, loc. cit.; Röhl, *Germany without Bismarck*, pp. 84 and 86; William II to Queen Victoria, 6 March 1892, *QVL*, series 3, volume II, p. 106.

13 Malet to Salisbury, 2 April 1892, SP 63/no. 93: Ponsonby to Malet, 24 June 1892, *QVL* series 3 volume II, p. 125.

14 Magnus, *Edward VII*, p. 240: William II to Queen Victoria, 28 January 1893, *QVL*, series 3, volume II, pp. 133–4.

15 Ibid., pp. 290–3. There is a full account of the 1893 visit to England in Eulenburg's journal, as printed in his *Erlebnisse*, I, pp. 212–45.

16 Langer, *Diplomacy of Imperialism*, pp. 44–5; Eulenburg, loc. cit.; *GP*, VIII, nos. 1752–4, pp. 107–10; Lee, *King Edward VII*, I, p. 707. See also the article by Vagts on William II and the Siam Crisis, *AHR*, 45, especially pp. 839–40.

17 Nichols, op. cit., pp. 280–2: Haller, I, pp. 245–6.

18 Caprivi's remarks on the advantages of the crisis are contained in a minute he added to *GP*, VIII, no. 1753, p. 108. Cf. Röhl, *Germany without Bismarck*, p. 105, and Haller, I, pp. 249–50.

19 Röhl, op. cit., pp. 108–10; Nichols, op. cit., pp. 325–7: Rich, *Holstein*, I, pp. 403–5 and 408–15.

20 William II to Queen Victoria, 24 April 1894, *QVL*, series 3, volume II, p. 395.

21 Nichols, op cit., p. 330.

22 Röhl's article citing a document of 1892 on Germany, Russia and Poland, *HJ*, VII, p. 144. William's sketch of a cruiser, Steinberg, *Yesterday's Deterrent*, facing p. 32.

23 Rich, op. cit., I, pp. 424–45; Haller, I, p. 261.

24 Ibid., pp. 261–2; A. Ponsonby, *Henry Ponsonby*, pp. 362–3.

Chapter 6 OPERETTA GOVERNMENT

1 Hohenlohe, *Denk.*, p. 4.

2 Reference to 'operetta government', Holstein to Eulenburg, 11 November 1894, Rich, *Holstein*, II, p. 486 (cf. Röhl, *Germany without Bismarck*, p. 128). See, also, other exchanges in Rich, loc. cit., pp. 484–8: Eulenburg to Holstein, 11 January 1895, *HP*, III, p. 489.

3 William's help to Nicholas II over his marriage difficulties, A. Ponsonby, *Henry Ponsonby*, p. 306. The 'Willy-Nicky' correspondence: 'curse of God stricken the French', Grant, *Letters*, p. 5; 'defend Europe', ibid., p. 11; praise for a capital speech, ibid., p. 7.

4 Waldersee's journal, 7 February 1895, Waldersee, *Denk.*, II, p. 338; Steinberg, *Yesterday's Deterrent*, pp. 72–3.

5 William II to Bigelow, 26 May 1894, facsimile of telegram reproduced in Carlisle Taylor, *Mahan*, facing p. 130.

6 Hohenlohe diary, 2 November, 1894, Hohenlohe, *Denk.*, pp. 7–8; Hohenlohe to Marschall (enclosing message from William II), 17 November, 1894, *GP*, IX, no. 2219, pp. 245–6.

7 Röhl, op. cit., p. 135: Marschall's diary, 11 November and 25 December 1895, cited ibid, pp. 137 and 161.

8 William II to Salisbury, 30 July 1895, uncatalogued telegram, SP.

9 For the Cowes Regatta, see *The Times*, 6, 7, 8 and 9 August 1895; Kiderlen-Waechter to Holstein, 7 August, *HP*, III, pp. 537–9; exchange of letters between Queen Victoria and Lord Salisbury, 8 August, *QVL*, series 3, volume II, pp. 544–8; Grenville, *Lord Salisbury and Foreign Policy*, pp. 37–9.

10 Projected visit to Hatfield, Kiderlen-Waechter letter cited above, p. 538. Kaiser and *Standard* article, Swaine to Barrington (Salisbury's secretary), 4 September 1895, SP 122/no. 90.

11 Hatzfeldt to Holstein 30, 31 July and 5 August 1895, *GP*, x, nos. 2371, 2372 and 2381, pp. 9–13 and 22–3; Hatzfeldt to Bülow, 7 August, ibid., no. 2385, pp. 25–7.

12 Gosselin to Salisbury, 30 August 1895, enclosing memorandum by Swaine, FO 64/1351/no. 194.

13 William II to Marschall, 25 October 1895, *GP*, XI, no. 2579, p. 10.

14 Malet to Salisbury, 26 October 1895, SP 120/no. 5; Gosselin to Salisbury, 4 and 29 November 1895, SP 120/nos. 7 and 18.

15 Princess Louise Sophie, *Behind the Scenes at the Prussian Court*, pp. 102–19.

16 Röhl, *Germany without Bismarck*, pp. 137–46; Hohenlohe, *Denk.*, pp. 114–15 and 124–44; Craig, *Politics of the Prussian Army*, pp. 246–7; Steinberg, *Yesterday's Deterrent*, pp. 81–3.

17 Lascelles to Salisbury, 21 December 1895, FO 64/1351/no. 317; William II to Hohenlohe, 21 December 1895, *GP*, x, no. 2572, pp. 251–5.

18 Journal of 29 December 1895, Hohenlohe, *Denk.*, pp. 146–7: Holstein to Eulenburg, 21 December 1895, *HP*, III, pp. 576–8; Eulenburg to Holstein, 30 December, ibid, p. 578; William II to Eulenburg, 25 December, cited from the Koblenz archives by Röhl, op. cit., p. 158: Rich, *Holstein*, II, pp. 500–1.

19 William II to Nicholas II, 2 January 1896, Grant, *Letters*, p. 30. For German reactions in general, see Rich, op. cit., pp. 466–70.

20 Waldersee, *Denk.*, II, pp. 363–4: Journal of 3 January 1896, Hohenlohe, *Denk.*, p. 151.

21 Ibid., Rich, op. cit., pp. 469–70; Röhl, op. cit., p. 165. Telegram to Kruger, 3 January 1896, is in *GP*, XI, no. 2610, pp. 31–2; cf. *QVL*, series 3, vol. III, p. 7.

22 Queen Victoria to William II, 5 January 1895, ibid., pp. 8–9.

23 Queen's Journal, 10 January 1896, ibid., pp. 17–18; William II to Queen Victoria, 8 January, Hohenlohe, *Denk.*, pp. 154–6; Lee, *King Edward VII*, I, p. 726.

24 Röhl, op. cit., pp. 167–9; Steinberg, op. cit., pp. 86–91; Hohenlohe, *Denk.*, p. 156; Lascelles to Salisbury, 20 February 1896, SP 120/no. 53.

25 William's conversation with Grierson (3 March) was reported by Lascelles to Salisbury on 6 March, FO 64/1376/no. 61 (cf. Macdiarmid, *Grierson*, p.

117). For William's visit to the embassy, see Lascelles to Salisbury, 4 and 6 March 1896, FO 64/1376/nos. 59 and 63.

26 Lascelles' telegram to Salisbury, 5 May 1896, FO 64/1381/no. 22 and his despatch, 8 May, FO 64/1377/no. 124; Macdiarmid, op. cit., p. 119; Queen Victoria to Salisbury, 6 May, QVL, series 3, volume III, p. 43.

27 Röhl, op. cit., p. 189; Hohenlohe, Denk., pp. 228–31.

28 Röhl, op. cit., pp. 190–4.

29 Eulenburg to Bülow, 10 December 1896, Haller, I, p. 362; cf. Röhl, op. cit., p. 202.

30 Eulenburg's diary for 19 March 1890, quoted, ibid., p. 30.

31 Lascelles retrospective survey on Germany sent from Berlin 24 May 1907, BD, III, Appendix C, p. 435.

32 Holstein to Bülow, 22 May 1897, HP, IV, p. 39; Hohenlohe, Denk., pp. 332–3.

33 The fullest treatment of the Kaiser's attempt to solve the constitutional crisis of 1897 is in Röhl, op. cit., pp. 229–46. See also Hohenlohe, Denk., pp. 345–64, passim and Haller, II, pp. 16–34.

Chapter 7 WORLD POWERS

1 Bülow, Memoirs 1897–1903, pp. 80–100; Bülow to German Foreign Ministry, 11 August 1897, GP, XIV (i), no. 3679, pp. 58–9; O'Conor to Salisbury, 6 and 12 August 1897, FO 65/1533, nos. 179 and 188; Nicholas II to Marie Feodorovna, 1 August 1897 (O.S.), Bing, Letters of Tsar Nicholas and Empress Marie, pp. 129–31.

2 Hohenlohe, Denk., pp. 398 and 408–9 (includes Nicholas's telegram of 7 November); Bülow, op. cit., p. 180; GP, XIV (i), nos. 3688–90, pp. 68–70 (William's jubilant telegram is printed as no. 3690); Memorandum by Bertie, 18 November 1897, FO 17/1330.

3 Langer, Diplomacy of Imperialism, pp. 453–60; Holstein to Hatzfeldt, 13 November 1897, HP, IV, pp. 48–53; Bülow to Hatzfeldt, 2 December, ibid, pp. 56–8.

4 William II to Nicholas II, 14 January 1898, Grant, Letters, p. 45 (with facsimile facing p. 30); Hohenlohe to Holstein, 31 December 1897, HP, IV, p. 61.

5 Footnote to Hohenlohe, Denk., p. 425.

6 Steinberg, Yesterday's Deterrent, pp. 126–9, 144–6, 160–1 and 208–23; Berghahn, Tirpitz-Plan, pp. 140–53.

7 Röhl, Germany without Bismarck, pp. 253–4; Steinberg, op. cit., p. 133; Bülow, op. cit., pp. 109–10 and 133; William II to Hohenlohe, 27 March 1898, Hohenlohe, Denk., p. 437.

8 Stettin speech, Johann, Reden des Kaisers, pp. 80–1. For the Navy League,

Steinberg, op. cit., pp. 137–8; Herwig, pp. 7–8; Berghahn, op. cit., pp. 137–8; Kehr, *Primat den Innenpolitik*, pp. 146–7.

9 Marder, *British Naval Policy*, pp. 292–5 and 301.

10 Steinberg article on the German invasion plan, *HJ*, volume 6: text of memorandum of 12 November 1897, pp. 115–19.

11 Grenville, *Lord Salisbury and Foreign Policy*, pp. 31–2 and 150–1.

12 Hatzfeldt to German Foreign Ministry, 25 and 29 March, 1 and 3 April, 1898, *GP*, XIV (i), nos. 3781, 3782, 3784 and 3785, pp. 195–207; Holstein to Hatzfeldt, 3 April 1898, *HP*, IV, pp. 68–70. William's marginal comment on Hatzfeldt to Hohenlohe, 7 April 1898, *GP*, XIV (i), no. 3789, pp. 216–17.

13 Hatzfeldt to Salisbury, 15 April 1898, SP 122/no. 45: Salisbury to Hatzfeldt, 19 April, SP 122/no. 46.

14 Salisbury to Lascelles, 11 May 1898, FO 64/1436/no. 109(a); note in *GP*, XIV (i), p. 230; Holstein to Hatzfeldt, 31 May, *HP*, IV, pp. 81–2; Greville, op. cit., pp. 166–8; William II to Nicholas II, 30 May, Grant, *Letters*, pp. 50–5; Nicholas II to William II, telegram, 3 June, *GP*, XIV, no. 3803, p. 250.

15 William II to the Empress Frederick, 1 June 1898, *HP*, IV, pp. 82–4.

16 Empress Frederick to Queen Victoria, 15 July 1898, *QVL*, series 3, volume III, pp. 258–9; Memorandum by William II, 22 August 1898, *GP*, XIV (i), no. 3865, pp. 333–8; Bülow to William II, 24 August, ibid., no. 3866, pp. 339–42; Lascelles to Balfour, 23 August 1898, *BD*, I, pp. 100–1.

17 William II, *German Emperor's Speeches*, pp. 318–22. The fullest contemporary account of the Kaiser's journey is in Gaulis, *La Ruine d'un Empire*, pp. 156–242. See also Bülow, op. cit., pp. 237–66.

18 Marie Feodorovna to Nicholas II, 21 November 1898 (O.S.), Bing, op. cit., p. 136.

19 William II to Nicholas II, 9 November 1898, Grant, *Letters*, pp. 65–70; William II to Queen Victoria, 5 November, *QVL*, series 3, volume III, p. 311.

20 Herzl had two audiences with William II in the autumn of 1898: the first was at Constantinople on 19 October (Lowenthal, *Diaries of Herzl*, pp. 266–7); the second was outside Jerusalem on 28 October (ibid., p. 282).

21 Damascus Speech, Johann, *Reden*, p. 81; Damascus visit, Gaulis, op. cit., pp. 185–6; *Punch* on 'Cook's Crusader', 15 October 1898.

22 Fischer, *Germany's Aims*, pp. 20–1; comments on Cecil Rhodes, Lascelles to Bertie, 17 March 1899, SP 121/no. 23.

23 Queen Victoria to Salisbury, 24 October 1898, SP 122/no. 123: William II to Queen Victoria, *QVL*, series 3, volume III, p. 311.

24 Salisbury to Queen Victoria, 17 November 1898, ibid., p. 312; Lascelles to Salisbury, 21 and 24 December 1898, FO 64/1439/no. 339 and SP 121/no. 20; Holstein to Hatzfeldt, 22 December 1898, *HP*, IV, p. 101.

25 Lascelles to Salisbury, 20 January 1899, FO 64/1469/nos. 13 and 16.

26 Queen's Journal, 27 January 1899, *QVL*, series 3, volume III, p. 336; Queen Victoria to Nicholas II, 1 March 1899, ibid., pp. 343–4.

27 Report by Bülow, 25 February 1899, cited Fischer, *War of Illusions*, p. 50.

28 Exchanges between William II and Queen Victoria, with comments by Salisbury, 27 May to 12 June 1899, *QVL*, series 3, volume III, pp. 375–82 *passim*.

29 Salisbury to Lascelles, 10 May 1899, SP 122/no. 15; Grenville, op. cit., p. 277.

30 Ibid., pp. 274–7; Bülow, op. cit., p. 281.

31 Ibid., pp. 305–9; William II to Bülow, 29 October 1899, *GP*, XV, no. 4300, pp. 406–8; Memorandum by Bigge, 20 November 1899, SP 85/no. 89.

32 Garvin, *Chamberlain*, III, pp. 506–13; Bülow, op. cit., pp. 353–4; Grenville, op. cit., pp. 281–3; Lascelles to Salisbury, 13 December 1899, FO 64/1471/no. 315; Kehr, *Schlachtflottenbau*, pp. 177–82.

33 Berghahn, *Tirpitz-Plan*, pp. 205 and 248.

34 Herwig, p. 18.

35 Cricket parallel, correspondence in Lee, *King Edward VII*, I, pp. 756–9 (the Kaiser referred to Australia's victory in 'the cricket match last year'; as usual, five Test matches were played in the summer of 1899, but only the Lords' Test produced a result). On Germany, Russia and the Boer War, see ibid., p. 769 and *QVL*, series 3, volume III, pp. 499 and 503; cf. Grenville, op. cit., pp. 285–8.

36 For 'noodles' remark, Lascelles to Salisbury, 3 March 1900, SP 121/no. 40; for comparison of Louis XVI and Nicholas II, the same to the same, 9 March, SP 121/no. 48; for 'devotion to the Queen' remark, the same to the same, 10 March, SP 121/no. 50.

37 Rich, *Holstein*, II, pp. 619–20; *GP*, XVI, nos. 4598–600, pp. 80–3; Barrington (Salisbury's private secretary) to Salisbury, 18 July 1900, SP 122/no. 87; Barrington to Brodrick, 5 August 1900, SP 96/no. 111.

38 Bülow, op. cit., p. 356; Langer, op. cit., p. 699. There are many edited versions of the speech. I have followed the collated version printed by Professor Michael Balfour, *The Kaiser and his Times* (revised Penguin edition), pp. 226–7. See, also, Spitzemberg, p. 400 (Journal, 11 August 1900).

39 Amery, *Chamberlain*, IV, pp. 138–40 and 159; *BD*, II, nos. 8, 9 and 11; Journal of Sir Ernest Satow, 20 August 1900, PRO 30/33, file 16/3.

40 Langer, op. cit., pp. 702–3; Memorandum by Bertie, 13 September 1900, FO 17/1446 (cf. *BD*, II, no. 12).

41 Eckardstein, II, p. 235–6; Benson, *Kaiser and English Relations*, pp. 176–8.

42 Ibid., pp. 178–81; William II, *My Memoirs*, pp. 98–100; Waters, *Potsdam and Doorn*, pp. 30–1; Brett, *Esher Journals*, I, p. 279; Ponsonby, *Recollections of Three Reigns*, p. 82; Eckardstein, loc. cit.

43 *The Times*, 6 February 1901, with verse tribute on p. 8.

Chapter 8 ADMIRALS ALL

1 Bülow, *Memoirs, 1897–1903*, pp. 498–500; Lee, *King Edward VII*, II p. 11; Waters, *Potsdam and Doorn*, pp. 30–1.

2 Rich, *Holstein*, II, pp. 630–1; Grenville article, *Bulletin of the Institute of Historical Research*, XXVII (1954), pp. 201–13.

3 Ponsonby, *Recollections of Three Reigns*, p. 110; Magnus, *Edward VII*, pp. 299–300.

4 Ibid., p. 264.

5 For William and his family, see Dorpalen article, *AHR*, LVIII, pp. 20–1; and, in general, the first two chapters of Viktoria Luise, *The Kaiser's Daughter*. On Hohenlohe's resignation see the undated memorandum, probably of mid-September 1900, in Hohenlohe, *Denk.*, p. 582, and Bülow, op. cit., pp. 372–93.

6 L. Cecil, *Ballin*, pp. 102–8.

7 Hellige article in *Geschichte in Wissenschaft und Unterricht*, no. 19, pp. 542–3. On William II's attitude towards anti-semitism, see Stern, *Gold and Iron*, pp. 447–9 and 544.

8 Eulenburg, *Erlebnisse*, II, pp. 327–36: H.S.Chamberlain to William II, 15 November 1901, Chamberlain, *Briefe*, II, pp. 132–41, and William's reply of 31 December, ibid., pp. 141–3.

9 William II to Nicholas II, 3 January 1902, Grant, *Letters*, pp. 80–6.

10 Ibid., pp. 91, 101, 108; Bülow, *Memoirs 1897–1903*, pp. 572–3.

11 Marder, *British Naval Policy*, pp. 463–7; Woodward, *Great Britain and the German Navy*, p. 52; Magnus, op. cit., p. 307.

12 Memorandum by William II, 22 March 1904, *GP*, XXI, no. 6481, pp. 169–70; Albertini, *Origins of War of 1914*, I, p. 149; Spitzemberg, p. 439 (Journal, 15 April 1904).

13 *Flying Dutchman* episode, Zedlitz-Trützschler, *Twelve Years*, p. 89 (Journal, 3 November 1904); Memorandum by Lichnowsky, 19 April 1904, *GP*, XIX (i), no. 6031, pp. 174–5; Schlieffen to Bülow, 20 April 1904, ibid., no. 6032, pp. 175–6; Fischer, *War of Illusions*, p. 53; Berghahn, *Tirpitz-Plan*, p. 494.

14 Marder, op. cit., pp. 477 and 479–81; Hough, *Louis and Victoria*, p. 185.

15 Montagu to William II, 17 October 1904, MK, XXIV, Reel 7/00688.

16 William II to Nicholas II, 27 October 1904, *GP*, XIX (i), no. 6118, pp. 303–4; Nicholas II to William II, 29 October 1904, ibid., no. 6119, pp. 304–5; Rich, *Holstein*, II, p. 689.

17 Ibid., p. 691; William II to Nicholas II, 30 November and 17 December 1904, Grant, *Letters*, pp. 129–37 and 142–8. The reference to the French President will be found in a similar letter of 21 December, ibid., p. 152. See also William II to Bülow, 28 December 1904, *GP*, XIX, I, no. 6146, pp. 346–7.

18 Bülow, *Memoirs 1903–09*, pp. 106–7; Kühlmann, *Erinnerungen*, p. 225; Rich,

op. cit., pp. 694–5; Hallgarten, *Imperialismus*, I, pp. 623–31. Exchanges between William II and Bülow, 20–26 March 1905, *GP*, xx (i), nos. 6564–6 and 6574–5, pp. 263–5 and 272–3.

19 Schoen, *Memoirs of an ambassador*, pp. 19–23.

20 Hough, op. cit., p. 188.

21 Taylor, *Struggle for Mastery*, pp. 430–32; Bülow, op. cit., pp. 108–19; Rich, op. cit., pp. 696–713; Albertini, *Origins*, I, pp. 154–7; Fischer, *War of Illusions*, pp. 54–7.

22 William II to Bülow, 25 July 1905, *GP*, xix (ii), no. 6220, pp. 458–60; Bülow, op. cit., pp. 131–2.

23 Ibid., pp. 133–41.

24 Ibid., pp. 141–43.

25 Bülow to Foreign Ministry, 8 September 1905, *GP*, xx (ii), no. 6803, pp. 562–3.

26 Monger, *End of Isolation*, pp. 268–70; Taylor, op. cit., pp. 436–7.

27 Nicholas II to William II, 7 October 1905, GP, xix (ii), no. 6247 pp. 512–13; William II to Bülow, 26 November, 1905, ibid., no. 6255, pp. 524–5.

28 It should be noted that these much-quoted remarks, from the Kaiser's 'Christmas candles' letter, depend purely on the testimony of Bülow (op. cit., p. 191). He was not always the most scrupulous of reporters.

29 Rich, op. cit., p. 751: Bülow, op. cit., pp. 205–6. There is a stimulating survey of the problems raised by the Algeciras Conference in Hallgarten, op. cit., I, pp. 664–76.

30 K. on N., p. 221 (English, p. 199); cf. William II, *My Memoirs*, pp. 103–6.

Chapter 9 SCANDALS AND KAISER CRISIS

1 Berghahn, *Germany and the Approach of War*, pp. 57–9. *The Times* (on German prince's birth) 5 and 7 July 1906. Full-page advertisement for William Le Queux's novel, *The Times*, 13 March 1906, p. 11. Questions in House of Commons reported in the following day's edition. On the sales of *Seestern*, Tower to Grey, 24 January 1906, *BD*, III, no. 413, p. 354.

2 Magnus, *Edward VII*, pp. 380–1; Ponsonby, *Recollections*, p. 182; Bülow, *Memoirs, 1903–09*, p. 238.

3 Randolph S. Churchill, *Winston S. Churchill*, II, pp. 195–7.

4 Zedlitz-Trützschler, *Twelve Years*, pp. 199–200 (for 'big cold' episode); Holstein diary, 11 November 1906, *HP*, IV, p. 447.

5 Holstein to Radolin, 19 January 1906, ibid., p. 389.

6 Rich, *Holstein*, II, pp. 758–69.

7 Haller, *Eulenburg*, II, p. 197.

8 Ramm, *Germany 1789–1919*, pp. 411–12; Bülow, op. cit., p. 271.

9 Rich, op. cit., pp. 772–8.

10 William, Crown Prince, *Memoirs*, p. 106.

11 Haller, II, pp. 203–5.

12 Harden to Holstein, 20 June 1907, *HP*, IV, p. 485.

13 The same to the same, 25 November 1907, ibid., p. 506; Rich, op. cit., p. 785.

14 Eulenburg to Crown Prince William, 22 May 1888, Röhl, *Eulenburgs Pol. Korr.*, I, no. 176, p. 294.

15 Ibid., p. 53.

16 Berghahn, *Tirpitz-Plan*, pp. 419–48 and 458–60; Dumas (British naval attaché) to Lascelles, 9 January 1907, *BD*, VI, no. 1, pp. 2–3.

17 Montagu to William II, 7 May 1907, MK, XXIV, Reel 7/00766; Bülow, op. cit., p. 290.

18 Berghahn, *Tirpitz-Plan*, pp. 505–8; Marder, *Dreadnought to Scapa Flow*, I, pp. 132–3.

19 Bülow, op. cit., p. 284; Steinberg article on the 'Copenhagen complex', *JCH*, I, no. 3, especially pp. 23 and 40–6.

20 Bülow, op. cit., p. 296; *The Times*, 17, 21, 24, 26, 28 and 29 October 1907.

21 Brett, *Esher Journals*, II, pp. 254–5; form of presentation for honorary degree at Oxford, Bodleian Library, Bod. Ms. Oxon c. 32(7).

22 Tyrrell to Stuart-Wortley, 8 November 1907, Bod. Ms. Eng. Hist. d. 256, folios 1–2.

23 Daphne Fielding, *The Duchess of Jermyn Street*, pp. 71–2.

24 William II to H.S.Chamberlain, 23 December 1907, Chamberlain, *Briefe*, II, pp. 226–7.

25 Private letters from Stuart-Wortley to his wife, relating the Kaiser's conversations, 1, 2 and 7 December 1907, Bod. Ms. Eng. Hist. d. 256, folios 3–22.

26 Woodham-Smith, *Florence Nightingale* (1952 edition), p. 431; William II to H.S.Chamberlain, 23 December 1907, loc. cit.; William II to Stuart-Wortley, (? 15) December 1907, Bod. Ms. Eng. Hist. d. 256, folio 60; Montagu to William II, 29 December 1907, MK, XXIV, Reel 7/00783.

27 Woodward, *Great Britain and the German Navy*, pp. 155–7.

28 The original letter from William II to Lord Tweedmouth of 14 February 1908 is in the Bodleian Library, Oxford (Bod. Ms. Eng. Hist. c. 264). The file also contains correspondence between the Admiralty and the Foreign Office concerning the letter, and relevant material from a later date. This paragraph is based on the file as a whole. The letter is printed in *GP*, XXIV as no. 8181, pp. 32–5. See, also, Woodward, op. cit., pp. 158–9 and Brett, *Esher Journals*, II, pp. 285–6.

29 Metternich to Bülow, 8 March 1908, *GP*, XXIV, no. 8193, pp. 44–6.

30 William II to Bülow, 13 August 1908, *GP*, XXIV, no. 8226, pp. 126–9;

Bülow, op. cit., pp. 312–14; Memorandum by Hardinge, 16 August 1908, *BD*, VI, no. 117, pp. 184–90.

31 Exchanges between Stuart-Wortley and William II in September 1908, Bod. Ms. Eng. Hist. d. 256, folios 31–4. William II to Stuart-Wortley, 15 October, 1908, ibid., folios 42–6.

32 *Daily Telegraph*, 28 October 1908; Schüssler, *Die Daily-Telegraph-Affaire*, pp. 13–16. Editor's letter to Stuart-Wortley, Bod. Ms. Eng. Hist. d. 256, folio 53.

33 Woodward, op. cit., p. 501 (extract from *The Economist*); *The Times*, 29 October 1908; Albertini, *Origins*, I, pp. 318–20; Stuart-Wortley to William II, 31 October 1908, Bod. Ms. Eng. Hist. d. 256, folio 58.

34 Bülow, op. cit., p. 347.

35 Zeppelin speech of 10 November 1908, Johann, *Reden*, pp. 122–3; Spitzemberg, p. 496; William II to Bülow, 9 November 1908, *GP*, XXIV, no. 8270, pp. 199–202.

36 Bülow, op. cit., pp. 355–8; Schussler, op. cit., p. 66; Kürenberg, *War Alles Falsch?*, pp. 247–9.

37 Zedlitz-Trützschler, *Twelve Years*, pp. 271–2.

38 William II to Francis Ferdinand, 16 December 1908, Kann article, *AHR*, LVII, p. 328.

39 Jonas, *Crown Prince William*, pp. 47–8; Dorpalen article on the influence of the Empress, *AHR*, LVIII, pp. 22–3. See also Goschen to Grey, 13 November 1908, *BD*, VI, no. 136, pp. 217–18, an interesting and detailed analysis of German reactions to the whole crisis.

Chapter 10   THE DANGER ZONE

1 K. on N., p. 303 (English version, p. 281); Albertini, *Origins*, I, pp. 228–9; Taylor, *Struggle for Mastery*, pp. 451–3 and 455–7; Fischer, *War of Illusions*, pp. 59–60.

2 William II to Francis Ferdinand, 31 December 1908, Kann article, *AHR*, LVII, p. 330.

3 Conrad von Hötzendorf, *Aus meiner Dienstzeit*, I, pp. 379–84.

4 Lyncker quoted by Zedlitz-Trützschler, *Twelve Years*, p. 266 (Journal entry for 26 March 1909).

5 Bülow to Pourtales, 21 March 1909, *GP*, XXVI (ii), no. 9460, pp. 693–5.

6 Eyck, *Wilhelm II*, pp. 515–16; Fischer, *Germany's Aims*, p. 23.

7 Bülow, *Memoirs 1903–1909*, pp. 500–3; William II to Francis Ferdinand, 13 August 1909, Kann article, loc. cit., p. 339.

8 Dorpalen article on the influence of the Empress, *AHR*, LVIII, p. 23; Jarausch, *Enigmatic Chancellor*, pp. 64–8; Fischer, *World Power or Decline*, pp. 9–13.

9 Memorandum on discussion in the chancellery, 3 June 1909, *GP*, XXVIII,

no. 10306, pp. 167–78; Berghahn, *Germany and the Approach of War*, pp. 91–2; Marder, *Dreadnought to Scapa Flow*, I, p. 173; Hallgarten, *Imperialismus*, II, pp. 119–21.

10 William II on Edward VII's funeral, see *My Memoirs*, pp. 125 and 129 and William II to Bethmann-Hollweg, 20, 21 and 23 May 1910, *GP*, XXVIII, nos 10388, 10389 and 10390, pp. 324–30. See also *The Times*, 20 and 21 May 1910, and Brett, *Esher Journals*, III, p. 4. William II to George V, 15 February 1911, Nicolson, *King George V*, p. 125.

11 K. on N., p. 366 (English version, p. 344).

12 Jarausch, op. cit., p. 111; Gooch, *Studies in Diplomacy*, p. 140.

13 K. on N., p. 416 (English version, p. 395).

14 Gooch, op. cit., pp. 140–2; Hallgarten, op. cit., pp. 235–40.

15 Gooch, op. cit., pp. 49–50; Spitzemberg (Journal 27 April 1911), p. 528; William II to Bethmann-Hollweg, 22 April 1911, *GP*, XXIX, no. 10538, p. 89.

16 Kiderlen-Waechter to William II, 3 May 1911, ibid., no. 10549, pp. 101–8; Jäckh, *Kiderlen-Waechter*, II, p. 122: Joanne Mortimer article on Agadir, *HJ*, 10, pp. 442–4.

17 William II, *My Memoirs*, p. 141; Nicolson, op. cit., pp. 182–5; Memorandum by Bethmann-Hollweg, 23 May 1911, *GP*, XXIX, no. 10562, pp. 120–1.

18 Kiderlen-Waechter to German Foreign Ministry, 26 June 1911, *GP*, XXIX, no. 10576, p. 152.

19 Fischer, *War of Illusions*, pp. 74–5 and 78–9; Robbins, *Sir Edward Grey*, p. 242. Cf. Taylor, *Struggle for Mastery*, p. 471 and the article by Cosgrove on Lloyd George's speech, *HJ*, 12, pp. 698–9.

20 Jäckh, op. cit., II, pp. 128–34; Fischer, op. cit., p. 82.

21 Ibid., pp. 83–5; Moltke to his wife, 19 August 1911, Moltke, *Erinnerungen*, p. 362; Görlitz, *Der Kaiser . . .* , p. 88.

22 Ibid., p. 92 (6 September 1911); Tirpitz, *Aufbau*, pp. 200–9; Hubatsch, *Ära Tirpitz*, pp. 91–2; Ritter, *S and S*, II, pp. 172–3.

23 Note on William's Hamburg speech, 27 August 1911, *GP*, XXXI, pp. 3–4.

24 Jonas, op. cit., p. 71; Fischer, op. cit., p. 92.

25 On the elections, ibid., pp. 95–111. Franz Mehring, 'Ein aufgeklärter Despot?', translated extract in Peter Paret (ed.), *Frederick the Great*, p. 222.

26 Görlitz, op. cit., p. 101.

27 Fischer, op. cit., pp. 118–19.

28 Ibid., p. 120; Berghahn, op. cit., p. 129.

29 Montagu to William II, 6 November 1911, MK XXIV, Reel 8/00011.

30 Speech aboard the *Hohenzollern*, 1912, cited from the Michaelis Papers by Herwig, pp. 22–3.

31 William II to Francis Ferdinand, 6 December 1911, Kann article, *AHR*, LVII, p. 344.

32 Cecil, *Ballin*, pp. 188–9; Woodward, *Great Britain and the German Navy*, pp. 323–5; Randolph S. Churchill, *Winston S. Churchill*, II, pp. 560–1; Memorandum by Bethmann-Hollweg, 29 January 1912, *GP*, XXXI, no. 11347, pp. 97–8.

33 Haldane's diary, *BD*, VI, no. 506, pp. 676–84; Robbins, op. cit., pp. 256–8; Tirpitz, op. cit., pp. 286–8; Cecil, op. cit., pp. 189–92; Hubatsch, op. cit., pp. 107–12; Woodward, op. cit., pp. 329–37.

34 Randolph S. Churchill, op. cit., pp. 563–4.

35 Cecil, op. cit., pp. 195–7.

36 Dorpalen article on the influence of the Empress, *AHR*, LVIII, pp. 23–4; Metternich to Bethmann-Hollweg, 20 December 1911 and 17 March 1912, *GP*, XXXI, nos 11344 and 11403, pp. 81–6 and 181–3.

37 Albertini, *Origins*, I, pp. 364–96; Berghahn, op. cit., pp. 138–9; Görlitz, op. cit., pp. 121 and 122 (Müller's journal, 19 October and 5 November, 1912); William II to Kiderlen-Waechter, 21 November 1912, *GP*, XXXIII, no. 12405, pp. 373–4.

38 Francis Ferdinand to Berchtold, 22 November 1912, *O-UA*, IV, no. 4571, p. 979.

39 Nicolson, op. cit., pp. 207–9; Lichnowsky to Bethmann-Hollweg, 3 December 1912, *GP*, XXXIX, no. 15612, pp. 119–23.

40 Fischer, op. cit., pp. 161–4; Görlitz, op. cit., pp. 124–6; Röhl article on Admiral von Müller, *HJ*, 12, pp. 661–2; Röhl, *1914, Delusion or Design?*, pp. 29–30.

41 Fischer, op. cit., pp. 179–82. On Germany, Britain and the naval problems, see also the article by Langhorne, *HJ*, 14, especially pp. 359–62 and 369–70.

42 Fischer, op. cit., 174–7.

43 William II to Nicholas II, 18 March 1913, Grant, *Letters*, p. 278.

44 Viktoria Luise, *Ein Leben als Tochter des Kaisers*, pp. 93–103 and *Im Glanz der Krone*, pp. 199–201 (cf. the selected English translation from these books, *The Kaiser's Daughter*, pp. 67–74); James Pope-Hennessy, *Queen Mary*, p. 480; Nicolson, op. cit., p. 216; *Illustrated London News*, 30 May 1913; William II to Francis Ferdinand, 27 May 1913, Kann article, *AHR*, LVII, p. 349.

Chapter 11 NOW OR NEVER

1 Viktoria Luise, *Kaiser's Daughter*, pp. 75–6; Topham, *Memories of the Kaiser's Court*, p. 238; Fischer, *War of Illusions*, pp. 220, 221 and 247.

2 An extract from Gebsattel's memorandum, together with the Kaiser's critical appraisal of it, has been published in translation by J.C.G.Röhl, *From Bismarck to Hitler*, pp. 49–52.

3 Tabouis, *Jules Cambon*, p. 244.

4 Kitchen, *German Officer Corps*, pp. 197–218; Rosenberg, *Imperial Germany*, pp. 56–8; Craig, *Politics of the Prussian Army*, pp. 252–3.

5 Jarausch, *Enigmatic Chancellor*, p. 71; Berghahn, *Germany and the Approach of War*, pp. 163–5.

6 Ibid., p. 186; Fischer, op. cit., pp. 371–85.

7 Stolberg to Jagow, 18 October 1913, *GP*, xxxvi (i), no. 14176, pp. 398–9.

8 Berchtold to Francis Joseph, 28 October 1913, *O-UA*, vii, no. 8934, pp. 512–15; Dedijer, *Road to Sarajevo*, pp. 156–8.

9 Fischer, *War of Illusions*, pp. 226–9; Eyck, *Wilhelm II*, p. 692; Tabouis, op. cit., pp. 240–4.

10 Fischer, op. cit., p. 334; Hallgarten, *Imperialismus*, ii, pp. 429–41.

11 Fischer, op. cit., pp. 334–5 and 346–8; Berghahn, op. cit., pp. 142–4.

12 William ii's comment on Pourtalès to German Foreign Ministry, 13 December 1913, *GP*, xxxviii, no. 15483, p. 256.

13 Cited, from Soviet sources, by Fischer, op. cit., p. 336.

14 Ibid., pp. 385–8.

15 Ritter, *The Schlieffen Plan*, pp. 144–8 and 292; Barnett, *The Swordbearers* (Penguin edition), p. 33.

16 Tschirschky to Bethmann-Hollweg, 23 March 1914, and Treutler to Jagow, 24 March, *GP*, xxxix, nos. 15715 and 15716, pp. 333–4 and 336–7. For an analysis of Tisza's views on the relations between Germany and Hungary, see Norman Stone's article, *JCH*, i, no. 3, especially pp. 154 and 167–8.

17 Treutler to Jagow, 27 March 1914, *GP*, xxxix, no. 15720, pp. 342–3; Tschirschky to Jagow, 10 May 1914, ibid, no. 15732, pp. 358–60; Fischer, op. cit., pp. 416–17; Albertini, *Origins*, i, pp. 508–9.

18 Tschirschky to Bethmann-Hollweg, 17 June 1914, *GP*, xxxix, no. 15735, p. 364; Treutler to Zimmermann (with accompanying report), 15 June 1914, ibid, no. 15736, p. 365. William ii to Francis Ferdinand, 14 June 1914, telegram, cited from the Austrian archives by Dedijer, op. cit., p. 158.

19 On Lichnowsky, see the introduction to Röhl, *1914, Delusion or Design?*, pp. 44–5 and Lichnowsky's own testimony, ibid, pp. 98–9; Lichnowsky, *Heading for the Abyss*, pp. 33–40; Nicolson, *Carnock*, pp. 391–3.

20 Gilbert, *Sir Horace Rumbold*, p. 105.

21 Görlitz, *The Kaiser and his Court* (journal of Admiral von Müller, 1914–18), p. 2.

22 Marginal comment on Tschirschky to Bethmann-Hollweg, 30 June 1914, *DD*, i, no. 7, pp. 10–11.

23 Szögyeny to Berchtold, 5 July 1914, *O-UA*, viii, no. 10058, pp. 306–7.

24 Falkenhayn to Moltke, 5 July 1914, *DD*, i, p. xii (also, Geiss, pp. 77–8); Albertini, *Origins*, ii, pp. 141–2.

25 Fischer, op. cit., p. 478.

26 See William's marginal comments on the relevant documents printed in Geiss, pp. 106, 108 and 114–16.

27 Telegrams exchanged between William II and Jagow, 11 July 1914, *DD*, I, nos. 30a and 32a, p. 52; Tabouis, op. cit., p. 245.

28 Geiss, pp. 89–101.

29 Görlitz (Müller's diary, 19 July 1914), op. cit., p. 4.

30 Ibid., pp. 6–8; Horn, *The Private War of Seaman Stumpf*, pp. 18–20; Nicholas II to William II, telegram, 29 July 1914, *DD*, II, no. 332, pp. 48–9.

31 Fischer, op. cit., pp. 483–4; Geiss, pp. 220 and 231–2.

32 See three documents dated 28 July 1914, William II to Jagow, Bethmann-Hollweg to William II and Bethmann-Hollweg to Tschirschky, *DD*, II, nos 293, 308 and 323, pp. 18–19, 29–30 and 39.

33 Exchange of telegrams, Nicholas II and William II, 28–29 July 1914, *DD*, II, nos 332–5, pp. 48–51.

34 Geiss, pp. 267–8; Fischer, op. cit., pp. 492–4.

35 William II to Nicholas II, 1 August 1914, *DD*, III, no. 600, pp. 92–3. The selection of documents in Geiss, pp. 260–349, gives a clear picture of events in the last days of peace.

36 Tirpitz, *Deutsche Ohnmachtspolitik*, pp. 2–3; Fischer, op. cit., pp. 494–5; Nicolson, op. cit., pp. 245–7. See also the article by Kurt Jagow on George V and Prince Henry, *Berliner Monatshefte*, volume 16, especially pp. 683–5 and 689–91.

37 Cf. Ritter, *S and S*, III, p. 37.

38 William II's comments on Lichnowsky to Jagow, 29 July, *DD*, II, no. 368 and on Pourtales to Jagow, 30 July 1914, *DD*, II, no. 401, pp. 130–3.

39 Moltke, *Errinnerungen*, pp. 18–21; Geiss, pp. 336–7.

40 Bethmann-Hollweg to Lichnowsky, 3 August 1914, *DD*, IV, no. 790, pp. 37–8; Jagow to Bülow, 3 August, ibid, no. 791, p. 38; Grey to Goschen, 4 August 1914, *BD*, XI, p. 573; Goschen to Grey, 6 August, ibid, p. 671.

41 Gilbert, op. cit., p. 122.

Chapter 12   WAR LORD ON SUFFERANCE

1 Ryder, *German Revolution*, p. 43; Masur, *Imperial Berlin*, pp. 265–6; Conrad, *Aus meiner Dienstzeit*, III, pp. 469–70.

2 E. Blücher, *An Englishwoman in Berlin*, p. 137; Görlitz, *The Kaiser and his Court*, p. 18.

3 Fischer, *Germany's Aims*, p. 121.

4 Görlitz, op. cit., pp. 22–4.

5 Wheeler-Bennett, *Hindenburg*, pp. 13–18; Hindenburg, *Out of my Life*, p. 103.

6 Wheeler-Bennett, op. cit., pp. 24–8, 33 and 49: Ritter, *S and S*, III, pp. 52–3.

7 Fischer, op. cit., p. 99; Zechlin article, *HZ*, 199, p. 405.

8 Görlitz, op. cit., pp. 28–9; Barnett, *Swordbearers*, pp. 100–1.

9 Ibid., pp. 107–12. There are succinct accounts of the battles of Tannenberg and the Marne in Frankland and Dowling, *Decisive Battles*, pp. 11–34.

10 Ritter, *S and S*, III, pp. 40–2 and 47–8.

11 Görlitz, op. cit., pp. 41–2.

12 William II to H. S. Chamberlain, 25 November 1914, Chamberlain, *Briefe*, II, p. 244. Müller's diary (Görlitz, op. cit., pp. 35–56) gives a good impression of life at Charleville.

13 Ibid., p. 57; Fischer, op. cit., pp. 124 and 128.

14 House missions, Ritter, *S and S*, III, pp. 137–40 and 152–7.

15 Cecil, *Ballin*, pp. 276–80; Fischer, op. cit., pp. 192–3 and 196–7; Jarausch, *Enigmatic Chancellor*, pp. 236–8.

16 Herwig, pp. 20–9.

17 Ibid., p. 177.

18 William's comments on a letter from Tirpitz, 24 August 1915, quoted from the naval archives by Dr Herwig, ibid, p. 179; Hubatsch, *Ära Tirpitz*, pp. 129–30.

19 Dorpalen article, *AHR*, LVII, pp. 25–6.

20 Görlitz, op. cit., p. 138.

21 Ibid., p. 147; Herwig, p. 184; Fischer, op. cit., pp. 285–6.

22 The fullest and finest account of Verdun is in Alistair Horne's *The Price of Glory*. See also his succinct narrative of the battle in Frankland and Dowling, op. cit., pp. 36–47.

23 Görlitz, op. cit., pp. 145 and 156.

24 Ibid., pp. 168–70; Ritter, *S and S*, III, p. 264; Herwig, pp. 185–6.

25 Horn, *Private War of Seaman Stumpf*, pp. 211–12.

26 Ritter, *S and S*, III, p. 50.

27 Wheeler-Bennett, op. cit., pp. 70–1; Görlitz, op. cit., p. 198.

28 Dorpalen article, *AHR*, LVIII, p. 26.

29 Cited from the Michaelis papers by Herwig, op. cit., p. 29.

Chapter 13 NEMESIS

1 Horne, *Price of Glory*, pp. 302–3.

2 Ritter, *S and S*, III, pp. 279–88; Fischer, *Germany's War Aims*, pp. 295–302; Jarausch, *Enigmatic Chancellor*, pp. 250–4.

3 Fischer, op. cit, p. 301, footnote 2.

4 Ritter, *S and S*, III, pp. 312–16; Görlitz, *Kaiser and his Court*, pp. 230–1.

5 Easter Message: Görlitz, op. cit., pp. 255–6; Jarausch, op. cit., pp. 331–6; Fischer, op. cit., pp. 315–18.

6 Jarausch, op. cit., pp. 369–80; Ritter, *S and S*, III, pp. 478–83; Dorpalen article, on the influence of the Empress, *AHR*, LVIII, p. 28.

7 Wheeler-Bennett, *Hindenburg*, pp. 107–8; Görlitz, op. cit., p. 286; Fischer, op. cit., p. 401.

8 Ritter, *S and S*, III, p. 483.

9 Fischer, op. cit., p. 439; Ritter, *S and S*, IV, pp. 15–17 and 397.

10 Görlitz, op. cit., 290–307.

11 Ibid., pp. 313–14; Lorenz, *Kaiser Karl*, pp. 416–17.

12 Wheeler-Bennett, op. cit., pp. 126–7; Görlitz, op. cit., pp. 310–23; Ritter, *S and S*, IV, pp. 82 and 103.

13 Fischer, op. cit., pp. 366–9; Ritter, *S and S*, III, pp. 403–4 and 573–4.

14 Summers and Mangold, *File on the Tsar*, p. 281; Waters, *Potsdam and Doorn*, pp. 255–7.

15 Fischer, op. cit., p. 478.

16 Czernin, *In the World War*, p. 228.

17 Görlitz, op. cit., pp. 320–1 for William's visit to the front; and Ritter, *S and S*, IV, p. 95 for Rupert's comment.

18 Ibid., pp. 100–1; Kühlmann, *Erinnerungen*, pp. 537–8 and p. 548; Dorpalen article on the Empress, *AHR*, LVIII, pp. 29–30.

19 Johann, *Reden*, pp. 128–9; Görlitz, op. cit., p. 330.

20 Ibid., pp. 332–3; Ritter, *S and S*, IV, pp. 106–9; Kühlmann, op. cit., p. 547; Fischer, op. cit., pp. 501–3.

21 Wheeler-Bennett, *Brest-Litovsk*, *passim*, with treaty text printed as an appendix; Görlitz, op. cit., p. 340.

22 Ibid., pp. 344 and 346; Barnett, *Swordbearers*, pp. 337–49.

23 Summers and Mangold, op. cit., pp. 281–90.

24 Kühlmann, op. cit., pp. 572–4; Ritter, *S and S*, IV, pp. 310–12; Dorpalen article, *AHR*, LVIII, p. 31.

25 Görlitz, op. cit., p. 374.

26 Ritter, *S and S*, IV, pp. 323–4; Niemann, *Kaiser und Revolution*, pp. 42–5.

27 Cecil, *Ballin*, pp. 336–8; Dorpalen article, *AHR*, LVIII, pp. 31–2.

28 Ilsemann, I, p. 17; Görlitz, op. cit., pp. 387 and 389 (Krupps), and 394–5 (Kiel); Niemann, op. cit., pp. 79–82; Fischer, op. cit., pp. 634–5; Wheeler-Bennett, *Hindenburg*, pp. 161–3.

29 Ritter, *S and S*, IV, pp. 345–7; Maximilian of Baden, *Memoirs*, II, p. 15.

30 Ritter, *S and S*, IV, pp. 350–4.

31 Niemann, op. cit., pp. 100–5; Baumont, *The Fall of the Kaiser*, pp. 3–4.

32 Memorandum by William II, 14 October 1918, printed by F. Gregory Campbell, *CEH*, II, pp. 379–83.

33 Ritter, *S and S*, IV, p. 376; Max of Baden, op. cit., p. 137.

34 Herwig, pp. 242–9; Waldeyer-Hartz, *Hipper*, pp. 236–7.

35 Hipper's diary for 31 October 1918, quoted by Herwig, p. 258.

36 Ilsemann, I, p. 30; Ritter, *S and S*, IV, p. 376; Dorpalen article, *AHR*, LVIII, p. 36.

37 Ritter, *S and S*, IV, p. 474; Balfour, *Kaiser and his Times*, p. 402; Baumont, op. cit., p. 22.

38 An account of Groener's mission to Berlin, written by the representative of the Supreme Command attached to the Foreign Ministry (Colonel von Haeften) is printed in translation by Dr Röhl in *From Bismarck to Hitler*, pp. 82–4.

39 Herwig, p. 259; Horn, *German Naval Mutinies*, p. 254.

40 Wheeler-Bennett, *Wreath to Clio*, pp. 154 and 176; Baumont, op. cit., pp. 94–112; Westarp, *Das Ende der Monarchie*, pp. 42–50; Niemann, op. cit., pp. 136–47.

41 Ilsemann, I, pp. 36–43; Jonas, *Crown Prince*, pp. 119–20; Baumont, op. cit., pp. 129–31; Wheeler-Bennett, loc. cit.; Westarp, op. cit., pp. 59–60.

42 Ibid., pp. 92–5.

43 Herwig, p. 261.

44 Ilsemann, I, pp. 43–5; Westarp, op. cit., p. 97.

Chapter 14   AMERONGEN AND DOORN

1 Ilsemann, I, pp. 45–7; Westarp, *Ende der Monarchie*, p. 97.

2 Bentinck, *Ex-Kaiser in Exile*, pp. 14–16 and 22–5; Ilsemann, I, p. 48.

3 Ibid., p. 49; William II to the Empress, 13 November 1918, Viktoria Luise, *Ein Leben als Tochter des Kaisers*, pp. 212–13 (reproduced in facsimile facing p. 209).

4 Gilbert, *Winston S. Churchill*, IV, p. 166.

5 On possible trial of the Kaiser, see Hankey, *Supreme Council*, pp. 114, 116 and 190. On intruders at Amerongen, see Ilsemann, I, p. 143 and Küremberg, *War Alles Falsch?*, pp. 391–6.

6 Ilsemann, I, contains the most detailed account of the Kaiser's daily life at this time: for 'Gorgon' entry, see p. 96.

7 Ibid., p. 149.

8 Purchase of Doorn, ibid., pp. 112–14 and 154–5; history of Doorn, Scheurleer, *Huis Doorn*, pp. 5–10.

9 Viktoria Luise, *Im Strom der Zeit*, pp. 136–7; Jonas, *Crown Prince*, pp. 135–6; Ilsemann, I, p. 161.

10 Ibid., pp. 173–8; Viktoria Luise, *Ein Leben als Tochter*, p. 232.

11 Jonas, op. cit., pp. 145–6; Viktoria Luise, *Im Strom*, pp. 144–50; Ilsemann, I, pp. 218 and 250–4; Daisy of Pless, *From my Private Diary*, p. 290.

12 Ilsemann, I, p. 275.

13 Ilsemann, II, pp. 18–19; Wheeler-Bennett, *Hindenburg*, pp. 240–3 and 265–7.

14 Nicolson, *Lord Carnock*, pp. 166 and 167; K. on N., p. 187.

15 Ilsemann, II, pp. 152–9 and 191–6.

16 Swastika symbolism, William II, *Die chinesische Monade*, pp. 191–2.

17 Reading habits, personal observations on visits to Doorn museum; reference to film, Anna Neagle, *There's Always Tomorrow*, p. 241.

18 William II to Queen Mary, 1 October 1938, Pope-Hennessy, *Queen Mary*, p. 592.

19 Phipps to Eden, 21 January 1936, FO 372/3186/ Telegram 18, and subsequent inter-departmental correspondence preserved in the same file.

20 Memorandum by Ashton-Gwatkin and correspondence with Professor Schairel, 9 February 1938, FO 371/21660. For Kleist's visit, see Gilbert, *Winston S. Churchill*, V, pp. 963–5 and Wheeler-Bennett, *Nemesis of Power*, pp. 410–12.

21 *Daily Telegraph*, 8 and 10 December 1938, with correspondence relating to the report in FO 371/21665. Boyd-Carpenter to Caccia, 20 March 1939, FO 371/23081. For the influence on the Kaiser of Dr W. Boyd-Carpenter when Bishop of Ripon, see Major, *Life and Letters of W. Boyd-Carpenter*, pp. 233–49. On William's anger at the Nazi persecution of the Jews, see Ilsemann, II, p. 313.

22 Wheeler-Bennett, *Wreath to Clio*, p. 181: Bruce Lockhart, *Comes the Reckoning*, pp. 35–40.

23 Viktoria Luise, *Ein Leben als Tochter*, p. 287. On question of asylum, see Halifax to Bland, 13 November 1939, FO 371/23127/ Telegram 179. On the transference of the Kaiser's personal funds to Switzerland, see Bland to Halifax, 27 January 1940, FO 371/24422/ No. 56.

24 Eric Seal (Principal Private Secretary to Churchill as First Lord of the Admiralty) to R.C.S.Stevenson of the Foreign Office, 10 May 1940, FO 371/24422. This file includes further related correspondence on 11, 12 and 13 May.

25 Ilsemann, II, pp. 340–1; Viktoria Luise, *Im Strom*, p. 285 and *The Kaiser's Daughter*, pp. 203–4; Bland to Halifax, 12 May 1940, FO 371/24422.

26 Ilsemann, II, p. 345; Viktoria Luise, *Ein Leben als Tochter*, p. 290.

27 William's remarks over the war flag at Versailles, Viktoria Luise, *Im Strom*, p. 286. (This passage is not included in the abridged single volume English translation of the Duchess of Brunswick's memoirs.)

28 Viktoria Luise, *Ein Leben als Tochter*, pp. 293–4 and *Im Strom*, p. 288; Ilsemann, II, pp. 346–8.

29 Ibid., pp. 348–9; Jonas, op. cit., p. 202; Viktoria Luise, *Ein Leben als Tochter*, pp. 295–8, and *Im Strom*, p. 246 and *The Kaiser's Daughter*, pp. 208–10.

List of Sources

Abbreviations used in the Reference Notes are shown in square brackets.

I UNPRINTED MATERIAL

This book is based primarily on printed sources. I have, however, used the following archival material:—

Papers of the third Marquess of Salisbury, Hatfield House, Hertfordshire. [SP].

Papers of the second Earl of Selborne, Bodleian Library, Oxford.

Papers of Sir Ernest Satow, Public Record Office, London. [PRO 30/33].

Microfilm of the 'Montagu File' in the German Marinekabinette archives, Naval Historical Branch of the Ministry of Defence, London [MK].

Papers concerning the *Daily Telegraph* 'Interview' of 1908, Bodleian Library, Oxford [Bod. MS., Eng. Hist d. 256].

Papers concerning the 'Tweedmouth Letter', Bodleian Library, Oxford [Bod. Ms. Eng. Hist. c. 264].

Papers concerning Kaiser Wilhelm II and the University of Oxford, Bodleian Library, Oxford [Bod. Ms. Oxon c. 32(7)].

Foreign Office Correspondence, Public Record Office, London [FO]. (Crown copyright material reproduced by permission of the Controller of H.M. Stationery Office.)

I have also used marginal comments made by the Kaiser in 1931 on a copy of Harold Nicolson's *Die Verschwörung der Diplomaten* in my possession. These comments have not been quoted or printed before. In the reference notes I have shown them by the abbreviation 'K. on N.', followed by a page reference to the German edition and, in brackets, the corresponding page reference to the original English version of the book, *Lord Carnock*.

II OFFICIAL PRINTED COLLECTIONS OF DOCUMENTS

BITTNER, Ludwig, PRIBRAM, Alfred, SRBIK, Heinrich and UEBERSBERGER Hans: *Oesterreich-Ingarns Aussenpolitik von der Bosnischen Krise 1908 bis zum Kriegsausbruch 1914* (Vienna, 1930) 8 vols [*O-UA*].

GOOCH, G.P. and TEMPERLEY, H.: *British Documents on the Origins of the War* 11 vols (London, 1927–38) (vol. XI edited by J.W.Headlam-Morley) [*BD*].

FRANCE Ministère des Affaires Étrangères: *Documents diplomatiques françaises, 1871–1914*; second series from 1901; third series from 1911 (Paris, 1929–).

KAUTSKY, K., SCHUCKING, W. and MONTGELAS, M.: *Die Deutschen Dokumente zum Kriegsausbruch*, 3 vols (Berlin, 1919) [*DD*].

LEPSIUS, J., MENDELSOHN-BARTHOLDY, A. and THIMME, F.: *Die Grosse Politik der Europäischen Kabinette*, 39 vols (Berlin, 1922–7) [*GP*].

III BOOKS

ALBERTINI, Luigi: *The Origins of the War of 1914*, 3 vols (Oxford, 1952) [Albertini, *Origins*].

AMERY, Julian: *Life of Joseph Chamberlain*, vol. IV (London, 1951).

ARONSON, Theo: *The Kaisers* (London, 1971).

BALFOUR, Michael: *The Kaiser and His Times* (London, 1964).

BARKELEY, R.: *The Empress Frederick* (London, 1956).

BARNETT, Correlli: *The Swordbearers* (London, 1963).

BAUMONT, Maurice: *The Fall of the Kaiser* (London, 1930).

BELL, G.K.A.: *Randall Davidson*, vol. I (London 1935).

BENNETT, Daphne: *Vicky, Princess Royal of England & German Empress* (London, 1971).

BENSON, E.F.: *The Kaiser and English Relations* (London, 1936).

BENTINCK, Lady Norah: *The Ex-Kaiser in Exile* (London, 1922).

BERGHAHN, V.R.: *Der Tirpitz-Plan* (Düsseldorf, 1971).

—— *Germany and the Approach of War in 1914* (London, 1973).

BIGELOW, Poulteney: *The German Emperor* (London and New York, 1892).

—— *Prussian Memories, 1864–1914* (New York, 1915).

—— *Seventy Summers*, 2 vols (London and New York, 1925).

BING, E.J.: *The Letters of Nicholas II to the Empress Marie Feodorovna* (London, 1937).

BISMARCK, Otto von: *Erinnerung und Gedanke*, definitive edition of his memoirs, published as volume XV of *Die Gesammelten Werke Bismarcks* (Berlin, 1935) [*GW*, XV].

BLÜCHER, Princess: *An Englishwoman in Berlin* (London, 1920).

BRETT, M.V.B.: *Journals and Letters of Viscount Esher*, 4 vols (London, 1934–6).

BROOK-SHEPHERD, Gordon: *The Last Habsburg* (London, 1968).

BUCHANAN, Meriel: *Queen Victoria's Relations* (London, 1954).

BÜLOW, Prince von: *Memoirs*, 4 vols (London and New York, 1932).

BUSSMANN, W.: *Staatssekretar Graf Herbert von Bismarck* (Göttingen, 1964).

CECIL, Lady Gwendolen: *Life of Robert, Marquis of Salisbury*, vols 3 and 4 (London 1931–2).

CECIL, Lamar: *Albert Ballin* (Princeton, 1967).

CHAMBERLAIN, Houston Stewart: *Briefe, 1882–1924, und Briefwechsel mit Kaiser Wilhelm II* (Munich, 1928).

CHURCHILL, Randolph: *Winston S. Churchill*, vol. II, 1901–14 (London, 1967).

CHURCHILL, Winston S.: *The World Crisis*, 4 vols (London, 1923–31).

—— *Great Contemporaries* (London, 1937).

CONRAD VON HÖTZENDORF, F.: *Aus meiner Dienstzeit 1906–1918*, 5 vols (Vienna, 1922).

CORTI, E.E.C.: *Wenn* (Graz, 1954).

—— *Alexander von Battenberg* (London, 1954).

—— *The English Empress*, a revised translation of *Wenn* (London, 1967).

COWLES, Virginia: *The Kaiser* (London, 1963).

CRAIG, Gordon, A.: *The Politics of the Prussian Army* (Oxford, 1955).

CZERNIN, Count Ottokar: *In the World War* (London and New York, 1919).

DAVIS, A.N.: *The Kaiser I Knew* (London, 1920).

DEDIJER, Vladimir: *The Road to Sarajevo* (London, 1967).

DUGDALE, Blanche E.C.: *Arthur James Balfour*, vol. I (London, 1936).

ECKARDSTEIN, H. von: *Lebenserinnerungen und politische Denkwürdigkeiten* (Leipzig, 1920) [Eckardstein].

EULENBURG, Furst Philipp zu: *Aus 50 Jahren* (Berlin, 1925).

—— *Ende König Ludwigs II und andere Erlebnisse I* (Leipzig, 1934).

—— *Erlebnisse an deutschen und fremden Höfen, II* (Leipzig, 1934).

EYCK, Erich: *Das persönliche Regiment Wilhelms, II* (Zurich, 1948).

FALKENHAYN, E. von: *General Headquarters, 1914–16 and its Critical Decisions* (London, 1919).

FIELDING, Daphne: *The Duchess of Jermyn Street* (London, 1964).

FISCHER, Fritz: *Germany's Aims in the First World War* (London, 1967).

—— *War of Illusions* (London, 1975).

—— *World Power or Decline* (London, 1975).

FISCHER, Henry (ed.): *The private lives of William II and his consort* (London, 1904).

FRANKLAND, Noble and DOWLING, Christopher (eds): *Decisive Battles of the Twentieth Century* (London, 1976).

FREDERIC, H.: *The Young Emperor* (London, 1892).

FULFORD, Roger (ed.): *Dearest Child*, letters between Queen Victoria and the Princess Royal, 1858–61 (London, 1964).

—— *Dearest Mama*, 1861–65 (London, 1968).

—— *Your Dear Letter*, 1865–71 (London, 1971).

—— *Darling Child*, 1871–76 (London, 1976).

GARVIN, J.L.: *Life of Joseph Chamberlain*, vol. III (London, 1934).

GEISS, Imanuel, (ed.): *July 1914*, selected Documents (London, 1967) [Geiss].

GILBERT, Martin: *Winston S. Churchill*, vols. III, IV and V (London, 1971, 1975, 1976).

—— *Sir Horace Rumbold, Portrait of a Diplomat, 1869–1941* (London, 1973).

GÖRLITZ, Walther (ed.): *The Kaiser and his Court* (London, 1961).

—— *Der Kaiser . . . Aufzeichnungen des Chefs des Marinekabinetts Admiral Georg Alexander von Müller* (Göttingen, 1965).

GOOCH, G.P.: *Studies in Diplomacy and Statecraft* (London, 1942).

GRANT, N.F. (ed.): *The Kaiser's Letters to the Tsar* (London, 1920) [Grant, *Letters*].

GRENVILLE, J.A.S.: *Lord Salisbury and Foreign Policy* (London, 1964; revised paperback, 1970).

GREY OF FALLODON, Viscount: *Twenty-Five Years*, 2 vols (London, 1925).

HALLER, J.: *Philip Eulenburg, the Kaiser's Friend*, 2 vols (London, 1930) [Haller].

HALLGARTEN, G.W.F.: *Imperialismus vor 1914*, 2 vols (Munich, 1963).

HANKEY, Lord: *The Supreme Control at the Paris Peace Conference 1919* (London, 1963).

HARDEN, Maximilian: *Köpfe*, 2 vols (Berlin, 1913).

HERWIG, Holger H.: *The German Naval Officer Corps* (Oxford, 1973) [Herwig].

HINDENBURG, Field-Marshal Paul von: *Out of My Life* (London, 1920).

HINZPETER, G.: *Kaiser Wilhelm II, eine Skizze nach der Natur gezeichnet* (Bielefeld, 1888).

HOHENLOHE-SCHILLINGSFURST, Fürst Chlodwig zu: *Denkwürdigkeiten der Reichskanzlerzeit* (Stuttgart and Berlin, 1931) [Hohenlohe, *Denk.*].

HORN, Daniel: *The Private War of Seaman Stumpf* (London, 1969).

—— *The German Naval Mutinies of World War I* (New Brunswick, N.J., 1969).

HORNE, Alastair: *The Price of Glory* (paperback, London, 1964).

HOUGH, Richard: *Louis and Victoria, the First Mountbattens* (London, 1974).

HUBATSCH, Walther: *Die Ära Tirpitz* (Göttingen, 1955).

ILSEMANN, Sigurd von: *Der Kaiser in Holland*, 2 vols (Munich 1967, 1968) [Ilsemann].

JÄCKH, E.: *Kiderlen-Waechter* (Berlin and Leipzig, 1924).

JARAUSCH, Konrad H.: *The Enigmatic Chancellor, Bethmann Hollweg and the Hubris of Imperial Germany* (New Haven and London, 1973).

JONAS, Klaus W.: *The Life of Crown Prince William* (London, 1961).

KEHR, Eckart: *Schlachtflottenbau und Parteipolitik, 1894–1901* (Berlin, 1930).

—— *Der Primat der Innenpolitik* (posthumously edited by H-U Wehler) (Berlin, 1965).

KITCHEN, Martin: *The German Officer Corps, 1890–1914* (Oxford, 1968).

KLUCK, A. von: *The March on Paris and the Battle of the Marne, 1914* (London, 1920).

KOELTZ, L.: *Documents allemands sur la bataille de la Marne* (Paris, 1930).

KÜHLMANN, Richard von: *Erinnerungen* (Heidelberg, 1948).

KÜRENBERG, Joachim von: *War Alles Falsch? Das Leben Kaiser Wilhelms II* (Bonn, 1951).

KURTZ, Harold: *The Second Reich* (London, 1970).

LANGER, William L.: *The Diplomacy of Imperialism, 1890–1902* (New York, rev. edn, 1950).

LEE, Sir Sidney: *King Edward VII*, 2 vols (London, 1925 and 1927).

LICHNOWSKY, Prince: *Heading for the Abyss* (London, 1928).

LLOYD GEORGE, D.: *War Memoirs*, 6 vols (London, 1933–5).

LOCKHART, R. Bruce: *Comes the Reckoning* (London, 1947).

LONGFORD, Elizabeth: *Victoria R.I.* (London, 1964).

LORENZ, Reinhold: *Kaiser Karl* (Graz, Vienna and Cologne, 1959).

LOUISE SOPHIE, Princess of Prussia: *Behind the Scenes at the Prussian Court* (London, 1939).

LOWE, C.J.: *Salisbury and the Mediterranean 1886–96* (London and Toronto, 1965).

LOWENTHAL, M. (ed.): *Diaries of Theodor Herzl* (London, 1958).

LUCIUS VON BALLHAUSEN: *Bismarck-Erinnerungen* (Stuttgart and Berlin, 1921).

LUDENDORFF, General Erich: *My War Memoirs 1914–18* (London, 1919).

LUDWIG, Emil: *Kaiser Wilhelm II* (London, 1926).

MACDIARMID, D.S.: *Life of Lieutenant-General Sir James Moncrieff Grierson* (London, 1923).

MAGNUS, Philip: *King Edward the Seventh* (London, 1964).

MAJOR, H.D.A.: *Life and Letters of W. Boyd Carpenter* (London, 1925).

MARDER, Arthur J.: *British Naval Policy, 1880–1905* (London, 1941).

—— *From the Dreadnought to Scapa Flow*, 3 vols (London, 1961–6).

MASUR, Gerhard: *Imperial Berlin* (London, 1971).

MAX VON BADEN, Prince: *Memoirs* (London, 1928).

MOLTKE, H. von: *Erinnerungen, Briefe, Dokumente 1877–1916* (Berlin, 1922).

MONGER, G.W.: *The End of Isolation* (London, 1963).

NEAGLE, Dame Anna (Mrs Herbert Wilcox): *There's Always Tomorrow* (London, 1974).

NEWTON, Lord: *Lord Lansdowne* (London, 1921).

NICHOLS, J.A.: *Germany after Bismarck, the Caprivi Era* (Cambridge, Mass., 1958).

NICOLSON, Harold: *Lord Carnock* (London, 1930).

—— *King George V* (London, 1952).

NIEMANN, Alfred: *Kaiser und Revolution* (Berlin, 1922).

NOWAK, Karl; *Kaiser and Chancellor* (London, 1930).

—— *Germany's Road to Ruin* (London, 1932).

PAGET, Walburga: *Embassies of Other Days*, 2 vols (London, 1923).

PALMER, Alan: *Bismarck* (London, 1976).

PARET, Peter: *Frederick the Great, a profile* (London, 1972).

PLESS, Daisy, Princess of: *Princess Daisy of Pless, by Herself* (London, 1928).

—— *From My Private Diary* (London, 1931).

—— *What I Left Unsaid* (London, 1936).

PONSONBY, Arthur: *Henry Ponsonby, his life from his letters* (London, 1942).

PONSONBY, Sir Frederick: *Recollections of Three Reigns* (London, 1951).

—— (ed.): *Letters of the Empress Frederick* (London, 1928) [*LEF*].

POPE-HENNESSY, James: *Queen Mary* (London, 1959).

RAMM, Agatha: *Germany, 1789–1919* (London, 1967).

—— *Sir Robert Morier* (Oxford, 1973).

RATHENAU, Walther: *Der Kaiser, eine Betrachtung* (Berlin, 1923).

RICH, Norman: *Friedrich von Holstein*, 2 vols (Cambridge, 1965).

RICH, Norman and FISHER, M.H. (eds.): *The Holstein Papers*, 4 vols (Cambridge, 1955–63) [*HP*].

RITTER, Gerhard: *The Schlieffen Plan* (London, 1958).

—— *The Sword and the Sceptre*, 4 vols (London, 1972) [Ritter, *S and S*].

RÖHL, John C.G.: *Germany without Bismarck* (London, 1967).

—— *From Bismarck to Hitler* (London, 1970).

—— *1914: Delusion or Design?* (London, 1973).

—— (ed.) *Philipp Eulenburgs Politische Korrespondenz*, vol. 1 (Boppard, 1976).

ROSENBERG, Arthur: *The Birth of the German Republic* (Oxford, 1931) (reprinted as paperback, *Imperial Germany*, 1970).

RUMBOLD, Horace: *The War Crisis in Berlin, July–August 1914* (London, 1940).

RYDER, A.J.: *The German Revolution of 1918* (Cambridge, 1967).

SAZONOV, S.D.: *Fateful Years 1909–1916* (London, 1928).

SCHEURLEER, Th. H. Lunsingh: *Huis Doorn* (Doorn, 1952).

SCHOEN, W. von: *Memoirs of an ambassador* (London, 1930).

SCHUSSLER, Wilhelm: *Die Daily-Telegraph-Affaire* (Göttingen, 1952).

SPEARS, E.L.: *Liaison, 1914* (London, 1930).

STEINBERG, Jonathan: *Yesterday's Deterrent* (London, 1965).

STEINER, Zara S.: *The Foreign Office and Foreign Policy* (London, 1970).

STERN, Fritz: *Gold and Iron; Bismarck, Bleichröder, and the Building of the German Empire* (New York and London, 1977).

SUMMERS, Anthony and MANGOLD, Tom: *The File on the Tsar* (London, 1976).

TABOUIS, Geneviève: *Jules Cambon* (London, 1928).

TAYLOR, A.J.P.: *The Struggle for Mastery in Europe* (Oxford, 1954).

TAYLOR, Carlisle C.: *The Life of Admiral Mahan* (London, 1920).

TIRPITZ, A. von: *Erinnerungen* (Leipzig, 1919).

—— *Der Aufbau der deutschen Weltmacht* (Stuttgart, 1924).

—— *Deutsche Ohnmachtspolitik im Weltkriege* (Hamburg, 1926).

TOPHAM, Anne: *Memories of the Kaiser's Court* (London, 1914).

VICTORIA, Queen: *Letters*, First Series, vol. 3, edited A.C.Benson and Viscount Esher (London, 1907); Second and Third Series, edited G.E.Buckle (London, 1926 and 1930) [*QVL*].

VIKTORIA LUISE, Herzogin: *Ein Leben als Tochter des Kaisers* (Göttingen, 1965).

—— *Im Glanz der Krone* (Göttingen, 1968).

—— *Bilder der Kaiserzeit* (Göttingen, 1969).

—— *Im Strom der Zeit* (Göttingen, 1975).

—— *The Kaiser's Daughter* (an abridged translation of her three volumes of memoirs) (London, 1977).

VIERHAUS, Rudolf (ed.): *Das Tagebuch der Baronin Spitzemberg* (Göttingen, 1960) [Spitzemberg].

WALDERSEE, Alfred von: *Denkwürdigkeiten*, 3 vols, edited by H.O.Meissner (Berlin and Stuttgart, 1922–3) [Waldersee, *Denk*.].

WALDEYER-HARTZ, H.E.H. von: *Admiral von Hipper* (Berlin, 1933).

WATERS, W.H.H.: *Secret and Confidential* (London, 1926).

—— *Potsdam and Doorn* (London, 1935).

WESTARP, Count Kuno von: *Das Ende der Monarchie am 9 November 1918* (Berlin, 1952).

WHEELER-BENNETT, John W.: *Hindenburg, The Wooden Titan* (London, 1936, revised edn, 1967).

—— *Brest-Litovsk, The Forgotten Peace* (London, 1938).

—— *The Nemesis of Power* (London, 1953).

—— *A Wreath to Clio* (London, 1967).

WILHELM II, German Emperor and King of Prussia: *The Word of the Lord upon the waters*, Sermons 1890–91 (London, 1892).

—— *The German Emperor's Speeches* (London and New York, 1904).

—— *Comparative Tables* (London, 1921).

—— *My Memoirs* (London, 1922).

—— *Erinnerungen an Korfu* (Berlin and Leipzig, 1924).

—— *My Early Life* (London, 1926) [*EL*].

—— *Die chinesiche Monade* (Leipzig, 1934).

WILHELM, Crown Prince of Germany: *Memoirs* (London, 1922).

WILSON, Lawrence: *The Incredible Kaiser* (London, 1963).

WOLF J.B.: *The Diplomatic History of the Bagdad Railway* (New York, 1936).

WOODHAM-SMITH, Cecil: *Queen Victoria, Her Life and Times 1819–1886* (London, 1972).

WOODWARD, E.L.: *Great Britain and the German Navy* (Oxford, 1935).

YAMOLINSKY, A.: *Memoirs of Count Witte* (London, 1921).

ZEDLITZ-TRÜTZSCHLER, R.: *Twelve Years at the German Court* (London, 1924).

ZEMAN, Z.A.B.: *The Break-up of the Habsburg Empire, 1914–1918* (Oxford, 1961).

ZENTLER, Kurt: *Kaiserliche Zeiten* (Munich, 1964).

IV CONTEMPORARY NEWSPAPERS AND PERIODICALS

I have used *The Times*, *The Illustrated London News* and *Punch* over a considerable period of time and selected files from other daily newspapers and reviews. Details are given in the reference notes.

V HISTORICAL PERIODICALS

American Historical Review, published Washington, D.C. [*AHR*].

A. Vagts, 'William II and the Siam Episode', xv, 4 (1940), pp. 834–41.

R. A. Kann, 'Emperor William II and Archduke Francis Ferdinand in their Correspondence', LVII, 2 (1952), pp. 323–51.

A. Dorpalen, 'Empress Augusta Victoria and the Fall of the German Monarchy', LVIII, 1 (1952), pp. 17–38.

Berliner Monatshefte, published Berlin.

Kurt Jagow, 'Das "Königswort" Georges V', 16 (2), July 1938, pp. 683–91.

Bulletin of the Institute of Historical Research, published London.

J.A.S. Grenville, 'Lansdowne's abortive proposal of 12 March 1901 for a secret agreement with Germany', 27 (1954), pp. 201–13.

Central European History, published Atlanta, Georgia [*CEH*].

F. Gregory Campbell, 'The Kaiser and *Mitteleuropa* in October 1918', 2, no. 3 (September 1969), pp. 376–83.

H.H. Herwig, 'Admirals versus Generals; the War Aims of the Imperial German Navy', 5, no. 3 (September 1972), pp. 208–33.

K.H. Jarausch, 'The Illusion of Limited War; Bethmann-Hollweg's Calculated Risk, July 1914', 2, no. 1 (March 1969), pp. 48–76.

Geschichte in Wissenschaft und Unterricht, published Munich.

H.D. Hellige, 'Wilhelm II und Walter Rathenau', no. 19 (1968), pp. 538–44.

Historical Journal: published Cambridge [*HJ*].

Richard Cosgrove: 'Lloyd George's Speech at the Mansion House, 21 July 1911', 12, no. 4 (1969), pp. 698–701.

Richard Langhorne: 'Naval Question in Anglo-German Relations 1912–14', 14, no. 2 (1971), pp. 359–70.

Joanne S. Mortimer: 'Commercial interests and German diplomacy in the Agadir Crisis', 10, no. 3 (1967), pp. 440–56.

J.C.G. Röhl: 'A document of 1892 on Germany, Prussia and Poland', 7, no. 1 (1964), pp. 142–8.

—— 'The Disintegration of the *Kartell* and the Politics of Bismarck's Fall from Power', 9, no. 1 (1966), pp. 60–89.

—— 'Admiral von Müller and the Approach of War, 1911–14', 12, no. 4 (1969), pp. 651–73.

J. Steinberg: 'A German Plan for the Invasion of Holland and Belgium, 1897', 6, no. 1 (1963), pp. 107–15.

Historische Zeitschrift, published Munich [*HZ*].

V.R. Berghahn: 'Zu den Zielen des deutschen Flottenbaus unter Wilhelm II', 210 (1970), pp. 34–100.

K. Lehmann: 'Zu Kaiser Wilhelms II England-Politik', 147 (1933), pp. 553–8.

E. Zechlin: 'Deutschland zwischen Kabinettskrieg und Wirtschaftskrieg', 199 (1964), pp. 347–458.

Journal of Contemporary History, published London [*JCH*]. Volume 1, number 3 (July 1966) of this periodical contains ten stimulating articles on the coming of the First World War. The following of them are cited in my reference notes:

Jonathan Steinberg, 'The Copenhagen Complex', pp. 23–46.

Norman Stone: 'Hungary and the Crisis of 1914', pp. 153–70.

Journal of Modern History: published Chicago. [*JMH*].

Paul M. Kennedy: 'German World Policy and the Alliance Negotiations with England', 45, no. 4 (December 1973), pp. 605–73.

Krasny Arkhiv: published Moscow.

A. Savin: 'Some letters from Prince William of Prussia to Alexander III' (commentary in Russian, letters in the original French, with a Russian translation), 2 (1922), pp. 118–29.

Index

Abbreviation used: W for Kaiser William II

INDEX

Portsmouth: W visits as a child, 7; W reports on fortifications of, 23
Potsdam: W's confirmation at, 14; accent of, 16–17; W's military life in, 20–2, 24–5; W's speech to recruits at (1891), 54; W at during Sarajevo crisis, 168–9; W's last visit to, 208–9; Kaiserin buried at, 218; W's funeral instructions and, 226
Pravda, Bolshevik newspaper: German funds for, 198, 201
Prittwitz, General Max von, commander of German Eighth Army: 177, 178
Prussia: Queen Victoria criticizes, 4, 5, 9: military traditions of, 7–9, 34–5, 56; constitution of, 36–7, 140; minister-president ('prime minister') of, 37, 57, 64
Pula: W visits, 139, 197
Punch, British periodical: 'Dropping the Pilot', 50; on W's Brandenburg speech, 56–7; 'Cook's Crusader', 92

Queen, Ellery, novelist: books in W's library, 222

racialism: W's views on, 105–6, 157, 220
railways: W's travels on, 38, 182, (into exile) 211, 212–13; Russians build in Poland, 41; Germans build in Middle East, 92–3; in China, 94
Rathenau, Walther, German industrialist: 105
Reich: *see* Germany
Reichstag: suffrage for, 36, 64; elections to, (1890) 44, 47–8, (1907) 123, (1912) 147–8; and army, 59, 79, 151, 157–8, 159; W and, 70, 150, 175; and navy, 78, 79, 85–6, 97, 151; W criticized in, 81, 135; government attacked in, 117, 147, 148; and Eulenburg circle, 122; in World War I, 175, 193, 195
Reinsurance Treaty (1887): 41, 53
Reval: 107
revolution: Germany foments, 176, 198; in Germany 201, 209–11
Rhoades J., contributor to *The Times*: verses praising W (1901), 101
Rhodes, Cecil, prime minister of Cape Colony: 69; visits Berlin, 93
Richter Eugen, liberal deputy: criticizes W, 81
Richthofen, Otto von, State Secretary for Foreign Affairs: 104
Riddle of the Sands (Childers): 108
Riga: W visits (1917), 196

Roberts, Earl, British Field Marshal: 130, 134
Rodd, Sir James Rennell, British diplomat: 129
Roman Catholic Church: feared, 48; and schools, 55, 57; and peace, 195
Romanov dynasty: 198, 203
Roosevelt, Theodore, President of the United States: 113, 117
Rosebery, Archibald Philip Primrose, Earl of, British foreign secretary: 58–60, 70
Rosyth: British establish naval base at, 107
Roumania: at war with Germany, 190, 192
Rudolph, Crown Prince of Austria: 14
Rumbold, Sir Horace, counsellor at British embassy in Berlin: 165–6, 174
Rupert, Crown Prince of Bavaria: criticizes Hindenburg cult, 199–200; visited by Princess Hermine, 219
Russia: W's attempts to estrange from Britain and France, 68, 73, 78–9, 94, 98, 138, 161–2; danger to Germany, 41–2, 49, 159, 162–3, 166; and China, 82–3, 84; and possible Anglo-German alliance, 88, 89, 90; war with Japan, 109, 110–11; proposed alliance with Germany, 111; Björkö treaty and, 114, 116; revolutionary disturbances in, 116, 176; sponsors peace conference, 127; in Balkan affairs, 137–9, 152–3; prepares for war, 168, 170–1; in World War I, 171, 177, 178–9, 183–4; revolution of 1917 in, 198–9; makes peace at Brest-Litovsk, 201–2

St Petersburg (*after 1914 see* Petrograd): W visits (1884), 22–3, 38, 53; (1897) 82
Salisbury, Robert Gascoyne Cecil, Third Marquess of, British prime minister: views on W, 32, 39, 95, 99; relations with W, 58, 70–2, 73–4, 75, 101; and Kruger telegram, 77; and Triple Alliance, 79; and France, 87; and possible Anglo-German alliance, 89, 93; and Russia, 94, 98
Samoa: Anglo-German dispute over, 94–5
Sandringham: W visits, 23, 96, 107
San Remo: W's parents at, 31–2
Sarajevo Crisis (1914): 166–70
Saturday Review, British periodical: 87
Sayers, Dorothy L. British author: short stories in W's library, 222
Scheer, Admiral Reinhard von, commander-in-chief High Seas Fleet: and Jutland, 188–9; in 1918, 208, 211
Scheidemann, Philipp, socialist deputy: 158
Scheldt estuary: W considers naval plan for seizing (1897), 88